FAN PHENOMEN

HARRY POTTER

EDITED BY
VALERIE ESTELLE FRANKEL

Credits

First published in the UK in 2019 by Intellect Books,
The Mill, Parnall Road, Fishponds, Bristol, BS16 3JG, UK

First published in the USA in 2019 by Intellect Books,
The University of Chicago Press, 1427 E. 60th Street,
Chicago, IL 60637, USA

Copyright © 2019 Intellect Ltd

Editor: Valerie Estelle Frankel

Production Editor: Naomi Curston

Copy Editor: Emma Rhys

Typesetting and Cover Design: Aleksandra Szumlas

Inside front cover image: Shana Mosella, *Anime Los Angeles*.
Ontario, CA, 2017. Photo by Michael Benedict.

Inside back cover image: Ray Bender aka Aunt Tessy Cosplay
plays Boggart-Snape at *Comic-Con*. San Diego, CA, 2018.
Photo by Valerie Estelle Frankel.

A catalogue record for this book is available from
the British Library

Fan Phenomena Series
ISSN: 2051-4468
eISSN: 2051-4476

Fan Phenomena: Harry Potter
ISBN: 978-1-78938-070-5
ePDF: 978-1-78938-072-9
ePUB: 978-1-78938-071-2

Printed and bound by
Hobbs, UK.

Contents

Introduction
The State of *Potter* Today

→ *Harry Potter*, as well as being the bestselling children's book series (Rowling, 1997–2007) of all time, has defined the meaning of fandom. As it debuted around the same time as the Internet came to popularity, fanfiction, fanart and fanvids showed what this new tool could offer. Wizard rock crowded Myspace and Bandcamp, even as YouTube, DeviantArt and FanFiction.net welcomed all comers with their creativity.

In the midst of all this, the massive, celebrated fansites like The Leaky Cauldron and MuggleNet were the place to be. In fact, in a gesture of basically unprecedented support for her fan community, J. K. Rowling invited the webmasters of these two sites, Emerson Spartz of MuggleNet and Melissa Anelli of The Leaky Cauldron, to Scotland to read book six and interview her. Rowling also showed support for these and other websites with the J. K. Rowling Fan Site Awards, saluting the fans who put so much effort into celebrating her works.

Of course, in person fans could really strut their stuff. Aside from general fantasy conventions, from *Comic-Con* to *Worldcon*, several tracks of specifically *Potter* conferences suddenly materialized. These, sponsored by HP Education Fanon, Inc. (*Nimbus 2003*, *The Witching Hour*, *Lumos*, *Prophecy 2007*, *Portus*, *Azkatraz*, *Infinitus* and *Ascendio 2012*) and by the educational group Narrate Conferences (*Phoenix Rising 2007* and *Terminus 2008*), focused heavily on academic papers and speculation on how the series would end. This was the height of Potterdom, with Rowling's clues and twist endings providing endless fuel for speculation. Enterprising fans mapped out Hogwarts or described Ginny's mythic roots in everything from King Arthur to Red Riding Hood. Held only weeks after book seven was published, *Prophecy 2007* saluted the perished characters with shrines, where fans could leave spontaneous gifts of socks for Dobby and hotel bottles of shampoo for Professor Snape. While some actors attended these conferences, the real stars were *Potter* and fan culture professors like John Granger and Henry Jenkins. They taught actual *Potter* classes back at their universities too, leading to a new level not just of scholarship but also of academic respect for the Potterheads. Books like *Hog's Head Conversations* (Prinzi, 2009) and *Teaching with Harry Potter* (Frankel, 2013) emphasized new avenues for fandom as popular culture gained a new respect in academics.

The conferences also offered a place to celebrate the lighter side of *Potter* – fanfiction and art, cosplay and wizard rock concerts far into the night. Some conferences pushed this to the logical conclusion and structured the conference like a school, with crafting class, dance class, History of Magic, mythology, writing and anything else that fit the bill. Balls, fashion shows and unusual experiments like Water Quidditch and parody plays gave the fans delightful places to show off. *MISTI-Con* (2013–ongoing) a deliberately small New England gathering, kicked off a steady intimate get-together, while a

Introduction
Valerie Estelle Frankel

Figure 1: Yuki the Destroyer, Online Comic and @HagridCosplay at Comic-Con 2018.

few cities and universities began annual *Potter* fairs. Adding the theme parks, computer games, films and Pottermore itself, the official world was expanding into... well, an entire world indeed. The unofficial events expanded alongside it.

Still, some parts of the Potterverse ran their course and began to fade. The yearly music festival 'Wrockstock' stretched from 2007 to 2013, but some of the wrockers began retiring. Meanwhile, the conferences faded into the less academic *LeakyCons* (begun in 2009 by The Leaky Cauldron and still ongoing in 2018), which invited young adult authors to help celebrate an expanding world beyond the Potterverse. *LeakyCon* began to fill with crossover fans sporting mockingjay pins and Camp Half-Blood T-shirts as teen dystopia and Percy Jackson novels succeeded Harry's legacy.

Fan groups in major cities persevered, with the staff changing but the trivia nights, gaming afternoons and cosplay adventures stretching for decades. Even as the New York wizards skated in costume at the Rockefeller Center and the Los Angeles branch headed off to the beach to visit Shell Cottage – or the theme park after it opened – the fandom was going strong. The Harry Potter Alliance (HP Alliance), a social action group founded by Andrew Slack in 2005, continued to engage millions of fans with over a hundred international chapters. Quidditch, founded at colleges across the world, lasted as a sport, with an annual Quidditch Cup. Themed camps for younger kids across the US – heavy in crafts and Quidditch – helped them share in the love of *Potter*. Libraries

Figure 2: Ray Bender aka
Aunt Tessy Cosplay plays
Boggart-Snape at
Comic-Con 2018.

hosted parties and events, especially to coincide with Harry's birthday or the release of new material in 2016.

This included the London and Broadway play *Harry Potter and the Cursed Child* (Rowling, Thorne and Tiffany, 2016) and the new film franchise *Fantastic Beasts*, along with the new backstory of Ilvermorny, the American school of magic, presented on Pottermore (admittedly amid some controversy about cultural appropriation). After the drought since 2007, fans finally had new stories. These too produced special celebrations at the conventions as the attendees at *LeakyCon 2016* dressed in 1920s fashion and read the best *Cursed Child* scenes onstage. Once more, art, fanvids, fanfiction, music and so on had expanded to welcome new series.

This book celebrates it all – the costumers, writers, artists and wrockers. More, it delves into the stories behind the fans' most marvellous creations. Theme park design writer Erin Pyne carries readers inside the Wizarding World of Harry Potter, explaining the storyline and plan behind it. Matt Maggiacomo, executive director of the HP Alliance, details how *Potter* fans across the world are fighting for social justice in Harry's name. There are also interviews with creators of the fan films *The Greater Good* (Zagri, 2013) and *Snape and the Marauders* (Zagri, 2016), as well as Team StarKid, who wrote the beloved *A Very Potter Musical* (Lang, Lang and Holden/Team StarKid, 2009) and its sequels – parodies performed at *LeakyCons* to the delight of thousands of fans.

César Alfonso Marino considers the licensed computer games, finishing with Warner Bros. Interactive Entertainment's 2018 *Harry Potter: Hogwarts Mystery* app and the evolution of the gaming platforms. Paralleling this, S. Even Kreider lays out fans' efforts to adapt the series for roleplaying games (RPGs) and explains the benefits and pitfalls of each system. Gazing over the early history, Emily E. Roach describes the journey of the fans from LiveJournal to Tumblr, seeking better mediums for communication.

Moving on to new material, my own chapter examines Rowling's post-*Deathly Hallows* (2007) works, from *Casual Vacancy* (2012) to *Fantastic Beasts and Where to Find Them* (2016), and considers why these aren't striking the fans as publishers and producers had hoped. For something unique,

Introduction
Valerie Estelle Frankel

Valerie Guempel invites readers to follow her to the 2018 *Cursed Child* Broadway premiere as she reveals through intimate details why the play must be watched, not just read. Katryn Alessandri considers the play from another angle, tracking the fans' hostility to black Hermione and how this reflects a growing backlash against diversity, evident in other fandoms from Marvel's *Avengers* to *Star Wars*.

Indeed, crossover fandoms and derivative works have often commented deeply and thoughtfully on the Potterverse, expanding through the years to reveal new insights. Jessica Hautsch examines fans' Sorting of *Hamilton* (2015), *Buffy* (1997-2003) and *Game of Thrones* (books: Martin, 1996–ongoing; TV series: 2011-ongoing) characters into Hogwarts Houses, and what that art form conveys. Joel Hawkes analyses *The Unwritten* (2009-15), a parody/commentary comic that riffs on many *Potter* themes. Meanwhile Ariel Birdoff, author of *Nerd!Verse* (2014), describes why she combined so many fandoms into a single poetry volume, even as she shares her history founding the band Madam Pince and the Librarians; throwing *Potter* events with her library and fan group; and finally celebrating it all with the perfect *Potter* wedding.

Rowling's world continues to grow, with new theme parks, new games and now a *Fantastic Beasts* spin-off franchise that's only just beginning. As fans celebrate the books' twentieth anniversary and match the official offerings with their own merchandizing, art and dazzling fanworks, it becomes clear that there's no end to *Potter*, just as there's no end to the power of the imagination. ●

GO FURTHER

Books
Teaching with Harry Potter
Valerie Estelle Frankel
(Jefferson, NC: McFarland, 2013)

Harry Potter's *Bookshelf: The Great Books Behind the Hogwarts Adventures*
John Granger
(London: Penguin Group, 2009)

Hog's Head Conversations
Travis Prinzi
(Allentown, PA: Winged Lion Press, 2009)

Harry Potter and the Philosopher's Stone
J. K. Rowling
(London: Bloomsbury, 1997)

Harry Potter and the Chamber of Secrets
J. K. Rowling
(London: Bloomsbury, 1998)

Harry Potter and the Prisoner of Azkaban
J. K. Rowling
(New York: Scholastic, 1999)

Harry Potter and the Goblet of Fire
J. K. Rowling
(New York: Scholastic, 2000)

Fantastic Beasts and Where to Find Them
J. K. Rowling
(New York: Arthur A. Levine Books, 2001)

Quidditch Through the Ages
J. K. Rowling
(New York: Arthur A. Levine Books, 2001)

Harry Potter and the Order of the Phoenix
J. K. Rowling
(New York: Scholastic, 2003)

Harry Potter and the Half-Blood Prince
J. K. Rowling
(New York: Scholastic, 2005)

Introduction
Valerie Estelle Frankel

Harry Potter and the Deathly Hallows
J. K. Rowling
(New York: Scholastic, 2007)

The Tales of Beedle the Bard
J. K. Rowling
(New York: Scholastic, 2008)

Harry Potter and the Cursed Child
J. K. Rowling, Jack Thorne and John Tiffany
(Crawfordsville, IN: Pottermore, 2016)

Hogwarts: An Incomplete and Unreliable Guide (Kindle edn)
J. K. Rowling
(USA: Pottermore, 2016)

Short Stories from Hogwarts of Heroism, Hardship and Dangerous Hobbies
(Kindle edn)
J. K. Rowling
(USA: Pottermore, 2016)

Short Stories from Hogwarts of Power, Politics and Pesky Poltergeists
J. K. Rowling
(USA: Pottermore, 2016)

Online
'Potter Puppet Pals: The Mysterious Ticking Noise'
Neil Cicierega
YouTube. 23 March 2007, https://www.youtube.com/user/potterpuppetpals.

'Harry Potter Friday Parody'
The Hillywood Show
YouTube. 30 June 2011, https://www.youtube.com/watch?v=qvgVMecNpOc.

'Ilvermorny School of Witchcraft and Wizardry'
J. K. Rowling
Pottermore, https://www.pottermore.com/writing-by-jk-rowling/ilvermorny.

Websites
DeviantArt, https://www.deviantart.com/tag/harrypotter
FanFiction.net, https://www.fanfiction.net
Fiction Alley: Creativity is Magic, http://www.fictionalley.org/authors
Harry Potter and the Methods of Rationality, http://www.hpmor.com
Harry Potter's Realm of Wizardry, http://www.harrypotterrealm.com
MuggleNet, http://www.mugglenet.com
Pottermore, https://www.pottermore.com
The Harry Potter Alliance, https://www.thehpalliance.org
The Leaky Cauldron, http://www.the-leaky-cauldron.org
The Sugar Quill, http://www.sugarquill.net
Wizards in Space, https://wizardsinspacemag.com

Film/Television
Harry Potter and the Philosopher's Stone/Sorcerer's Stone, Chris Columbus, dir. (USA: Warner Bros, 2001).

Harry Potter and the Chamber of Secrets, Chris Columbus, dir. (USA: Warner Bros, 2002).

Harry Potter and the Prisoner of Azkaban, Alfonso Cuarón, dir. (USA: Warner Bros, 2004).

Harry Potter and the Goblet of Fire, Mike Newell, dir. (USA: Warner Bros, 2005).

Harry Potter and the Order of the Phoenix, David Yates, dir. (USA: Warner Bros, 2007).

Harry Potter and the Half-Blood Prince, David Yates, dir. (USA: Warner Bros, 2009).

Harry Potter and the Deathly Hallows – Part 1, David Yates, dir. (USA: Warner Bros, 2010).

Harry Potter and the Deathly Hallows – Part 2, David Yates, dir. (USA: Warner Bros, 2011).

The Greater Good, Justin Zagri, dir. (USA: Broad Strokes, 2013).

Introduction
Valerie Estelle Frankel

Fantastic Beasts and Where to Find Them, David Yates, dir. (USA: Warner Bros, 2016).

Severus Snape and the Marauders, Justin Zagri, dir. (USA: Broad Strokes, 2016).

Fantastic Beasts: The Crimes of Grindelwald, David Yates, dir. (USA: Warner Bros, 2018).

Theatre
Harry Potter and the Cursed Child, J. K. Rowling, Jack Thorne, John Tiffany and Imogen Heap (Palace Theatre, London, 30 July 2016–ongoing; Lyric Theatre, New York, 16 March 2018 – ongoing).

Musicals
A Very Potter Musical, Matt Lang, Nick Lang and Brian Holden (University of Michigan, Ann Arbor: Team StarKid, 9–11 April 2009).

A Very Potter Sequel, Matt Lang, Nick Lang and Brian Holden (University of Michigan, Ann Arbor: Team StarKid, 14–16 May 2010).

A Very Potter Senior Year, Matt Lang, Nick Lang and Brian Holden (Chicago: Team StarKid, 11 August 2012).

Music
It's a Slytherin World
Draco and the Malfoys
(Draco and the Malfoys, 2009)
http://evilwizardrock.com

Harry and the Potters and the Power of Love
Harry and the Potters
(Eskimo Laboratories, 2006)
http://harryandthepotters.com

Stacked!
Madame Pince and the Librarians
(Madam Pince and the Librarians, 2010)
https://librarywrock.bandcamp.com/

The Triwizard LP
Ministry of Magic
(Indytronic Records, 2007)

Huffleriot CD
Tonks and the Aurors
(Steph Anderson Music, 2018)
https://www.tonksandtheaurors.com/blog

Wizard Party Forever
The Whomping Willows
(The Whomping Willows, 2010)
https://thewhompingwillows.bandcamp.com

Video games
Harry Potter and the Philosopher's Stone/Sorcerer's Stone [Game Boy Advance, Game Boy Color, OS X, PC, PlayStation]
(Electronic Arts, 2001)

Harry Potter and the Chamber of Secrets [Game Boy Advance, Game Boy Color, GameCube, PC, PlayStation, PlayStation 2, Xbox]
(Electronic Arts, 2002)

Harry Potter and the Philosopher's Stone/Sorcerer's Stone [GameCube, PlayStation 2, Xbox]
(Electronic Arts, 2003)

Harry Potter and the Prisoner of Azkaban [Game Boy Advance, GameCube, PC, PlayStation 2, Xbox]
(Electronic Arts, 2004)

Harry Potter and the Goblet of Fire [Game Boy Advance, GameCube, PC, PlayStation 2, PlayStation Portable, Xbox]
(Electronic Arts, 2005)

Harry Potter and the Order of the Phoenix [Game Boy Advance, GameCube, Mac OS X, Nintendo DS, PC, PlayStation 2, PlayStation 3, PlayStation Portable, Wii, Xbox 360]
(Electronic Arts, 2007)

Harry Potter and the Half-Blood Prince [mobile, Nintendo DS, PC, PlayStation 2, PlayStation 3, PlayStation Portable, Wii, Xbox 360]
(Electronic Arts, 2009)

Harry Potter and the Deathly Hallows – Part 1 [mobile, Nintendo DS, PC, PlayStation 3, Wii, Xbox 360]
(Electronic Arts, 2010)

Introduction
Valerie Estelle Frankel

Harry Potter and the Deathly Hallows – Part 2 [mobile, Nintendo DS, PC, PlayStation 3, Wii, Xbox 360]
(Electronic Arts, 2011)

Harry Potter: Hogwarts Mystery [Android and iOS]
(Warner Bros. Interactive Entertainment, 2018)

Part 1
Real World

Chapter
01

The Wizarding World of Harry Potter: Bringing the Books to Life

Erin Pyne

→ On 18 June 2010, the Wizarding World of Harry Potter (WWoHP) opened to 40,000 fans waiting at the gate! The Wizarding World became THE destination for fans to immerse themselves in the Potterverse. For millions of readers, entering Universal's Islands of Adventure realm was like walking into their own imaginations. J. K. Rowling's world came to life, complete with the sights, sounds, smells, textures and tastes of the real world of Harry Potter.

Figure 1: The theme park invitation (2014).

Rumours and speculations

When the WWoHP was announced, Universal teased information, and rumours of the new realm spread through the Internet with fans speculating on the different rides, attractions and merchandise. Fan-created websites dedicated message boards to discussing the reports and rumours of the upcoming *Harry Potter* theme park. People imagined the Wizarding World to be a dream come to life, as close as they could get to really entering the Wizarding World. Universal's Wizarding World (WW) website held contests, teased artwork and had fans fill out questionnaires. I loved reading the rumours, ideas and hopes on the discussion boards, but of course I was not allowed to say anything. I walked through the construction site of Hogsmeade Village, watching how all the details from the designs and scripts were integrated to create a world as authentic to the vision of J. K. Rowling as possible.

In September 2009, Tom Felton announced the opening date (spring 2010)

The Wizarding World of Harry Potter:
Bringing the Books to Life
Erin Pyne

during a live webcast and the first details of Hogwarts Castle and other rides were released. I was able to have dinner with Tom and he described being blown away by the park, which was still under construction. A funny detail about this announcement is that the marketing team had built a full set of the Gryffindor common room for the webcast. Tom Felton walked in and looked very uncomfortable and said he didn't belong there! (He is a Slytherin after all!)

By February, fans watching the WW website were treated to the menu for the Three Broomsticks and showcased some of the merchandise for sale.

As the opening day approached in May, thousands of fans had already pre-booked vacation packages, and Universal kept up the media blitz with videos of the movie stars touring Hogsmeade. Daniel Radcliffe, Tom Felton, Warwick Davis, Emma Watson, Rupert Grint, Michael Gambon, Matthew Lewis, Robbie Coltrane and Oliver and James Phelps all walked the parks before the opening, drinking butterbeer and exploring the castle. Emma's wand even chose her in Ollivander's! J. K. Rowling herself came to visit and walked through Hogsmeade and Hogwarts – the places of her imagination, come to life.

Figure 2: Erin Pyne with Tom Felton (2010).

Grand openings
Universal is known for its extravagant grand openings, but the WWoHP was the most exceptional in the history of the company. Elaborate invitations went out, complete with a magic wand. As guests gathered in front of Hogwarts Castle, a full-scale Knight Bus drove out from beyond the castle and dropped off most of the movie actors. Soon after, Daniel Radcliffe and Rupert Grint drove up in the Weasley's Flying Ford Anglia! Daniel counted down from three, the crowd shouted, 'Lumos Maxima', and composer John Williams conducted the Orlando Symphony Orchestra in a live performance of the *Harry Potter* score as fireworks burst over Hogwarts Castle and stunning projection mapping lit up the building.

The WWoHP at Universal's Islands of Adventure (Orlando), featuring Hogsmeade Village, Hogwarts Castle and a Hippogriff ride in the Forbidden Forest, opened to amazing reviews. From the first bars of the theme song as everyone entered the gate, to the live smoke from the Hogwarts Express, fans were immersed in the world, able to buy candy in Honeydukes, sip butterbeer and pumpkin juice, mail letters at the Owl Post, grab dinner at the Three Broomsticks, wander into the forest and find Hagrid's hut. It was just like the movie set except that everything was touchable for a fully immersive experience. The thrilling ride in the castle, a mixture of digital and physical effects while riding on top of a giant robotic arm, transported guests into many of Harry's most iconic adventures, with Daniel Radcliffe and other stars filming new scenes for the ride. Even the hour-long queue line was mitigated by talking paintings, featuring the Hogwarts founders, a new Dumbledore scene and a realistic Sorting Hat animatronic singing a new song written by Jo Rowling herself!

Next came the expansion with Diagon Alley, Knockturn Alley and the Hogwarts Express at the main Universal Orlando park. Millions of *Harry Potter* fans flocked to experience the magic of Ollivander's, where the wand chooses the wizard; ride the magical Hogwarts Express; race through Gringotts Bank, facing Voldemort himself; and, of course, go shopping for all the wizard stuff in Diagon Alley and Hogsmeade. The success was so great, Universal quickly made plans to build more! In December 2011, Universal announced a planned Wizarding World in Los Angeles; in May 2012, they announced one in Osaka; and then the Universal Beijing WWoHP in 2015. Wizards have taken over the world! Is it weird that there are four Hogwarts Castles? Nah! The real one is still in Scotland.

And it isn't over yet! Universal continues its expansion of the Wizarding World with new rides and new realms. Universal Studios Japan created an amazing section of the evening parade featuring a Quidditch pitch float and a Great Hall float with projection-mapped Death Eaters attacking from the skies and wizard performers defending with sparking wands! Fans continue to speculate what new wonderful worlds they will soon be able to step into.

Every year from 2014 to 2017, Universal hosted the 'Celebration of Harry Potter', featuring movie stars, film creators and film-prop exhibitions where fans could meet the actors, artists and designers involved in the films and the theme park. This event also allowed fans to dress in full costumes (called cos-

**The Wizarding World of Harry Potter:
Bringing the Books to Life**
Erin Pyne

play) minus masks. Normally only wizard robes are permitted, but during the Celebration, fans could fully cosplay as their favourite characters! Every year I dressed differently, and it was always a surprise to see who would be featured. One year, the actual wand makers from the films came to demonstrate their craft. The graphic designers, Mina and Lima, took time meeting every guest and signing posters and artwork. Amid a backdrop of displayed film costumes, the costume designer of the films complimented fans on their cosplay and posed for pictures with them. Each year, the energy in the air was charged with positivity from fans all over the world who gathered for the massive three-day event, which was spread across the two theme parks.

Fandom celebrations

In response to the original theme park announcement, *Harry Potter*-convention organizers quickly determined that Orlando would be the next location! The *Infinitus 2010* symposium was held at the Universal Studios Resort specifically to celebrate the opening. In mid-July, the fandom gathered: this time, in addition to discussion forums, wizard rock and field Quidditch, attendees would experience the magic of the Wizarding World together. At a private party in Hogsmeade for attendees, called 'Night of a Thousand Wizards', the fandom was seen in full wizard robes and elaborate costumes, taking photos with the Hogwarts Express and walking through the hallowed halls of Hogwarts. Rides and shops were open all night, and the fans got special permission to come in costume. It was the first such event for fans.

As everyone awaited the 11 p.m. start, Snape, Lucius and Voldemort got their dance on, and other characters staged duels in the auditorium. It became clear that the fans could make the entertainment all on their own. While many braved the heat in white shirts and school ties, every imaginable full-on costume appeared, from original characters to perfect Mad-Eyes and Umbridges. Berni Farrant attended the event in a full handmade Hedwig costume featuring thousands of feathers. A Muggle-music dance party was held in front of the Three Broomsticks and the wizards danced and sang at the top of their lungs, 'Don't Stop Believing!' The theme park catered with treacle tarts, cauldron cakes, peanut-butter-strawberry ice cream and other snacks from the novels. With about 1700 fans finally showing up and rocking late into the night, it was unforgettable.

Figure 3: Erin Pyne and Rowan Pyne with the Hogwarts Express (2010).

The Wizarding World brought other *Harry Potter* fandom events to Orlando, including the *LeakyCon* and *Ascendio* symposiums, wizard rock shows and the International Quidditch World Cup, featuring dozens of college Quidditch teams from around the world. Universal hosted private night-time cosplay events in the park, and fans created special events and meetups to celebrate special days such as Harry's birthday and the 1st of September send-off of the Hogwarts Express to Hogwarts.

The 1st of September 2017 marked the year it would be 'nineteen years later', when Harry and his friends would send their own children off on the Hogwarts Express. This fan-created event featured people gathering in costumes and counting down the moment when the train would depart at 11 o'clock in the morning. It was an honour (and a full-circle journey) to be there with my own son, who dressed as Harry, and to ride the train to Hogwarts together. Later that evening, MuggleNet hosted a party in Diagon Alley ('Mugglenet Live – Nineteen Years Later'), featuring eight stars from the film, including Chris Rankin (Percy Weasley), Christian Coulson (Tom Riddle), Luke Youngblood (Lee Jordan) and Sean Biggerstaff (Oliver Wood). Ryan Turner (Hugo Weasley) was also there, as well as the big star of the night, Arthur Bowen, who played Albus Severus Potter. The actors hosted discussion panels and took questions from the fans before Diagon Alley opened for the private event. Guests with certain passes were also able to meet and get pictures with the actors.

The Leaky Cauldron catered the event, offering buffet-style food throughout Diagon Alley and unlimited butterbeer! The Gringotts Bank ride and the Hogwarts Express were open with no queues, and Celestina Warbeck and the Banshees performed fun jazzy numbers, including 'A Cauldron Full of Hot Strong Love', 'You Charmed the Heart Right Out of Me' and 'You Stole My Cauldron but You Can't Have My Heart' – all songs written by J. K. Rowling. My personal favourite of these is 'Beat Back Those Bludgers Boys and Chuck that Quaffle Here'. WADA – the Wizarding Academy of Dramatic Arts – also performed incredible puppet performances of stories from *The Tales of Beedle the Bard* (Rowling, 2008), including 'The Fountain of Fair Fortune' and 'The Tale of the Three Brothers'.

The Wizarding World of Harry Potter:
Bringing the Books to Life
Erin Pyne

Worried that you have missed out on Wizarding World fan events? There are so many more on the horizon!

Every wizard is a hero: A fan's experience in the Wizarding World of Harry Potter

A huge team at Universal Creative and designers from the *Potter* films (2001–11), including Stuart Craig and Alan Gilmore, helped design and create the look and feel of the park. Even the films' costume designer, Jany Temime, was involved in the design of the Universal employee *Harry Potter*-themed costumes. Thousands of people: writers, artists, architects, directors, producers, coordinators, lighting experts, audio/visual experts, costumers, prop builders, graphic designers, musical score composers, musicians, filmmakers and so many more worked for years to bring the Wizarding World to life! And at the heart of all that design was the guest experience.

So what does it take to make a guest feel like they are part of the Wizarding World? How do theme park designers engage all ages from all over the world? By making every guest the hero of the story!

Simply walking through an elaborately dressed set of Hogsmeade or Diagon Alley is not enough. It's passive. Theme park designers bring you into the story, making *you* the hero, using sensory stimuli to immerse each guest in the world with a 'Call to Adventure'.

The classic 'Hero's Journey' structure by Joseph Campbell is a blueprint for great storytelling. When applied to theme park design, each guest goes through the journey, creating a memorable, emotional experience.

Step One: Ordinary World – The story begins in the world of everyday life. An anchor of reality that serves to strengthen the transition to the extraordinary.

Before reaching Hogsmeade, guests walk through a common medieval village. In the same way, before entering Diagon Alley, everyone walks through London; before boarding the Hogwarts Express, passengers move through King's Cross station.

Step Two: Call to Adventure – The guest must be summoned. Music, smells, sound effects and even physical effects are used to create a portal.

A threshold one must cross. The Hero chooses to Refuse the Call or Bargain without Knowing. Most theme park visitors tend to go with Bargain without Knowing, and cross the threshold curious, excited and maybe even anxious about what will be on the other side!

Step Three: Crossing the First Threshold – *Crossing the threshold between worlds signifies the Hero's commitment to the journey and whatever it may have in store. Entering Hogsmeade, there is a large archway with a hanging wrought-iron sign engraved with the symbols of the town as well as an instruction, 'Please Respect the Spell Limits.' The moment you walk through the threshold, everything changes. The music of Harry Potter surrounds you, the steam from the Hogwarts Express fills the air, the smell of Honeydukes Sweet Shop wafts over you. You have entered a different world.*

Entering Diagon Alley, there is an unlabelled, inconspicuous entrance. Each visitor walks between brick pillars and around a brick wall to discover an opening in the brick. The sounds of moving bricks – straight from the film – fill your ears and as you pass through the threshold you are immersed in the grandeur of Diagon Alley, with the music playing, the movement in the shop windows and the call to move further in as the enormous dragon breathes fire from the rooftop of Gringotts Bank.

To board the Hogwarts Express from London, you discover the magical wall at Platform 9¾. First you witness others magically passing through a brick wall, then as you approach, there is no wall at all – it has magically opened for you and you hear the WHOOSH of magic as you pass through. Suddenly you emerge onto the magical platform of the Hogwarts Express, complete with music change and steam from the train. Even the employees are wearing Hogwarts Express conductor outfits, as opposed to the King's Cross uniforms worn just outside.

Once a guest has entered the new realm, he or she may feel overwhelmed and disoriented. The visual stimuli are stunning. Standing and watching people's reactions as they enter Diagon Alley is an attraction by itself. Most seem dazed, not knowing where to look. Some become overpowered by the transition into the Wizarding World and gasp or even cry.

Step Four: Meeting the Mentor and Receiving Supernatural Aid – *A centrepiece of the journey is Ollivander's with its true wizard experience: having*

The Wizarding World of Harry Potter:
Bringing the Books to Life
Erin Pyne

a wand choose you. A master Wand Keeper, filling in for Mr Ollivander, be-comes the Mentor, teaching guests about magic and the connection be-tween wand and wizard.

First, you enter Ollivander's, where thousands of wands fill the walls high up to the ceiling. Then you enter a small room where a Wand Keeper is silently waiting. The room is dark, silent and feels like entering a library. Everyone is quiet. This is a sacred space. The Wand Keeper speaks softly, talking about the connection between wand and wizard. Then he feels the magic in the room and selects one person, the person who is to be fitted for a wand. Echoing the experience of Harry, the wand chooses the wizard. The Wand Keeper allows the patron to try a couple of wands that create disas-trous magic in the shop, including causing flowers to droop, shelves to fall, drawers to bang and even a lightning storm inside! Finally, the Wand Keep-er selects a special wand, and as the chosen one touches it, a light from above glows bright; wind blows through the room; and the music swells in an emotional moment! That wand is repackaged and given to the wizard, and usually the person buys that $50 wand, because it chose them!

This personal connection is the catalyst that sends thousands of guests on a quest to discover magic throughout the realm. The interactive wands are a huge part of play and engagement in the Wizarding World. Following a map, practising magic and making physical and digital effects happen with a precise wave of the wand gives guests empowerment and increases their connection to the Hero's Journey.

The magic of the wands lies in a sensor on their tips, so when a wand is waved in a specific way it triggers another sensor to create a magical mo-ment. Only the interactive wands have the sensors. Areas where magic can happen are marked on an elaborate map styled after the Marauders Map. Each area has a bronze medallion on the ground with the name of the spell and a description of the motion to make with the wand. Areas can be any-where, from window displays to water fountains to shop signs! Hogsmeade, Diagon Alley and Knockturn Alley all feature spots for magic!

Some interactives are comical, such as flushing the toilet to watch the 'You-Know-Poo' sign go down the drain, or beautiful, such as watching the Tales of Beedle the Bard book open up and magically tell the story of 'The Fountain of Fair Fortune' through receding shadow boxes within! In Knock-turn Alley, more wand-waving challenges result in spooky or wicked outcomes such as a dancing skeleton you control with your body, an exploding bird and a door with a large eyeball that blasts you with air if you touch the handle!

Wizards line up in front of these magical spots, each waiting to take their turn to practise magic. Meeting the Mentor and receiving this supernatural aid is all a part of the Hero's Journey!

Step Five: Road of Trials – Once oriented, guests begin to explore, but looking at things is not enough to fully engage someone into believing they are part of the journey. They must be able to play in the world, be challenged by the world and rewarded. For this, every gift shop has items to play with: try on a robe in Madame Malkin's and stand in front of the talking mirror, which insists, 'Tuck in your shirt, scruffy.' Adopt a Pygmy Puff in Weasley's Wizard Wheezes and ring the big bell; exchange your Muggle money for real Gringotts gold; get attacked by a Monster Book of Monsters; hear Moaning Myrtle haunting the bathroom; practise Hippogriff riding; drink a butterbeer; watch a Beedle the Bard production; listen to the Toad Chorus or dance at a Celestina Warbeck concert. Of course, there's endless shopping for robes, books, bottles of pumpkin juice, chocolate frogs, Every Flavour Beans and other beloved products from the books. The Hero encounters villains here as well. In Knockturn Alley, guests enter the dominion of dark wizards and encounter greater challenges requiring bravery and fortitude (although many guests squee with giddy happiness walking through the entrance of Borgin and Burkes).

Entering Knockturn Alley, fans leave the sunlit streets of Diagon Alley and enter a dark alleyway that curves into an even darker courtyard where the sky is magically always night with grey clouds moving slowly overhead. Once the eyes adjust to the darkness, fans can make out shop signs, including Dystal Phalanges, the bone shop, featuring a full mermaid skeleton and a dancing ape skeleton controlled by passing wizards with interactive wands. Other shops (closed) include E.L.M. and Wizards Undertakers & Embalmers, Fledermaus and Tanner Bats & Skins, Markus Scarrs Indelible Tattoos and the White Wyvern Pub. The shop that is open to walk into is Borgin and Burkes, and the shop windows and interior display cases are filled with dark items and cursed objects – including props from the film – such as the Cursed Necklace and the Hand of Fate – which attempts

The Wizarding World of Harry Potter:
Bringing the Books to Life
Erin Pyne

to grab passers-by! A trunk under a table rumbles and rocks (perhaps there is a boggart in there?) and if you listen closely, a bird chirps from within the Vanishing Cabinet in the far corner. Just outside Borgin and Burkes is a window full of singing shrunken heads. A wave of the interactive wand and a 'Silencio' spell shuts them up. Once guests escape the maze of Knockturn Alley, they emerge back out into the bright, busy streets of Diagon Alley!

The Road of Trials is about new experiences and engaging in the world as if you are a part of it. You have magic! You wear the clothes, eat the food, carry the trinkets and know the language of the Wizarding World. You are accepted here. You belong.

Step Six: Ordeal/Crossing the Second Threshold – Whether you are in Hogsmeade or Diagon Alley, there is a key attraction that offers a secondary threshold within the land: a new Call to Adventure. Hogwarts Castle and Gringotts Bank are placed as centrepieces within these realms, respectively. Each attraction has its own Call to Adventure to face great villains but also gain strong allies; each attraction follows its own Hero's Journey but is part of the whole.

Entering Hogwarts, for example, guests accept a new Call to Adventure – cross the secondary threshold – and go through a series of trials, meeting the Mentor and Receiving Supernatural Aid!

Harry, Ron and Hermione persuade you to skip class to watch the Quidditch match, and Hermione conjures up a magical flying bench, so you can follow Harry on his broomstick. Unfortunately, Hagrid loses the Hungarian Horntail, wreaking havoc that sends your magical bench tumbling into the Forbidden Forest to face giant spiders, acromantulas and the Whomping Willow. Then Dementors attack! Luckily, Harry casts them away and you follow him back to the Great Hall a hero!

Gringotts has a spectacular threshold: a grand gilded bank lobby. You are on your way to open a vault in the bowels of Gringotts and go on a tour. Unfortunately, at the same moment, Harry, Ron, Hermione and Griphook the goblin break into Bellatrix's vault to steal the Horcrux goblet. Bellatrix arrives and accuses you of breaking into her vault (she has something against muggleborns). You are thrust into an adventure assisted by Ron's brother, Bill Weasley, a code breaker at Gringotts. Facing Voldemort himself, you are rescued by Harry riding on the back of a dragon! Hermione *blows out the walls and together you all escape Gringotts!*

In each adventure, a villain puts not only the lives of the characters on the line, but also the lives of the guests. The Hero must endure the dangers and draw upon powerful allies to overcome the challenges and fulfil his/her destiny at the journey's end. This is the highpoint of the Hero's story.

Step Seven: The Reward – The Hero has won the battle and now is primed for a reward! Thus… exit through a gift shop. With endorphins and adrenaline running high, guests are feeling really good after a ride. This results in impulsive decisions to obtain a special treat and feel more connected to the world, which means buying lots of cool stuff! The highly themed shops have everything from T-shirts and keychains to high-end replica costumes and props. It's a good thing you just went to Gringotts, 'cause you're going to need all your galleons!

Generally, a theme park designer will end here, bidding guests farewell at the highpoint resolution. However, because there are two parks to explore and many guests spend several days on vacation at the parks, while annual pass holders return again and again, the experience is designed to change each time and offers so many twists that accomplishing all the tasks in one or two days is quite a feat. The rest of the journey is the guest's emotional response to leaving the realm and returning home.

Step Eight: The Refusal to Return – The Hero may want to stay in this newly conquered realm to which he/she belongs and bask in the glory of a new identity. After all, what wizard can go back to the Muggle world without feeling a bit of a come down?

Step Nine: Return with the Elixir: Master of Two Worlds – At last, guests pass through the third threshold, the exit, where the extraordinary instantly transforms into the ordinary. The music, the smells of candy, the dazzling visuals, the magic inside the wand, fade away. Some fans have reported going through PPD – Post-Potter Depression – upon their return to the Muggle world. And this is normal, as the transition to ordinary life for the Hero who has just come back from the adventure is not easy and often comes with great hardship. But the guest carries the elixir or prize achieved on the quest: he or she leaves with new memories, photos, videos and Potter

**The Wizarding World of Harry Potter:
Bringing the Books to Life**
Erin Pyne

'stuff' that will soften their return to the ordinary world. Ultimately the Hero, master of two worlds, will return to where he started, but things will clearly never be the same again. ●

GO FURTHER

Books
The Hero with a Thousand Faces
Joseph Campbell
(New York: Princeton University Press, [1949] 1973)

Websites
Infinitus 2010, https://infinitus2010.wordpress.com
The Wizarding World of Harry Potter, https://www.universalorlando.com/web/en/us/universal-orlando-resort/the-wizarding-world-of-harry-potter/hub/index.html

'YER A WIZARD, HARRY'

RUBEUS HAGRID
(HARRY POTTER AND THE PHILOSOPHER'S STONE/SORCERER'S STONE)

Chapter
02

Surveying Fanworks: Art, Dance, Fic, Music and Community

Madeline Wilson

→ It's become something of a repeating cycle: creative people tend to become intensely passionate about the books, movies, TV shows and other media they enjoy, and fans who become tremendously invested in popular stories tend to be creative people.

We've seen fanfiction, community festivals, original songs, filks (the folk music of science fiction/fantasy) and more based on long-lasting entertainment franchises, such as the *Lord of the Rings*, *Pride and Prejudice* and *Star Wars*, for decades. But no single fandom has been as prolific as that of *Harry Potter*, and when we remember that it's only been about twenty years since *Harry Potter and the Philosopher's Stone/Sorcerer's Stone* (Rowling, 1997) was first published, the output of Potterverse fanworks becomes even more staggering.

Sites such as DeviantArt and Tumblr host several hundred thousand original works of fanart for the series. At the time of writing, FanFiction.net alone lists more than 785,000 *Harry Potter* stories, almost twice as many as that of the next largest collection (Naruto, at around 421,000), and that's not to mention the massive quantities found on other multifandom fanfiction websites and *Harry Potter*-specific ones, such as the Sugar Quill. There have been multiple short- and full-length musicals based on the Wizarding World, and wizard rock is the only long-lasting, still-thriving, fandom-based music movement to date. There's even been a *Harry Potter*-inspired choreography and dance education project, Dance Against the Dark Arts (DADA), founded by my sister and I.

As an eighteen-year *Harry Potter* fan and someone who is fascinated by the process of artistic inspiration, I have spent a lot of time thinking about the reasons behind this prodigious creative output. As Melissa Anelli, author of *Harry, A History* (2008), writes, the fact that the publication of *Sorcerer's Stone* more or less coincided with the introduction of the Internet into most people's daily lives certainly played a role. But many other fandoms that have sprung up since that time have either produced only a relative trickle of fanworks or have experienced brief booms of creativity without *Harry Potter*'s staying power. I wondered momentarily whether a multi-decade, worldwide Creativity Charm could be at work, but that seems unlikely. Ultimately, it seems, the real reason for the tremendous and continued output of Potterverse fanworks is three-fold: the intricate structure of the Wizarding World lends itself to nearly unlimited exploration; the *Potter* community is so tightly connected that previous art continues to inspire new projects; and J. K. Rowling has taken an open, encouraging attitude towards reimaginations of her stories, rather than being either strongly against or ambivalent towards her fans' creative works.

Without a doubt, *Harry Potter*'s Wizarding World is one of the most sprawling, sophisticated fictional worlds in all of literature. It delves into education,

Surveying Fanworks:
Art, Dance, Fic, Music and Community
Madeline Wilson

government, medicine, sports, scientific research, retail companies, international cultures and history going back over a thousand years, in addition to the creatures, potions and magical theory that make the Potterverse distinct from other stories about witches and wizards. The epilogue of *Harry Potter and the Deathly Hallows* (Rowling, 2007) and the recent addition of *Harry Potter and the Cursed Child* (Rowling, Thorne and Tiffany, 2016) provide a structure for the future following the original series, which fans can accept or ignore as they choose. The Pottermore interactive website imparts even more canon and backstory for devoted fans, and the *Fantastic Beasts* arm of the franchise has provided a whole new offshoot, with more to come over the next several years.

This sets the Wizarding World apart from many other sprawling universes that have large fandom audiences, such as *Star Wars*, Marvel and DC Comics. Those worlds have been shaped and reshaped by many creative minds over multiple decades. I asked my sister, Alicia Wilson, a multifandom artist and author of both *Harry Potter* and Marvel fanfiction, about the differences among her favourite franchises, and she said, 'Marvel and comics in general kind of AU [Alternative Universe] themselves all the time,' while *Harry Potter* has mostly been one finite set of stories for most of its existence, and even its new branches are all products of the same author's brain. When you compare a fandom universe in which Lois Lane might or might not be married to Superman at any given time and also might or might not have her own superpowers, as Nicholson points out; or one in which Captain America has both fought against and worked for the evil Hydra organization, as Riesman points out; with a *Harry Potter* universe in which characters only follow one arc in the canon, it's certainly much easier for members of the *Potter* fandom to agree on the elements that make a fanwork look and feel like it's a part of Rowling's cohesive world.

There are three avenues by which fan creators can explore the Potterverse: sticking strictly to the established canon; veering off into totally AU territory; and carving a middle path by using some ideas from the canon and others that are unspecified or clearly AU.

With so many well-developed primary and secondary characters, there are nearly endless possibilities for creating new scenarios about Harry, Ron, Hermione, Luna, Neville, Draco and more, without contradicting established facts. Sometimes this translates to retellings of events depicted in Rowling's stories. For example, 'Ascendio' (2007), a song by the now-defunct band Ministry of Magic, is a first-person summary of Harry's state of mind through the first several chapters of *Sorcerer's Stone*, from assuming his life will always be unhappy to finding out that he's a wizard to realizing that Hogwarts is his true home. Aaron Nordyke, who penned the song, says it's his favourite of his wizard rock creations, explaining in an e-mail on 19 February 2018: 'I love stories about a kid who discovers something special about [them]self. Rags-to-riches stories.' And another hugely popular wizard rock song, 'Potions Yesterday' (2005) by Draco and the Malfoys, relates a number of embarrassments that Harry experiences during *Harry Potter and the Chamber of Secrets* (Rowling, 2002), from Draco's self-righteous point-of-view.

In addition to showing familiar events from different perspectives, canon-based Wizarding World explorations can also take place between events depicted by Rowling. As a fanfiction author myself, I've written a few stories that I call 'missing moments'; one that I'm quite proud of depicts an argument and subsequent reconciliation between Molly and Arthur Weasley after Arthur gets into the altercation with Lucius Malfoy at Flourish and Blotts in *Chamber of Secrets*.

One might think that adhering closely to the established canon severely limits a fan artist's opportunities, but this isn't the case. While there are many canon-based *Potter* stories across the Internet, the Sugar Quill fanfiction site plainly states that it has only ever accepted 'creative stories written by authors with a true desire to improve their writing that fit within the universe of *Harry Potter* canon', and it still gathered several thousand stories during its nearly ten years of activity. Any story, song or piece of art centring on, say, the idea that Lupin and Tonks fall in love and get married, or that Ginny grows up to play professional Quidditch, or that young Tom Riddle spent the first part of his life in an orphanage, falls into the canon-based category and still leaves its creator plenty of room to imagine what conversations would have taken place and what choices would have been made. In a Facebook message on 19 February 2018, fan artist Ashley Parson told me that she finds herself drawn to the period of the Potterverse when the Marauders were young, particularly 'Hogwarts in an era before there was the constant threat of Voldemort', and is making plans to paint a simple scene of James and Lily on a date.

As the direct opposite of canon-based fanworks, Alternative Universe creations offer the most freedom to their makers, because they can go in almost

Surveying Fanworks:
Art, Dance, Fic, Music and Community
Madeline Wilson

any direction, as long as there are a few basic ties to Rowling's world. A well-known example is the 122-chapter 'Harry Potter and the Methods of Rationality' (2010–ongoing) by Eliezer Yudkowsky (under the pen name Less Wrong), which is summarized thusly on FanFiction.net:

> *Petunia married a biochemist, and Harry grew up reading science and science fiction. Then came the Hogwarts letter, [sic] and a world of intriguing new possibilities to exploit. And new friends, like Hermione Granger, and Professor McGonagall, and Professor Quirrell.*

Another notable example of an AU fic is 'Weasley Girl' (originally published in 2012) by author Hyaroo, which begins with Harry meeting the Weasleys at King's Cross station, just as it happened in *Sorcerer's Stone* – except Ron is replaced by Veronica 'Ronnie' Weasley. AU art gives its creators the opportunity to ask 'what if…?' about one or more characters that make up their fandom, and the depth of the Potterverse lends itself perfectly to those sorts of reimaginings.

Another reason for the popularity of AU *Harry Potter* fan creations is the large number of fans who dislike the epilogue of *Deathly Hallows* and part or all of *Cursed Child*. In a Facebook message on 12 March 2018, fanfiction connoisseur Michelle Fink told me, '[t]here is nothing that appeals to me about even considering reading the epilogue kids' era stories.' AU gives its authors the opportunity to change a choice made by Rowling that they didn't like and rearrange things to their satisfaction, and Michelle is drawn to such stories 'to explore different dimensions' of the Wizarding World.

Beyond this are the creators who take the dimensions of the Wizarding World, grab hold of them and run amok with them until they've twisted and turned and tied those dimensions up in ridiculous knots and created an incredible musical trilogy full of Red Vines and Zac Efron posters that still manages to honour the witches, wizards and magical beasts that inspired it – I'm talking, of course, about Team StarKid and their *A Very Potter Musical* (Lang, Lang and Holden/Team StarKid, 2009) and its two sequels, which first collided headlong with the larger *Potter* fandom in the summer of 2009. There are recognizable elements from the *Harry Potter* books in each, but it's as if they've been put into a blender. The first act of *A Very Potter Musical* is basically the plot of *Harry Potter and the Goblet of Fire* (Rowling, 2000), with

Quirrell as Defence Against the Dark Arts teacher instead of Moody, while the second act is a combination of *Harry Potter and the Order of the Phoenix* (Rowling, 2003) and *Deathly Hallows*. *A Very Potter Sequel* (Lang, Lang and Holden/Team StarKid, 2010) begins after Voldemort's defeat, but the characters take a Time-Turner back to Harry's first year at Hogwarts, and from there the story loosely follows the plot of *Harry Potter and the Prisoner of Azkaban* (Rowling, 1999) with Professor Umbridge thrown in. *A Very Potter Senior Year* (Lang, Lang and Holden/Team StarKid, 2012) begins with the students fighting Death Eaters at the Ministry of Magic (as they do in *Order of the Phoenix*), but the rest of the show is mostly based on *Chamber of Secrets* with a few elements from *Deathly Hallows*. And then there's all the silly stuff: Draco is secretly in love with Hermione, spends a lot of time rolling around on the floor and really wants to go to a school called Pigfarts, which is located on Mars. Ron is eating a snack in nearly every scene. Lavender Brown is Asian, and Cho Chang is a white girl with a Southern American accent. Lucius Malfoy dances everywhere he goes. The Sorting Hat is joined by the Scarf of Sexual Preference. Quirrell and Voldemort are played by two actors standing back-to-back inside one costume. Parts of the *Very Potter* shows are so AU that their only tie to the original books is that Harry Potter is standing onstage, yet overall they are one giant monument to their creators' love of the Potterverse.

Between the canon-centric and the AU lie creations that are a mix of the two extremes. Sometimes they mostly adhere to the canon but deviate in one or more notable ways, and sometimes they feature events and character relationships that are neither stated in the canon nor ruled out by it. In a video chat interview on 23 March 2018, Alicia Wilson told me she tends to prefer fanworks of the former type, because she dislikes certain aspects of the *Potter* canon but loves others. She can't see Ron and Hermione having a lasting, healthy relationship, but she is a 'ride or die Ginny/Harry' fan. And while I generally try to stick closely to canon in my fanfiction, it just doesn't make any sense to me that James Potter would suddenly have become Head Boy after one moment of heroic guilt, when he had never been a prefect and his entire school career had been marked by mischief and irresponsibility. Therefore, in my Marauders-era story, Remus Lupin is Head Boy alongside Head Girl Lily Evans.

Canon-adjacent works are a wonderful way to explore and further flesh out characters whom we see only a little of in Rowling's stories, or those whom we only see in limited circumstances. A perfect example is Nymphadora Tonks:

Surveying Fanworks:
Art, Dance, Fic, Music and Community
Madeline Wilson

while she makes several appearances in the last three novels, we almost never see her when she is not working as an Auror or using her Auror training to help the Order of the Phoenix. Yet Steph Anderson has written five full-length albums, an EP and numerous other songs released on her Bandcamp site or as part of charity projects for her band Tonks and the Aurors. In an e-mail exchange on 21 February and 25 March 2018, she told me, 'I pull from everywhere [...] I have to draw inspiration where I can.' So in addition to songs about the various aspects of being in love with a werewolf and the daily life of an Auror, Steph has penned tracks about Tonks having a closer relationship with her cousin Sirius than we see in the books; a description of Tonks and Lupin's wedding day, which gets only the briefest mention in *Deathly Hallows*; and Tonks grieving the loss of her father, a character whom we only see twice in the entire series. Further, she's created one of my favourite headcanons in all of the Potterverse – the idea that Tonks dated Charlie Weasley while they were at school together, but they split up because Charlie was too interested in dragons to be a good boyfriend. I asked Steph about how she came up with this pairing, and she explained:

> When I started my band I did A LOT of research. In that research I found out that Tonks and Charlie would have been at Hogwarts together [...] and possibly in the same year. I connected a few other dots, thinking that Molly is way too familiar with Tonks as an OotP member, so she had to have met her before [...] [so] I decided to make this familiarity because Tonks and Charlie dated.

Steph believes that fanworks are important because 'we can and really should expand upon the universe' of the Wizarding World, a sentiment obviously shared by millions of *Potter* fans around the world. Many of them experience a feeling expressed by fanfiction reader and writer April Simms. In an e-mail on 25 March, she told me, '*Harry Potter* isn't just some *thing* that I like. It almost feels like it's a part of who I am. What really inspired me to create things for this fandom was a yearning to be a part of that world' (original emphasis).

For some *Potter* fans, that yearning means mixing up aspects of characters with whom they identify on one level so they can connect with that character on other levels as well. Perhaps the most famous example of this is 'racebent Hermione', or the depiction of Hermione as a person of colour.

Although Emma Watson, a white actor, played Hermione in the films and the character is almost always depicted as white in official illustrations, her race is never definitively stated in the books. In the only explicit canon reference to her skin colour, she is described as 'very brown' in *Prizoner of Azkaban* after spending the summer on the sunny French coast, which would cause most people's skin to darken a bit, regardless of their natural hue. (She is also once described as 'white' when she is very scared in *Prisoner of Azkaban*, calling to mind non-race-related colloquial expressions such as 'white as a sheet' or 'white as a ghost'.) Because the *Harry Potter* series has touched lives literally all around the world, it's no surprise that there is a vast quantity of fanart depicting Hermione as non-white across the Internet, and, according to Bennett, there has been long before Noma Dumezweni was cast to play the character in *Cursed Child*.

For other fan creators, their longing to enter Harry's world translates into a desire to weave their own narrative within Rowling's by creating an original character and dropping him or her into some portion of Harry's story. Many fanfiction readers scoff at the innumerable variations on the theme of 'a mysterious American student arrives at Hogwarts during Harry's third year', which are often more indulgent than unique or clever. Still, people keep writing them, and April Simms enjoys seeing 'how the story changes around them and because of them'. Even when the original character is obviously a Mary Sue, a barely disguised stand-in for the author, April said, 'I love Mary Sues and there's nothing wrong with wish-fulfillment stories, because who doesn't wish to be a part of this world?'

Being part of a sprawling, worldwide fandom is, in many ways, almost as good as being an actual Hogwarts student, because an enormous variety of new creative fanworks keeps appearing. The stories and characters of Harry Potter's world are certainly the base inspiration for all the paintings, songs, scripts, fanfictions and more, but at this point, it's not at all surprising that older fanworks have begun sparking newer ones. Steph, for example, was already an independent musician and a *Harry Potter* fan when she found the band Harry and the Potters online. Nonetheless, she told me, 'I actually was a fan of wizard rock for years before I finally stopped talking about it and just DID IT.'

In some cases, creators had already done a little *Potter*-inspired creating but were encouraged to take their crafts seriously by discovering how much success other fan artists were achieving. Alicia Wilson has loved to draw since

Surveying Fanworks:
Art, Dance, Fic, Music and Community
Madeline Wilson

Figure 1: 'The Weasley Family' by Alicia Wilson, drawn for the fanfic 'Part of the Family' by Madeline Wilson (2010).

she was old enough to hold a pencil, and when she was introduced to the Potterverse at age 8, she began creating organically, drawing characters and scenes from the series just as she drew pictures of other things she liked. But she cites artist Frankie 'Frak' Franco III and his work as her inspiration for actually considering herself as a 'fan artist' and thinking of her wizarding creations as more than just doodles. In a similar way, Aaron Nordyke told me that he and his friends Luke Conard and Jason Munday had already been making 'nerdy electronica music' about topics such as World of Warcraft for some time when Luke happened to write a song about Ron and Hermione being in love. They were completely unaware of the phenomenon of wizard rock, but wrock fans found Luke's song, 'Accio Love' (2007), and 'filled him in [on] what was happening'. Aaron said, 'Luke told Jason and I about wizard rock, and he asked if we wanted to write a bunch of songs exclusively about *Harry Potter*. We said yes and ended up creating four albums of original music.'

Sometimes fan creations in one medium can inspire works in another. Unsurprisingly, it's quite common for fanfiction to inspire fanart and vice-versa. For example, the painting of Lily Evans and James Potter on a date that Ashley Parson is planning to create was directly inspired by a Marauders-era fanfiction that she really enjoyed. And after reading a short story I had written about the Weasleys at Christmastime when Teddy Lupin was a young boy, Alicia illustrated a perfectly imperfect Weasley family portrait, just as I had described it.

And then there's the art inspired by the realization that the fandom is lacking something. Attending *LeakyCon 2009* was my first big introduction to the fandom that existed outside of my sister and my adolescent group of friends. I saw my first wizard rock shows; walked through my first gallery of fanart; attended programmes about *Potter*-based social justice movements and met adults of all ages who took fanfictions as seriously as if they were original writing projects. There was even a performance of a short musical based on 'The Fountain of Fair Fortune' from *The Tales of Beedle the Bard* (Rowling, 2008). But as I looked around and saw nearly everything I had never realized I really wanted, I noticed a glaring lack of dancers in the fandom.

I took my first ballet class when I was in preschool and haven't stopped dancing since, eventually studying multiple styles multiple times a week. Further, I knew most of the friends I had made through dance were *Harry Potter* fans on some level. It was astonishing to me that I hadn't seen or heard anything about dancers at *LeakyCon*, and I mulled over that gaping hole in the fandom for weeks, from the convention in late May until late July when I drove to Chicago with my parents to pick my sister up from her summer intensive ballet programme. As we were heading back to Ohio after seeing an incredible *Harry Potter* exhibition at the Chicago Museum of Science and Industry, I told Alicia that she and I needed to start some kind of wizarding dance project. We brainstormed for much of the drive home, coming up with the name 'Dance Against the Dark Arts' and listing numerous wrock songs and pieces from the film soundtracks that we wanted to use for choreography. By the time *Leaky-Con 2011* rolled around (there wasn't one in 2010), we had developed and prepared to present a 50-minute-long dance workshop, featuring three dance combinations set to wizard rock and an exercise about using the tools of one's body to portray a variety of characters. We were hoping ten or twelve people would come, and we were blown away when more than twice that many turned up! Over the years we've created five more original Dance Against the Dark Arts workshops, and we've also presented pared-down versions of some of our programmes at community *Harry Potter* festivals. DADA has been on hiatus for a couple of years as Alicia and I have each got busy with jobs at dance studios and other elements of life, but we're both sure that we're not finished with our *Harry Potter* dance project.

Of course, hardly any of the vast creative output of the *Potter* fandom could have reached its audience without the blessing of J. K. Rowling. She has been notably permissive towards the use of her characters, settings and stories in semi-original works, which contrasts strikingly with the attitude taken by certain other authors. Anne Rice, author of the *Vampire Chronicles* series (1976-ongoing), has been vehemently and loudly opposed to fanfiction throughout her entire career, to the point of irritating many fan creators. After reading *The Queen of the Damned* (1988), the third instalment of the *Vampire Chronicles*, April Simms told me, 'I had this idea for a story. I wanted to write about it, but Anne Rice pursues people who create fanfiction with such malicious intent that it's not even worth it. It makes me dislike her writing.' Orson Scott Card, best known for writing *Ender's Game* (1985), has also been known for railing against fans creating their own interpretations of his works, despite the fact that he himself contributed a story to a collection of Isaac Asimov-inspired

Surveying Fanworks:
Art, Dance, Fic, Music and Community
Madeline Wilson

*Figure 2: Madeline Wilson,
Alicia Wilson and Emily
Edwards at* LeakyCon 2011.

fanfiction that was legally published in 1989. In 2004, he wrote on his official website that writing fanfiction based on his work was 'morally identical to moving into my house without invitation and throwing out my family'. However, he eventually changed his mind, although not necessarily for the purpose of championing creativity. In 2012, he created a contest for fanfictions about his work and told the *Wall Street Journal*: 'Every piece of fan fiction is an ad for my book. What kind of idiot would I be to want that to disappear?' (cited by Romano).

The *Potter* fandom is extremely fortunate, therefore, to have a chief architect who is so open to and encouraging of its creativity with her fictional world, a fact that most of its participants are well aware of and grateful for. Steph Anderson noted,

> We can't create fan works unless the creator is either agnostic or supportive of it. J.K. Rowling's encouragement of most fan works has helped, as the WB [Warner Brothers] was going to shut down all fan works and fan sites at one point, which most likely would have killed wizard rock.

Steph was referring to a series of events collectively known as 'PotterWar'. In the early days of the web, when the ability to transmit words and images to the other side of the globe in a second or less was brand new to most people, those with a vested interest in intellectual property rights quickly realized that laws protecting such rights were woefully behind the times. Further, the fact that anyone (children, teens or adults) would want to create whole websites about *Harry Potter*, often with a mishmash of original thoughts and content pulled straight from Rowling's books, was surprising to Rowling at first. She initially took a relaxed view of fans celebrating her work online, but she did worry about people who might infringe on her rights as a creator, so she was rather relieved when Warner Brothers acquired the rights to *Harry Potter* properties and told her they were going to 'corral, loosely, the fan sites', Anelli writes. However, when Warner Brothers sent out its standard cease-and-desist letters to numerous fansite webmasters, many of whom were kids, they read as if they were going to take away people's livelihoods and sue them for everything they had. After much furore, back-and-forths among lawyers on all sides and a flurry of critical press pieces, Warner Brothers 'backed off' (Anelli). In 2004, a spokesman for the Christopher Little Agency, which represents Rowling, stated that she was 'flattered by the fact there is such great interest in her *Harry Potter* series' and that she was only concerned that fanworks are not obscene, 'fans are not exploited, and [fanfiction] is not being published in the strict sense of traditional print publishing' (cited by Waters).

These days, while many fan creators still feel that Warner Brothers is too overzealous in labelling certain things as copyright infringement, the fandom as a whole has become pretty adept at negotiating potential pitfalls and educating newcomers on how to create without infringement, as well as how to protect their own fanworks. Rowling maintains her encouraging attitude towards fanworks, even wading into the controversial racebent Hermione debate, tweeting out: 'Canon: brown eyes, frizzy hair and very clever. White skin was never specified. Rowling loves black Hermione', in December 2015. Her continued support for her fans' creativity guarantees that the constant stream of *Harry Potter* fanworks isn't likely to stop any time soon. Ashley Parson said, 'I think it makes a huge difference knowing that she encourages fans to be [a part] of what she started. It makes me feel a level of acceptance that I haven't gotten with other fandoms'. Alicia Wilson agrees, saying Rowling's encouragement makes her 'appreciate [the Wizarding] world even more, because it makes me feel appreciated as a creator by the ultimate creator, even if she never sees my stuff'.

J. K. Rowling could easily have stopped writing after her first four books

Surveying Fanworks:
Art, Dance, Fic, Music and Community
Madeline Wilson

and she would have been set for life financially, but she continued with the se-ries and other *Potter*-related endeavours because she so loves the characters and the world she created. Given the amount of time that most fan creators spend brainstorming, planning, producing and promoting their works for lit-tle or no financial payoff, it's safe to assume they wouldn't keep coming back to *Harry Potter* if they didn't truly love the source material and the fandom itself. We've seen Harry's story, which began as nothing but literature, expand time and again until it encompassed literally all of the creative arts. And as the fandom continues to expand – as more and more people pick up *Sorcerer's Stone* and go on to discover *Potter* fanfiction, *A Very Potter Musical* and ar-chives of art and other creative projects – we certainly can't expect the output of fanworks to decrease. The creativity of the Potterverse and the volume of works it produces will continue as long as there are *Potter* fans – which is to say, forever. ●

GO FURTHER

Books
Harry, A History
Melissa Anelli
(New York: Pocket Books, 2008)

The Spectacular Sisterhood of Superwomen
Hope Nicholson
(Philadelphia: Quirk Books, 2017)

Harry Potter and the Prisoner of Azkaban
J. K. Rowling
(New York: Scholastic, 1999)

Online
'What a "Racebent" Hermione Granger Really Represents'
Alanna Bennett
BuzzFeed. 1 February 2015, https://www.buzzfeed.com/alannabennett/what-a- race-bent-hermione- granger-really-represen-.

'OSC Answers Questions'
Orson Scott Card
Hatrack River – The Official Website of Orson Scott Card. 19 July 2004, http://www.hatrack.com/research/questions/q0121.shtml.

'Harry Potter'
Chimera9
DeviantArt, https://www.deviantart.com/chimera9/art/Harry-Potter-67629678.

'Harry Potter Girls'
harry-potter-fanclub
DeviantArt, https://www.deviantart.com/harry-potter-fanclub/art/Harry-Potter-Girls-99259813.

'Weasley Girl'
Hyaroo
FanFiction.net. 17 December 2013, https://www.fanfiction.net/s/8202739/ 1/Weasley-Girl.

'Harry Potter: A Tribute'
MoPotter
DeviantArt, https://www.deviantart.com/mopotter/art/Harry-Potter-A-Trib-ute-228851619.

'Harry Potter tumblr sketchdump'
nastjastark
DeviantArt, https://www.deviantart.com/nastjastark/art/Harry-Potter-tumblr-sketch-dump-589027160.

Surveying Fanworks:
Art, Dance, Fic, Music and Community
Madeline Wilson

'When in Doubt, Go to the Library'
Peace of Seoul
Tumblr. 12 August 2018, http://peaceofseoul.tumblr.com/post/176928294149/when-in-doubt-go-to-the-library.

'Hogwarts students were about to face the worst test of…'
potterbyblvnk
Tumblr. n.d., http://blvnk-art.tumblr.com/post/160569595004/hogwarts-students-were-about-to-face-the-worst.

'First Captain America Became Evil, then the Comics World Erupted'
Abraham Riesman
Vulture. 27 June 2017, http://www.vulture.com/2017/06/marvel-hydra- captain-america-nick- spencer.html.

'A Guide to Fandom's Complicated Relationship with Orson Scott Card'
Aja Romano
Daily Dot. 7 May 2013, https://www.dailydot.com/society/orson-scott-card-enders-game-fandom-anti-gay/.

'Canon: Brown Eyes, Frizzy Hair and Very Clever. White Skin Was Never Specified. Rowling Loves Black Hermione :-* https://twitter.com/mauvedust /status/67585906528 5812224…'
J. K. Rowling (@jk_rowling)
Twitter. 21 December 2015, https://twitter.com/jk_rowling/status/678888094339366914?lang=en.

'POTTER'
Savannahrcb
DeviantArt, https://www.deviantart.com/savannahrcb/art/POTTER-507211189.

'Rowling Backs Potter Fan Fiction'
Darren Waters
BBC News. 27 May 2004, http://news.bbc.co.uk/2/hi/entertainment/3753001.stm.

'Harry Potter and the Methods of Rationality'
Less Wrong (Eliezer Yudkowsky)
FanFiction.net. 28 February 2010, https://www.fanfiction.net/s/5782108/1/Harry-
Potter- and-the-Methods-of- Rationality.

'Ask Madam Pince'. The Sugar Quill, 5 August 2007, http://www.sugarquill.net/index.
php?action=ask.

Websites
Dance Against the Dark Arts (DADA), https://www.facebook.com/DanceAgainstThe-
DarkArts/
FanFiction.net, https://www.fanfiction.net
Fiction Alley: Creativity is Magic, http://www.fictionalley.org/authors/
Harry Potter and the Methods of Rationality, http://www.hpmor.com
Harry Potter Fanfiction, https://harrypotterfanfiction.com/
The Sugar Quill, http://www.sugarquill.net
Tonks and the Aurors, https://tonksandtheaurors.bandcamp.com/

Musicals
A Very Potter Musical, Matt Lang, Nick Lang and Brian Holden (University of Michigan,
Ann Arbor: Team StarKid, 9–11 April 2009).

A Very Potter Sequel, Matt Lang, Nick Lang and Brian Holden (University of Michigan,
Ann Arbor: Team StarKid, 14–16 May 2010).

A Very Potter Senior Year, Matt Lang, Nick Lang and Brian Holden (Leakycon 2012:
Hilton, Chicago: Team StarKid, 11 August 2012).

Music
'Accio Love'
Luke Conard
In *The Triwizard LP*, Ministry of Magic (Indytronic Records, 2007).

Surveying Fanworks:
Art, Dance, Fic, Music and Community
Madeline Wilson

'Potions Yesterday'
Draco and the Malfoys
In *Draco and the Malfoys*, Draco and the Malfoys (2005).

'Ascendio'
Aaron Nordyke
In *The Triwizard LP*, Ministry of Magic (Indytronic Records, 2007).

'GIVE HER HELL FROM US, PEEVES!'

THE WEASLEY TWINS
(*HARRY POTTER AND THE ORDER OF THE PHOENIX*)

Fan Appreciation #1
A. J. Holmes (composer, Team StarKid)
Aya Esther Hayashi

A. J. Holmes' headshot (2009).

Team StarKid burst onto the *Harry Potter* fandom in the spring of 2009 when the young musical theatre troupe – helmed by University of Michigan–Ann Arbor theatre students Matt and Nick Lang – released and uploaded as a means to share the parody musical with their friends and family, *A Very Potter Musical (AVPM)* quickly spread among the online-networked *Potter* fan communities. The creative team realized that the musical had a much larger audience than anticipated, so they polished up its production and reuploaded it to YouTube in June 2009. The show was renamed *A Very Potter Musical*, to avoid any accusations of copyright infringement, and quickly went viral again. *A Very Potter Musical*'s Internet success allowed Team StarKid to catch the attention of the mainstream entertainment industry, and the musical made it onto *Entertainment Weekly*'s list of best viral videos of 2009. After graduating, the Langs – along with Darren Criss (later of *Glee* [2009–15] fame) and Brian Holden – consolidated Team StarKid into an official theatre company based in Chicago. In addition to the three productions created at the University of Michigan (*Me and My Dick* [2009] and *A Very Potter Sequel* [2010]), Team StarKid produced another eight parody musicals (including a third *AVPM* sequel, *A Very Potter Senior Year* [2012]), two concert tours and three sketch comedy shows through 2016.

A. J. Holmes is, perhaps, best known in the *Harry Potter* fandom for his work as a composer with Team StarKid, contributing music and lyrics to *A Very Potter Musical*, *Me and My Dick* and *A Very Potter Senior Year*, and serving as the sole composer for *Twisted: The Untold Story of a Royal Vizier* (2013). Musically trained from a young age, A. J. focused on jazz piano and improvisation and performed on a comedy improv team in high school. He attended the School of Music (now the School of Music, Theatre and Dance) at the University of Michigan, majoring in musical theatre performance, and it was there that he met Team StarKid's founding members, Nick and Matt Lang.

Since graduating, Holmes has worked as a professional actor, having spent the last five years with the company behind *The Book of Mormon* (2017–ongoing). Currently, he is starring as Elder Cunningham in the Sydney production. Through a series of fortunate events, I was able to interview him for my dissertation chapter on Team StarKid when he was starring in the London production back in 2014. Our acquaintance has continued over the years, and he graciously agreed to sit down to a Google Video interview, despite the significant time difference between New York City and Sydney, Australia.

Fan Appreciation #1
A.J. Holmes

Aya Esther Hayashi (AEH): Thank you so much for agreeing to do this interview, A. J. It'll help to rehash a bit from our first interview. How did your involvement with Team StarKid begin?

A. J. Holmes (AJH): It was in 2008, during my sophomore year of college at the University of Michigan–Ann Arbor. I was still a motivated student, and Basement Arts[1] were holding their annual 24-hour script challenge. I wanted to be the asshole who did a musical, but I would need a book writer. I asked the people setting it up if they knew a book writer, and they put me in touch with Matt [Lang]. And I just met him. He said, 'I have this idea about a play with a bunch of penises called *The Penis Play*.' And that night, we wrote a twenty-minute version of *The Penis Play*, which eventually became *Me and My Dick*. So yeah, that's how I met Matt. We came together a few times in the night. At the beginning, we talked through the whole thing, and then he went off, and I went off. We were basically alone the whole night trying to figure it out. We came together once and then kept going. *(Laughs)* That was a lot of fun.

After that, Matt and Nick Lang approached me about writing some songs for a *Harry Potter* musical. They knew they had Darren [Criss] writing the songs. But I think they realized that, knowing Darren, it could help to have other people writing some songs as well. So they said, 'would you write some songs for it too?' And that was that.

AEH: What were your expectations for the project?

AJH: Very little. It was just a lot of fun because nobody could have anticipated what it became.

AEH: Can you describe what writing for the project was like?

AJH: *A Very Potter Musical* had a much more serious start, and it became more ridiculous as the project went on. I initially wrote an opening number that was a lot sincerer. It went *(singing)*, 'I'm going back to Hogwarts / Back to Dumbledore / Some other halls are exciting and all, but there's one hall that's great, I'm sure / I'm going back to Hogwarts / Back to my home / Hogwarts, my home.' 'Different as Can Be' was the first song that made it into the production.

AEH: Did you and Darren work together on certain things?

AJH: Not really. I kind of look back and kick myself about it. I wrote my songs, and he wrote his songs and we brought them in. [As music director] I played all of the songs, so I had to learn his songs and teach them to the band and stuff. There was this one night, when he tried to teach us all 'Granger Danger'. It was like, two in the morning. I walk into Studio 1 and none of us had any music written down, so he was just trying to teach it to us by playing it. *(Laughs)* We were all just not getting it at all, and it took so much longer than it should have taken. Looking back on it, I get the song. It's in G-flat, and we were like, 'Ugh, this is taking so long!' *(Laughs)*

AEH: That's such a musical theatre thing to do, to write a song in G-flat.

AJH: Right? I should have been able to do it. It was a great song. It just took forever. So that was fun.

AEH: Do you have any other favourite rehearsal moments or songs?

AJH: My favourite song to write and teach was 'To Dance Again!' I had just finished the song the night before I taught it to the cast, and it was a cool experience to watch it get put into the scene immediately. I mean that's what was so cool. I would be furiously working on songs, bring them in and they would get put in immediately. I could see them transfer so quickly from my brain to the stage with the cast doing it. Also, 'Voldemort's Going Down' worked like that. That was less than a week before the show opened that I brought that in, and I remember going, 'Oh boy, here we go!' Everybody learned it so fast. The turnaround time was probably the coolest part.

AEH: What was the initial reaction to *The Harry Potter Musical*?[2] When did you start to notice that it had reached a larger audience?

AJH: Very enthusiastic. The performances all sold out, and lines formed around the whole building. It was the longest line I'd ever seen for a Basement Arts show. We were over the moon about it. I didn't realize the advertising had been that good for the show. I don't think it was, actually. Word just got out about a *Harry Potter* musical, so people who had never seen a Basement Arts show before, who had never been to the theatre school before, were showing up because they were *Harry Potter* fans. We actually added a performance, and all the actors cut into their spring break to do it.

Fan Appreciation #1
A.J. Holmes

AEH: When did you start to notice that it had reached a larger audience?

AJH: I didn't have anything to do with the decision to put it on YouTube. It was initially put up as a way for our friends and family to watch it, but then it blew up. We were following the comments online and watching it blow up in front of our eyes. We had a sense that it was becoming something almost from the moment it went online. Aside from that, I experienced very little of the fan following personally.

AEH: Did your Twitter followers increase?

AJH: Oh, by thousands. But it wasn't until *LeakyCon* [in 2012] that I experienced the Team StarKid fanbase in person, en masse, which was overwhelming in its own way.

AEH: You composed some of the music for *A Very Potter Senior Year*, and then went to *LeakyCon 2012* for the reading where you played Professor Lockhart. What was that whole experience like?

AJH: I wrote very few of the songs. I found that there was an online contest to write a song, and I was initially like, 'Hey, isn't that my job?' I was writing songs up until I left for Chicago. I wrote the wizard duel song ('The School Is Mine') all night before I went to Chicago. I also wrote 'Always Dance', which made sense since it was a musical follow-up to 'To Dance Again'. The actors were excited, started to memorize and not hold onto their scripts. We had full costumes and stuff. I finally said to Nick and Matt, 'We can either do a staged reading well or do a full production poorly.' If you're not holding a script, you're giving the impression that you're doing a full production, and we didn't have the time to prepare that. If you have a script in hand, it sets the bar, and the production could only get better from there. Obviously, for the more emotional moments, we put the scripts down.

We put the whole thing together in a few days at the convention. We had twelve-hour rehearsals, and it was like a five-hour play. It was also the largest audience I've ever performed for. I remember looking side-to-side and seeing the room packed.

AEH: I understand that Evanna Lynch joined you all and reprised her role as Luna Lovegood. What was it like working with her?

AJH: Evanna was wonderful to work with. We all loved hanging out with her. She had a big job of having the first solo in the whole show, so we all give her lots of kudos for that! Really just can't say enough good things about her.

AEH: Out of the four Team StarKid productions that you have worked on, what was your favourite or the most rewarding?

AJH: *Twisted*[3] is my favourite because I had Kaley [McMahon] as my lyricist, Justin [Fischer] as my music director and Andrew [Fox] as my orchestrator. It was *my* team, a full music team. I had the most time to work on it. In the most idealistic version of myself, I've always been trying to push Team StarKid towards the more fully integrated musical, using the music to advance the story. I really felt like we could flesh out the musical elements of that show more than any other show because we had the money to do it and the time to do it. I just really loved that show.

A Very Potter Musical was a mish-mash of [musical] styles, the most slapdash of the bunch. It was just thrown together, which created its own charm, and we had no idea what it would turn into. I had so much fun working with Matt and Nick on Lockhart's scenes in *A Very Potter Senior Year*. Gilderoy was the coolest part ever, and I wish we could have done a run of that show because I loved being that guy who ran to the piano, played and sang songs, and made fun of Darren [as Harry]. There was no time for drama with that show because we just had to put it together.

Usually, that's what bogs [the process] down. We're all kids, and we're all trying to be in charge of each other. It's hard. When you're being managed, you find anything to criticize.

Me and My Dick was also fun because I got to collaborate [on the music and lyrics] with Carlos Valdes. I still hope we can extend that one, one day. I think it's such a fun show. Basically, I liked all the shows but for different reasons.

Fan Appreciation #1
A.J. Holmes

AEH: Are there any plans to revise or give a future life to any of these shows beyond their initial incarnations?

AJH: There are none right now. We have talked about doing a 90-minute, one-act version of *Me and My Dick* that we think would work pretty well. Carlos and I even went to Chicago for a couple of weeks and worked on it. We wrote a new opening number. That's about as far as we got. And *Twisted*, we had dreams of doing it again.[4] At the moment, it's being licensed by random little companies all around the world, which is fine, but not what we hoped for with it. We still carry the disappointment of that. But I'm not *there*, so it's hard. I would love to do it again one day. I would love to do any of these again one day.

AEH: With the licensing, who is behind that?

AJH: It's the writers… me, Kaley, Eric [Kahn Gale], Matt and Nick. Making pennies on the dollar. There was a production in Germany, and there's one happening in the Bronx, a small theatre company.

AEH: What has been the craziest or most fun experience that you have had because of your affiliation with TSK?

AJH: Well, just yesterday, there were ten StarKid fans at the *Book of Mormon* stage door, which is crazy considering it's been nine years. Other than that, perhaps *LeakyCon*.

AEH: Has being involved with StarKid had an effect on your career as a working actor?

AJH: Not that I've experienced directly, but I have spent the last five years working on the same show [*Book of Mormon*]. I haven't tried a Kickstarter for my own work, but I'm interested in seeing the potential of the StarKid audience for that.

AEH: Are you currently working on any compositional projects? Or any that you're willing to talk about?

AJH: I have a musical project in works with Kaley, Matt and Nick. We're not ready to announce the topic, but we're working on it.

AEH: Is it similar to the parody that Team StarKid has done before?

AJH: No, this is an original musical comedy, not parody. We're not doing it through StarKid. We're letting it simmer slowly. We haven't touched it in a while, so we've got to check the oven soon. *(Laughs)*

AEH: Do you hope to do an independent Kickstarter sort-of-thing with it?

AJH: We haven't thought anything that far in advance. We just want to spend time writing something without focusing on a production at all really.

AEH: I assume that that was probably the most stressful part with *Twisted*?

AJH: Deadlines are helpful, but they're also... Musicals take time. *Book of Mormon* took five or six years to germinate before it got to Broadway. It would be nice to take the time to write something without needing to finish it in a slapdash way.

AEH: ... To really take the time to knit it together.

AJH: Yeah, to make it everything it can be, and then, go and get a production out of it.

AEH: Very cool. Well, to end this interview, I have some rapid-fire *Potter* fan questions for you. That okay?

AJH: Sure!

AEH: To start, what's your favourite *Harry Potter* novel?

AJH: *Prisoner of Azkaban* [Rowling, 1999]. That's when Sirius and Lupin were introduced, right?

AEH: Yep! This is, perhaps, an obvious question. Do you prefer the books or the films?

Fan Appreciation #1
A.J. Holmes

AJH: Books. I was given books one to three together in a set. After that, I went to all the midnight releases for books four through seven. To be honest, I actually haven't seen all the movies.

AEH: Who is your favourite character?

AJH: Sirius, the loving godfather.

AEH: To which Hogwarts House do you belong?

AJH: Gryffindor. I think I've always been the golden boy who wants to be the best. It's a pretty simple narrative structure. I appreciate the primary colours of Gryffindor too.

AEH: If you could attend Hogwarts, what magical course would you want to take?

AJH: Defence Against Dark Arts... but only with Lupin!

AEH: If you could have any creature as your Patronus, what would it be?

AJH: Wolf... or a dog.

AEH: Lastly, if we want to keep up with you and your career, where should we go?

AJH: You can follow me on Twitter (@ajholmesmusic), Instagram (@a.j.holmes) or just follow me on Facebook (https://www.facebook.com/AJ-Holmes-180763885365268/).

AEH: Fantastic. Thank you so much for your time! ●

~~~~~~~~~

GO FURTHER

Online
'The 10 Best Viral Videos of 2009'
Margaret Lyons
Entertainment Weekly. 29 December 2009,
http://www.ew.com/article/2009/12/29/best-viral-videos-of-2009.

Website
StarKid Songbook, http://starkidsongs.blogspot.com

Musicals
A Very Potter Musical, music and lyrics by Darren Criss and A. J. Holmes, book by Matt Lang, Nick Lang and Brian Holden
(University of Michigan, Ann Arbor: Team StarKid, 9–11 April 2009).

Me and My Dick, music and lyrics by A.J. Holmes, Carlos Valdes and Darren Criss, book by Matt Lang, Nick Lang, Brian Holden and Eric Kahn Gale
(University of Michigan, Ann Arbor: Team StarKid, 29–31 October 2009).

A Very Potter Sequel, music and lyrics by Darren Criss, book by Matt Lang, Nick Lang and Brian Holden
(University of Michigan, Ann Arbor: Team StarKid, 14–16 May 2010).

A Very Potter Senior Year, music and lyrics by Clark Baxtresser, Pierce Siebers, A. J. Holmes and Darren Criss, book by Matt Lang, Nick Lang and Brian Holden
(Leakycon, Chicago Hilton: Team StarKid, 11 August 2012).

Twisted: The Untold Story of a Royal Vizier, music by A. J. Holmes, lyrics by Kaley McMahon, book by Matt Lang, Nick Lang and Eric Kahn Gale
(Chicago Greenhouse Theatre: TeamStarKid, 4–28 July 2013).

Notes
[1] Basement Arts is a student-run theatre organization on campus. Aspiring writers can participate in annual challenges like the '24-Hour Play' and submit their works to be considered for full productions during the academic year. If accepted, creators receive a $100 budget to produce their work at the Studio One Theatre on campus.

[2] *A Very Potter Musical* was originally titled *The Harry Potter Musical*. The Langs decided to change the name after the production's video went viral on YouTube to avoid copyright infringement claims.

[3] Featuring a book by Matt Lang, Nick Lang and Eric Kahn Gale, *Twisted* was Team StarKid's seventh full production. Analogous to the relationship between Stephen Schwartz's megamusical *Wicked* (2003) and Frank L. Baum's *The Wonderful Wizard of Oz* (1900) and its iconic 1939 film adaptation, *Twisted* reframes the story of Disney's *Aladdin* (1992) by making Ja'far (spelling of name adjusted for copyright reasons) the hero of the story. He is a well-meaning city official who, despite his best efforts, is blamed for the failings of the kingdom's government. It does not alter any of the original plot, but it offers unseen moments before, during and after the movie as well as different interpretations of overlapping events.

[4] In March 2014, the music team also produced an abridged concert version of *Twisted* at Studio 54 in New York City, which sold out both nights. They hoped to find a producer to finance an Off-Broadway production, but sadly, nothing came of it.

Part 2
Virtual World

Chapter
03

Polyjuice and Potterheads: The Changing Face of Fandom from LiveJournal to Tumblr

Emily E. Roach

→ The *Harry Potter* fandom is an increasingly fragmented space in 'the era of the un-death', as Alanna Bennett writes. Instead of disappearing into obscurity following the release of the final film, the series has been reinvigorated by the emergence of new material, most notably the five projected *Fantastic Beasts* films, the first of which was released in 2016 (Yates, dir.), and the two-part play *Harry Potter and the Cursed Child* (Rowling, Thorne and Tiffany, 2016), which was first staged in London in the same year.

Figure 1: Shana Mosella, Anime Los Angeles 2017 in Ontario.

These new releases have contributed to the sense of disconnect, as they have proved divisive. For some, the new material offers a welcome and exciting supplement to a much-loved canon. Others have criticized the new additions for failing to offer meaningful diversity, for poor casting decisions and narrative arcs that seem at odds with the ethos of the book series, with its messages of inclusion and J. K. Rowling's public support of marginalized communities. *Fantastic Beasts* and *Cursed Child* were both released to much media furore. Still, although the heightened activity in 2016 has certainly made it feel as though there is a new wave of *Potter*-related content, post-canon additions are not exactly new. Following the publication of the final book in 2007 and the release of the final film in 2011, a steady stream of post-canon information has been fed to the public in snippets, through J. K. Rowling's digital publishing news company, Pottermore, and her personal Twitter feed. The magic of the Potterverse has lost a little of its lustre and some fans who grew up with *Harry Potter* are questioning their continued investment in the series. In her article, 'The *Harry Potter* Fandom Is at a Crossroads' (2016), Bennett identifies the 'growing pains that come with a fandom that has, by and large, become adults', and notes that 'the fandom that made Harry Potter an icon is now deciding if the continued investment that began in 1997 is worth it'. As new fans enter the community and old fans grapple with their place within it, there is something of a crisis moment at which a disparate group of people operating across multiple platforms are looking for that robust sense of fellowship that the *Harry Potter* world has always provided.

As one of the Internet's oldest behemoth fandoms, *Harry Potter* is also experiencing a spatial disconnect due to the emergence of, and migration to, new online platforms. The increasingly immersive spaces of microblogging and blogging platforms like Twitter and Tumblr have attracted new participants who operate exclusively on these platforms. Moderated fandom communities, fests designed to encourage content creation based around a theme or 'ship' (parlance for relationship) and individual participants are being faced with an increasingly disparate array of platform options for fandom participation. Some of those who started out operating on older Internet plat-

Polyjuice and Potterheads:
The Changing Face of Fandom from
LiveJournal to Tumblr
Emily E. Roach

forms are struggling to reconcile the Tumblr-oriented style of fandom with the way it operated on the journals such as the popular Livejournal, while some who started on Tumblr view the journals as archaic and not particularly user-friendly. Participants from various corners of the *Harry Potter* fandom and my own observations as an active writer, fest and community moderator all reveal where the fandom is heading. In fact, early studies of trends in changing platforms suggest that *Harry Potter* fandom is at something of a crisis point with constantly evolving content and online spaces. I conclude by taking a (tea) leaf from Sybil Trelawny's book and offering some thoughts on the future.

Owls, howlers and the restricted section: Mailing lists and early archives
Rebecca Busker notes that 'participatory media fandom, defined as those fan activities and communities centered around the creation, consumption, and discussion of fannish product [...] has used a variety of media and technology to facilitate these activities and communities over its history'. Francesca Coppa echoes this observation, explaining that 'fans have [...] always been early adopters of technology, and so have communicated with each other via every conceivable platform'. *Harry Potter* fandom is certainly no exception. It was one of the first and certainly best-known early fandom communities to originate almost entirely online. Unlike other large media fandoms that preceded it (e.g. *Blake's 7*, *Star Trek*, *Starsky and Hutch* and *Man from U.N.C.L.E.*), *Harry Potter* fanzines and *doujinshis* (Japanese self-published works) were the exception, rather than the norm. The book series coincided with Internet usage becoming increasingly commonplace, and as such, the part of the community focused on facilitating transformative works of fanart, fanfiction, fanvids and roleplaying games (RPGs) has always primarily operated in digital spaces. Although it is difficult to be certain of precise dates, the first piece of *Harry Potter* fanfiction is believed to have been published around 1999 by Gypsy, who was also the first *Harry Potter* archivist at harrypotterrealm.com. Other notable early authors were Katie Bell, Elizabeth Notrab and Flourish Klink. With an online legacy spanning nearly two decades at the time of writing this article, it is no surprise that such an immense, long-lived fandom has experienced a certain flux in terms of the online spaces it occupies, as Internet platforms with new technological capabilities have becoming increasingly attractive.

Like many, *Harry Potter*'s online fan community evolved through mailing lists, newsgroups and other online technologies that facilitated real-time discussion, such as instant messenger (IM). Early online activity includes the Harry Potter for GrownUps (HP4GU) mailing list (1999); the newsgroup alt. fan.harry-potter (1999); the fan-run website that remains active today, MuggleNet (1999) and other popular sites such as the Harry Potter Lexicon (2000) and the Leaky Cauldron (2000). Kelly Chambliss has been active in the community since 2008, and participates as a writer, reader, forum moderator and reccer (recommender). Although Kelly joined after the close of the book canon, she recalls the experience of newsgroups from her first fandom, *Star Trek: Voyager* (1995–2001). Kelly says that '[u]senet newsgroups (ngs) ruled', but found that beyond discussions around specific fanfics, there was 'no real community'. The mailing lists also tended to take a fic-centric discussion focus, which some fans found useful. Amorette, who has been writing fanfiction since the pre-Internet days of the print 'zines, recalls that pre-journal user groups were spaces where posted fiction resulted in an exchange of 'in-depth commentary, some of which I still have filed away twenty years later because it was so helpful'. However, others found a sense of community difficult to foster when the lists focused on specific fics. Flourish Klink notes that there was a tension when 'people would start up a list for discussion of their fanfic'. The list 'really was more of a community hub/chatter location than anything – it filled a need for space for people to socialize [...] but the nature of [fic specific] lists prioritized a person and a fanfic'.

Flourish Klink is the chief research officer and partner at Chaotic Good Studies and works with people in the entertainment industry, helping them to learn, think and strategize about fan culture. She is also the co-host of popular fandom podcast, *Fansplaining*, and one of the earliest notable participants in the fandom. Although it is almost unthinkable in today's sprawling community, Flourish provides an important early fandom context, noting that 'before LJ [LiveJournal] the *Harry Potter* community was SMALL', with roughly '500 really active non-lurking people on sites like HP4GU, etc'. Flourish notes that in 1998, when *Harry Potter* fandom first began to emerge, 'there wasn't a Fanfiction.net section yet, there was no Leaky Cauldron, the only way to contact other fans was through regular email'. As the fandom began to gain traction and more spaces opened in the late 1990s, Flourish notes that it was still a small space. Although the news sites have vast and active discussion forums today, they were 'much more bloglike' when they were first established. Flourish also stresses the importance of IM in the early days: 'IM was WHERE IT WAS AT. You knew you were

Polyjuice and Potterheads:
The Changing Face of Fandom from
LiveJournal to Tumblr
Emily E. Roach

actually friends with someone when you had their IM name, as opposed to them just being someone you saw around online'. This suggests that even from its inception, the fandom community has operated across platforms with different functionalities, seeking out more discursive, immediate systems to chat to other *Potter*-lovers beyond static posts, group message boards and blog-style posts.

Together with the mailing lists, news groups and news-related fansites, the archive has always been an important part of the community. The multifandom archive FanFiction.net (founded in 1998) was an early home for *Harry Potter* fanfiction, and the early 2000s saw a number of additional archives emerge that were dedicated to the series, such as FictionAlley founded by Flourish Klink, Heidi Tandy and others; the Sugar Quill, an archive dedicated to canon-compliant ships and the infamous and now-defunct Gryffindor Tower, for Harry/Ginny shippers, all of which were established in 2001. Fanfic authors also utilized multifandom archives. When FanFiction.net took steps to censor and delete explicit content in 2002, writers gravitated towards existing multifandom archives that allowed for explicit content, such as AdultFanFiction.org (2002), and new archives were established in response to FanFiction.net's content restrictions, such as the Restricted Section (2002). This history reveals how the fans adapted and evolved, responding to censorship and the impact that censorship had on the relevant platforms. The early trailblazers writing fanfic and creating archives to house transformative works in the late 1990s and early 2000s laid the foundations.

In her article 'My Life Is a WIP on My LJ: Slashing the Slasher and the Reality of Celebrity and Internet Performances' (2006), Kristina Busse explores how 'the postmodern nature of the Internet acts as a space for production of what Halberstam calls *counterpublics*, thus permitting more complex and multiple constructions of queer female spaces in an easily accessible public venue', and urges against characterizing the Internet as a 'space', instead suggesting that 'the Internet contains many spaces'. This nuanced distinction has support from those participants who engaged with *Harry Potter* fandom in the early days. Due to the small population, Flourish notes that

initial groups were forced together when they weren't on LJ, because there were too few people to really group out into smaller subcategories [...] as the fandom grew and LJ became available there were more opportunities to build different kinds of spaces.

Busker notes that in contrast with the mailing lists, which were very specifically 'organized around a particular topic', LiveJournal offered a series of 'interconnected spaces, most of which are focused on individual people'. Not only did a growing community lead to the emergence of subgroups forming around ships or characters, but the fandom utilized a number of diverse technologies offering different functionalities, in order to find the most cohesive, interactive and community-oriented experience.

The rise and fall of LiveJournal
Many enthusiasts were already operating on LJ in the early 2000s, but it was really around 2003 that the site became the primary home of *Harry Potter*. Many of the big *Harry Potter* fests and communities still have a home on LJ at the time of writing. LJ allowed fans to create their own personal journals, with varying levels of security, which enabled them to set posts, or their entire journals, to 'friends only'. Although this meant that establishing a journal-based community might take a little time, it had the positive impact of making people more comfortable sharing details of their lives. Kelly Chambliss notes that LJ 'continued the community feeling of Yahoo! Groups' but offered alternative and compelling features in terms of being part of a fandom community. She notes that on LJ 'I can open up, go beyond fan-related posts to talk about more general things'. In that sense, LJ provided a cohesive sense of community, bringing everyone together. Simultaneously the growth of the fandom on LJ enabled people to curate their own experience, allowing them to focus on communities and fests that aligned with their individual interests, thus creating multiple factions. It operated both to strengthen and fragment the community. Oli, an active participant, started out lurking and reading fics on LJ. A reader and Draco Malfoy/Harry Potter or 'Drarry' shipper, Oli is mainly active on Tumblr these days. However, he and his friends recall the LJ experience with affection: 'on LJ it felt like there were more discussions going on [...] that there was less drama [...] since many journals were friends-locked, it probably diminished the aggression'.

LJ provided the ideal platform for a growing fandom with disparate interests and preoccupations to foster their own community spaces under a broad umbrella in a centralized and interconnected place. Fan studies scholarship identified LJ not just as a community-oriented space, but as a queer space, where the practice of writing homoerotic 'slash' fiction was a contrib-

Polyjuice and Potterheads:
The Changing Face of Fandom from
LiveJournal to Tumblr
Emily E. Roach

uting factor in queer community development. Hampton notes that the

> performance of queerness through slash is evident not only in the repeated scenarios staged within the fic's narrative, but also in fans' performances of their roles as slash fans of Harry Potter, as users of LJ, and in their adherence to the practices and conventions of slash fandom [...] the rules and expectations for posting content, commenting etiquette, and so on.

Figure 2: Ronan Beltracchi and Nikolaus Dodsworth-Heath cosplay an affectionate Remus and Sirius (2018).

People were free to create transformative works that would often be hosted on LJ, on personal and fest journals, and participants would engage with those works in accordance with unspoken rules of fandom etiquette as the community grew.

As identified with respect to the deletion of NC-17 rated content from FanFiction.net, the community has a history of responding critically to attempts to censor content. The ability to create works relatively free from censure and censorship has always been an important feature of fandom space, whose creative output is free from the fetters of mainstream publication. Even as it increased in size, fandom was still a largely private endeavour and it didn't permeate public consciousness in the way it does today. To some extent this contributed to the development of non-mainstream creative content that felt 'safe' to publish within the protected community spaces. With a booming community offering a multitude of possible ships, there was a versatility to the transformative content creators were able to produce, and they would typically be able to find subgroups who enjoyed transformative works exploring similar ships, characters or themes. Content has historically spanned the full spectrum from dark to kinky to fluffy and sweet, and the fandom was large enough to accommodate most tastes. That is not to say there was no virulent opposition on occasion from within. Like all sizeable fandoms, this one was not free from ship wars, fandom wank and the burgeoning hierarchies of so-called 'Big Name Fans' or BNFs and the formation of cliques and 'Inner Circles' that had significant traction in terms of mobilizing support and content creation from within their own spaces. Nevertheless, LJ was a place where communities hosting uncensored content thrived, such as the porn-focused Pornish Pixies founded by switchknife in 2003.

The first big hit for LJ users concerned the censorship of fan-created content. In 2007, LJ attempted to crack down on the journals they deemed to be connected to child pornography, incest, paedophilia and rape. The so-called LJ 'Strikethrough' was followed by a similar 'Boldthrough' in the same year, which involved the deletion of hundreds of personal journals and communities without notice. This measure impacted a broad swathe of journals across the platform, from rape survival groups to book discussion groups, and fandom did not escape unscathed. Pornish Pixies was one of the deleted communities, together with a number of other journals and communities within the *Harry Potter* fandom. Strikethrough and Boldthrough left fans concerned about the utility of the platform, and many communities either migrated to the more pro-fandom LJ clone, InsaneJournal, or established mirror accounts there to protect themselves against another attempt by LJ to delete fandom journals.

The year 2007 is important for three further reasons. It is the year David Karp founded multimedia blogging site Tumblr, the year Russian company SUP Media acquired LJ, and it is also the year that FanLib.com, 'a for-profit, multifandom archive', sought to establish itself as a platform for fic writers to host their works (for free) while generating profit for the platform creators and those connected with it. Francesca Coppa explains how the emergence of a platform designed 'to commercialize fanfiction' with 'no particular understanding of fans or fan culture' was a defining moment that set the wheels in motion for the creation of not-for-profit fic archiving site Archive of Our Own (AO3) – a concept proposed by astolat (cited by Coppa) in direct response to FanLib.com.

Although LJ remained popular and the deleted accounts were reinstated, 2007 was the beginning of the end of LJ's position as a primary home for *Harry Potter* fandom. Dr Casey Fiesler, who has begun a wider project to analyse trends and shifts in platforms, notes that 'between 2007 and 2009, things were happening with LiveJournal that made people not like it anymore', but points out that 'there had to be critical mass elsewhere in order for [...] en masse [migration]'. In 2007, there was no meaningful alternative to LJ. Tumblr was too young and untested, and it would be several years before the *Harry Potter* fandom would fully embrace its style. Yet the tide was already turning.

Polyjuice and Potterheads:
The Changing Face of Fandom from
LiveJournal to Tumblr
Emily E. Roach

Together with the fear of journals being deleted without warning, participants were becoming increasingly uncomfortable with LJ's Russian connections. In the case of Russian fans, Rajagopalan writes that 'recent research strongly emphasizes slashers' own perceptions of working in a repressive environment and their growing anxiety that their activities will, in time, be completely silenced'. For those in other jurisdictions, historic actions taken by LJ to censor content and increased media visibility of anti-LGBT sentiment in Russia both fuelled concerns that content might be deleted without warning and raised ethical issues around the continued use of LJ.

In 2017, LJ introduced its new terms of service (TOS). By this point, a decade after Strikethrough and Boldthrough, but with the memory still fresh for older fandom participants, other platforms such as Tumblr offered a more mobile-friendly and aesthetically pleasing alternative to the dated LJ interface. A few, like the HD Erised fest, a seasonal fest based around *Harry Potter* fandom's popular Drarry slash ship, began operating across platforms with a presence both on LJ and a Tumblr blog established in 2013. For many, the updated TOS, revealing that the servers had been moved from California to Russia and required agreement with Russian domestic laws including anti-LGBT legislation, was the final nail in the coffin. Writing for the Mary Sue in 2017, Marykate Jasper notes that 'there's never been a better time to delete that old LiveJournal'. Although some were sceptical about the impact of the updated LJ TOS on fandom communities, connecting it to 'the beginning of a domestic pre-election political crackdown, rather than any sort of international censorship effort', the deepening nexus between LJ and Russia and the out-of-date platform led many to leave.

Unlike in 2007, in 2017 there were viable online alternatives. Besides Tumblr, the fandom archive Archive of Our Own had also boomed and it offered a user-friendly interface that was popular with fandom participants and community moderators. Many big *Harry Potter* fests and popular writers had already switched to hosting fanfiction on AO3, where the fanworks received heightened feedback, drawing readers in from Tumblr and the journals alike. A substantial number set up mirror accounts on the fandom-friendly Dreamwidth (founded in 2009). Both Tumblr and Archive of Our Own are now increasingly important platforms for *Harry Potter* fandom. Fiesler's seems to confirm the connection between the mounting dissatisfaction with LJ and the increased popularity of other platforms, explaining how the initial results of her research highlight how journal activities 'precipitously dip' in tandem with Tumblr and AO3 'climbing'. Fiesler comments, 'I think that [AO3 and Tumblr] had to get popular enough, enough people moving there so that those were a place for people to move to, because when there's nowhere for you to go, they don't go.'

NextGen: *Harry Potter* fandom on Tumblr

Many of the Internet's largest fandoms are Tumblr-originated, and it has become an increasingly popular platform for fandom activities. Tumblr offers a very different experience to the journals, but it has a lot of features that appeal to new people entering the fandom. Oli notes, 'I use Tumblr the same way I use Facebook – scroll, read, "like", share'. Silveredglass, a reader and writer who primarily ships Drarry and Remus Lupin/Sirius Black or 'Wolfstar', found *Harry Potter* fandom through Tumblr. She notes that the LJ interface is 'confusing' and, like Oli, finds Tumblr's 'scrolling dash familiar to most people from Facebook and Twitter easier to grasp as a new user'. Fans whose only experience is Tumblr have a variety of views on the journals. Silveredglass comments that it feels like the journals offered 'a more collaborative fandom experience' to the Tumblr fandom experience. For others, the journals have an air of 'the old guard' that can be off-putting for new participants trying to engage with the fandom community and its various subgroups. J. Rowland, a relatively new participant and an enthusiastic reader of slash fiction, specifically Drarry, says:

> I've hesitated to engage on LJ because it feels like crashing a party where everyone has known each other for three or five or ten years already. Absolutely nobody has been actively exclusionary to me; I'm just shy as hell.

In speaking to other Tumblr-only participants, this sense of the journals as places where communities, friendships and cliques have already been formed is not unusual. Combined with a clunky interface and the increasing number of Internet users who are accessing fandom content from mobile devices, there seems little impetus for newer participants to develop a presence there.

That is not to say that Tumblr is free from problems and it is not a platform for everyone. Kelly Chambliss mentions that her 'sense is that [Tumblr] is not a platform designed for community or fiction or discussion', and even those that use Tumblr struggle to engage with lengthy meta on the platform. The

Polyjuice and Potterheads:
The Changing Face of Fandom from
LiveJournal to Tumblr
Emily E. Roach

platform undoubtedly has an impact on the way that matters get discussed. For every thoughtful, detailed meta post I have seen on Tumblr, I have seen countless more pithy posts designed to garner notes as opposed to engage with the nuances of fan culture and canon. As a platform, Tumblr is not ideally suited to lengthy think pieces or to thoughtful engagement, as the pace of a constantly moving blogging platform can be difficult to thoughtfully respond to while it feels relevant. Discourse on Tumblr moves at a rapid pace. For the original poster (OP), the discussion becomes fragmented as more people reblog and add their own commentary and the discussion rapidly branches. Unlike on a journal platform like LJ or Dreamwidth that has nested comments, here the OP must invest an enormous amount of time and energy if s/he wants to engage with every response. Although engaging with meta on journals could, on a busy post, feel similarly exhausting, it was more manageable as the OP retained control of the original post and the comments were all easily accessed by those interacting with the post and the OP themselves. Those who didn't want to engage with the discussion could easily avoid doing so on the journals, without constant iterations of the same post cropping up on their dash. Goddess47 is a writer, prolific reader, reccer and moderator who is active in several fandoms and is primarily a Severus Snape/Harry Potter or 'Snarry' shipper. Active on LJ, Dreamwidth and a self-confessed Tumblr newbie, Goddess47 notes that 'the looping of posts is annoying', even for those not actively engaging with the discussion, as the replies and reblogs of a piece of particularly heated discussion soon clogs up a viewer's dash.

As noted from the outset of this article, an instrumental part of fandom is building and fostering a sense of community and Tumblr does not offer an easy community experience for all users. Silveredglass notes that

> Tumblr can be like yelling into a void, you never really know who's seeing your posts, if no one follows you then really no one is – it's not great for having larger conversations, so it's not great for building communities.

Goddess47 adds, 'Tumblr is great for reading and finding fic, but it's not a "community" the way LJ and even Dreamwidth have been'. Like many with experience of both platforms, Goddess47 found it harder to get a sense of community on Tumblr, noting: 'what's nice about LJ and Dreamwidth is that I have a core group of folk that not only post fic, but also talk about real life'.

Because it is harder to curate a more private, filtered experience, and posts can be reblogged ad infinitum, some Tumblr users are understandably more cautious about sharing private details or they do so in a series of tags that cannot be reblogged but that can be easily missed by someone scrolling through an active feed.

Just as early *Harry Potter* fandom employed different technologies to develop a broader sense of community, participants on Tumblr increasingly combine their interactions with real-time, chat-based groups. Discord (2015), a freeware Voiceover Internet Protocol (VoIP) application with designated channels, is popular. The Drarry Discord is one of *Harry Potter*'s largest, with several hundred members at the time of writing, despite only being established in mid-2017. Slack (2013) is another example that uses technology similar to Internet Relay Chat (IRC), and mobile-messaging app WhatsApp (2009) is also popular. A clear nexus between a growing Tumblr base and increased use of chat-based services suggests that the *Potter* community does not yet have a platform that ticks all the boxes, yet the fans' desire to combine different technologies to enhance their experience is nothing new. Not only was IM identified as instrumental to early participants, but Chatzy (2001), IRC channels and GChat (now Google Hangouts) were also popular with journal users before other alternatives became available.

With all this, *Harry Potter* fandom has a history of responding to outside censorship quickly, taking ownership of the spaces it occupies by creating or migrating to fan-friendly spaces that allow freedom of content, when the ability to 'freely fandom' in outside-owned spaces is threatened. Anne Jamison notes that 'fic communities can change and adapt and rewrite at a speed traditional publishing just can't match', and this adaptability and flexibility has been a defining feature. Today, Leora Hadas notes, the community faces the challenges of increased visibility and media scrutiny and it 'has been steadily losing its exclusivity under assault by the combined forces of marketing and technology'. Fan parlance such as 'shipping' has become part of everyday vernacular, understood and scrutinized by non-fannish media. Within fandom communities, platforms like Tumblr without journals that only friends can access and with massive open chat rooms increase the sense of being 'watched'. This combines with a cultural shift towards increased creator/fan interaction enabled by social media, a growing body of fan studies scholarship and communities turning critical lenses upon their own pursuits.

Polyjuice and Potterheads:
The Changing Face of Fandom from
LiveJournal to Tumblr
Emily E. Roach

Although it is important to interrogate fandom endeavours and to critically analyse the works created and consumed, there is a tension between thoughtful critique and self-censorship. In the case of this new age of *Harry Potter* fandom, there is an increasing trend towards the policing of content and, unlike the days when the threat was the corporation, I would argue that the biggest threat today is people within the fandom spaces themselves. Oli notes that on LJ it 'feels like the progressive thinking on feminism, queerness, ethnicity was less generalized' than on Tumblr, and identifies more stringent policing: 'Tumblr is full of voicing opinions [that] influences writers.' By way of example, once a 'little black dress' or staple, Severus Snape is having a particularly hard time on Tumblr. Despite being a divisive character, InsaneJournal and LJ had multiple communities dedicated to Snape and popular Snape ships, yet on Tumblr, negotiating Snape-related vitriol can be something of a logistical nightmare. Not only does the space encourage heightened levels of emotional engagement and thoughtless, toxic attacks, but the lack of control that individual bloggers have over their own posts can result in something they have created being reblogged by 'antis' who are keen to highlight the 'problematic' aspects of the content they have created and shame the OP into silence. The same thing can happen with content that is deemed problematic from a kink perspective or ships with 'unhealthy' relationship dynamics, such as incest or those with a significant age difference.

The puritanical few who have appointed themselves the fandom police may be a minority, but they are increasingly vocal. This kind of toxic callout comes at a time when the media spotlight is more firmly trained on fandom spaces than ever, and when communities are operating on platforms with greater unfiltered public access than the more private journals before them. The concern is that this combination of factors will foster an oppressive culture of silence and cookie-cutter sanitized content that has none of the rich, versatile, subversive and transformative potential. They, by contrast, have a long legacy of fighting to protect freedom of creative content and encouraging a largely female-centric fandom to take ownership of its online spaces.

Conclusion
Harry Potter fandom is currently in a state of flux. As Fiesler observes in the context of fandom spaces more broadly, 'as we've moved across all these platforms, we lose [*sic*] people, it's less tight-knit than it was'. Increased critique

of canon and objects of fandom have 'shifted [...] [fandom's] expectations and raised the moral bar on which [fans] judged their media' and in this sense, *Harry Potter* has been found to be lacking on several fronts. Writing for *Vox*, Aja Romano identifies 'a growing gap between Rowling's fans and her writing'. As the culture adapts, evolves and grows, Romano observes, the Potterverse might expand but there's little sense of evolution, a frustration that 'the wizarding world won't change to reflect the increasingly diverse world we live in'. Together with these divisive new canon additions and the struggle to find connections across a greater multitude of technologies than before, it is difficult to gauge the future direction of the fandom at present.

Perhaps an element of the fractious sense of feeling displaced within fandom is the disconnect between the so-called 'fandom olds' and the newbies. In the context of *Doctor Who* fandom, Hadas notes that 'the more experienced and involved fannish crowd, who are already past their learning stage, now must share their play space with a multitude of players still mastering the rules'. With every influx of new players, there is always going to be a teething period of sorts. However, when the platforms are shifting and evolving, and new players enter new spaces, this idea of a static set of rules and etiquette breaks down. The rules themselves are growing, changing and evolving and there is little interest in or awareness of the structures of a fandom that came before. In spaces where people seek to break down the binaries of sexuality and gender in a multitude of ways, there seems to be a danger in drawing too bright a line between 'them against us' with regards to journal-based communities and those with a preference for Tumblr. As Hampton notes, albeit in a somewhat different context, 'fans span a wide range of ideological subject positions [...] it is important not to slip into the trap of categorizing [...] oppositional binaries'. Rather than further fragmenting a fandom that is already thinly stretched across multiple online spaces, the quest is to bring the various pieces together. Although that might sound somewhat utopian, the one common thread is the desire to foster a community. The use of multiple platforms today suggests that no one platform currently offers the right kind of functionality for a fandom that is both meta and discourse-heavy on the one hand, and one that is increasingly interested in multimedia and aesthetics on the other.

There is no doubt that *Harry Potter* fandom has radically evolved from the fandom that originated in 1998. Leisa Clark notes that 'the *Harry Potter*

Polyjuice and Potterheads:
The Changing Face of Fandom from
LiveJournal to Tumblr
Emily E. Roach

experience is very different for those who first read the books and then anxiously awaited the movies, versus those who came to the fandom first through the films and consequently (sometimes) the books'. However, not only is the series 'profoundly culturally relevant', but the fandom is too. As one of the earliest and largest online fandoms, careful analysis of the increase in online *Harry Potter* devotees helps to formulate an understanding of fan communities in the digital age. An understanding of their history helps to map trends in fandom migration; enhances the way we think about the formation of online communities; and enables us to explore the social structures that develop and understand the way online communities adapt to and utilize constantly evolving technologies. Such studies are not only fruitful contributions to broader fan studies scholarship, but they also offer something to the fans themselves. They acknowledge and record a history where the people took ownership of the cyberspaces they occupied. In an increasingly immersive and fast-paced digital world, the force of fandom history is becoming a powerful tool in helping *Harry Potter* fans to adapt to future changes, in a manner that allows our still largely female-dominated community to keep fan spaces accessible, transformative and free from normative structures. ●

GO FURTHER

Extracts/Essays/Articles
'On Symposia: LiveJournal and the Shape of Fannish Discourse'
Rebecca Lucy Busker
In *Transformative Works and Cultures*, 1 (2008) [Online], http://dx.doi.org/10.3983/twc.2008.0049.

'My Life Is a WIP on My LJ: Slashing the Slasher and the Reality of Celebrity and Internet Performances'
Kristina Busse
In K. Busse (ed.). *Fan Fiction and Fan Communities in the Age of the Internet* (Jefferson, NC: McFarland, 2006), pp. 207–24.

'Preface'
Leisa Clark
In L. Clark and A. Firestone (eds). *Harry Potter and Convergence Culture: Essays on Fandom and the Expanding Potterverse* (Jefferson, NC: McFarland, 2018), pp. 1–6.

'An Archive of Our Own'
Francesca Coppa
In A. Jamison (ed.). *Fic: Why Fanfiction Is Taking Over the World* (Dallas, TX: Smart Pop, 2013), pp. 302–08.

'The Web Planet: How the Changing Internet Divided *Doctor Who* Fan Fiction Writers'
Leora Hadas
In *Transformative Works and Cultures*, 3 (2009) [Online], https://doi.org/https://doi.org/10.3983/twc.2009.0129.

'Bound Princes and Monogamy Warnings: *Harry Potter*, Slash, and Queer Performance in Livejournal Communities'
Darlene Hampton
In L. Bennett and P. J. Booth (eds). 'Performance and Performativity in Fandom', special issue, *Transformative Works and Cultures*, 18 (2015) [Online], http://dx.doi.org/10.3983/twc.2015.0609.

'Introduction'
Anne Jamison
In A. Jamison (ed.). Fic: *Why Fanfiction Is Taking Over the World* (Dallas, TX: Smart Pop, 2013), pp. 300–01.

'Slash Fandom, Sociability, and Sexual Politics in Putin's Russia'
Sudha Rajagopalan
In A. Kustritz (ed.). 'European Fans and European Fan Objects: Localization and Translation', special issue, *Transformative Works and Cultures*, 19 (2015) [Online], http://dx.doi.org/10.3983/twc.2015.0620.

Polyjuice and Potterheads:
The Changing Face of Fandom from
LiveJournal to Tumblr
Emily E. Roach

Online
'The *Harry Potter* Fandom Is at a Crossroads'
Alanna Bennett
BuzzFeed. 20 November 2016, https://www.buzzfeed.com/alannabennett/the-harry-potter-fandom-is-at-a-crossroads?utm_term=.njN7mk3wgX#.bgRzOGYxNX.

'Fandom Platform Use Over Time'
Casey Fiesler (cfiesler)
Tumblr. 13 March 2018, http://cfiesler.tumblr.com/post/171831912875/survey-results-fan-platform-use-over-time.

'It Might Be Time to Delete Your Livejournal'
Marykate Jasper
The Mary Sue. 8 April 2017, https://www.themarysue.com/livejournal-russian-federation-tos.

'The *Harry Potter* Universe Still Can't Translate Its Gay Subtext into Text. It's A Problem'
Aja Romano
Vox. 4 September 2016, https://www.vox.com/2016/9/4/12534818/harry-potter-cursed-child-rowling-queerbaiting.

'Why Did Fans Flee Livejournal, and Where Will They Go After Tumblr?'
Heather Schwedel
Slate. 29 March 2018, https://slate.com/technology/2018/03/why-did-fans-leave-livejournal-and-where-will-they-go-after-tumblr.html.

Websites
AdultFanFiction, http://www.AdultFanFiction.net
alt.fan.harry-potter, https://groups.google.com/forum/#!forum/alt.fan.harry-potter
Drarry Discord, https://discordapp.com/invite/EQ9w79Q
FanFiction.net, https://www.fanfiction.net
Fansplaining, www.fansplaining.com
Fiction Alley: Creativity is Magic, http://www.fictionalley.org/authors
Harry Potter for GrownUps (HP4GU), https://groups.yahoo.com/neo/groups/harrypotterforgrownups/info

Harry Potter's Realm of Wizardry, http://www.harrypotterrealm.com
MuggleNet, http://www.mugglenet.com
The Harry Potter Lexicon, https://www.hp-lexicon.org
The Leaky Cauldron, http://www.the-leaky-cauldron.org
The Restricted Section II, http://www.restrictedsection2.org
The Sugar Quill, http://www.sugarquill.net

Chapter
04

The Magic of Video Game Adaptation: The Admirer Becomes the Caster in *Harry Potter and the Philosopher's Stone/Sorcerer's Stone*

César Alfonso Marino

→ The release of the video game *Harry Potter and the Philosopher's Stone* - or *Sorcerer's Stone* in the United States (Electronic Arts, 2001), led to revolutionary exploration within the saga. If the film Harry offered and brought to life an inventory of magic tools, such as talking hats, wands, flying broomsticks, spellbooks and potions, the video game explored what the film did not show or could not afford to show, due to the limitations of time and money.

For the film, the visual language had to replace the language of words to create the imaginative magic and charm of the book. The arrival at Hogwarts, for example, accompanied by a myriad of other boats approaching the castle in an orchestrated formation, surrounded by magnificent reflections of light mingling with the water, did not require anything other than visual spectacle. The very interior of Hogwarts, with the welcoming banquet lit by hundreds of candles floating under a ceiling imitating the frosty, starry night and staircases falling back on themselves and changing places, was enough to confer a special touch of magic.

However, after the magical experience of the first film, expectations had been raised: what else could be shown of the Wizarding World? This question would prompt an endeavour to redefine many aspects of the Potterverse that framed the video game.

From book to film and film to video game
The adaptation of the book to the screen required many cuts for time. However, the video game supplemented the film by showing what it could not include. On-screen, could we imagine Harry going through the halls of Hogwarts again and again in order to complete a collection of chocolate frog cards? Or stopping in front of a wall, painting, vase or mirror and wondering whether the wall, painting, vase or mirror hid anything else? That would have been unbearable for a film viewer, but reasonable, even expected, by a video game player.

The book had allowed us to imagine Harry through words, sometimes offering illustrations that revealed the charm of Harry's world. The film, on the other hand, took a decisive step in materializing Harry and making him an identifiable pop culture reference. After the success of the film, hats, capes, wands and spellbooks were produced on a large scale specifically as the film had imagined them, merchandizing the film props, including the Sorting Hat. Even the eventual theme parks perfectly matched the films' imagery. In recreating a universe with its own rules, the first film was decisive in submerging the viewer within the world of magic. However, on a deep level, fans had been hoping for an approach that could not be experienced by simply watching the screen. The admirer who, for example, had bought a Quidditch broom, wanted to take the place of the protagonist.

The Magic of Video Game Adaptation:
The Admirer Becomes the Caster in *Harry Potter and*
the Philosopher's Stone/Sorcerer's Stone
César Alfonso Marino

A game and something more...

Playing a video game is equivalent to taking another's place, suspending our reality or the logic that governs it to let us enter another world. The one who plays abandons his usual role to travel into another reality, to replace the everyday world with the fantasy that another world can offer, a world where everyone can be a different person, free of risk. Playing games, in this sense, involves crossing a threshold, but, also, sometimes taking a step back in time. It means rediscovering the children we once were and recovering the enthusiasm of youth in the game.

In the *Harry Potter* video game, the child hero as well as his player is the one who explores, who pursues prizes or trophies, who wanders through countless corridors, who rides on a broomstick and waves a wand hoping to defeat the monsters of his nightmares. He is the one who faces challenges, who is not afraid of saying no or fighting evil to restore good, even though, in the real world, such a mission would be impossible. It is, in short, the child who daydreams a story in which the ending allows him or her to believe in the triumph of magic.

The adaptation of the *Harry Potter* universe to the format of the video game had this agency in mind from the beginning, as it sought to provide the player with another way of interacting, another way of incorporating the fantasy that the book first awoke and that the film was preparing to feed by giving it a tangible form. In fact, the film and video game premiered simultaneously in November 2001, emphasizing how they were built to work in tandem. The video game set out to present the story in a different way, by allowing the fan to make his/her own decisions about the adventure. As Hogwarts was explored, s/he practised spells with his/her wand or completed the requirements of the missions of the main plot. For the first time, readers could not only watch Harry's world come alive but also visit it fully and in fact have the opportunity to be Harry, in all his encounters: the game involved attending the same classes as he did, encountering the same blunders of his destiny and overcoming the same obstacles.

Changes and complements

In the world of video games, adaptations of films often offer anecdotal commentary on the plot. The admirer who approaches such games often ends up disappointed, as s/he had expected an experience similar to the fantasy that had filled the big screen. Some games are clumsily adapted, or the plot is too predictable or the puzzles too easy or too hard. Many gamers still recall *E.T.*'s (Spielberg, 1982) notorious tie-in game published by Atari (1982), for which creators' mistakes led to a game flawed on every level and a serious financial failure. On this occasion, however, the developers knew that *Harry Potter* fans wanted to wave their wand like Harry, practise his spells and ride his broom to win the annual Quidditch Cup. The biggest challenge was how to recreate those fantasies.

The path that Electronic Arts had to travel was to retrace the steps of failed video game adaptations. The idea was to create a narrative continuity that would no longer be read on a superficial level but instead go deeper, in an imitation of film aesthetics. In fact, the cinematography of Chris Columbus, his distinct use of lighting and the tones of the film colour palette, as well as the alternation of camera angles, was attempted in the video game. The effect of continuity worked strategically to give the player the opportunity to explore scenarios and recreate magical experiences similar to Harry's.

In short, the developers' idea was to create something more than a platform adventure puzzle game; they aimed at authentically imitating life at Hogwarts and, through excellent graphics, life in the universe imagined by J. K. Rowling. The idea of rewarding the player for completing a collection of cards or mastering all the Hogwarts' classes comprised a large part of the redefinition of the traditional platform game, in order to offer fans a complex sense of progression. The possibility of prolonging or extending what could not be shown onscreen was maintained in order to imitate a truly natural experience of the antinomic world of magic. That is, the developers did not set out to imitate Harry's world by reproducing his encounters or most iconic character features, but by capturing the essence of Hogwarts students' day-to-day lives, surrounded by the wizards, fairies, goblins, ghosts, centaurs and monsters that roam outside and inside Hogwarts Castle. However, after gathering several collector cards and discovering the stories of all the characters, the player often ended up wondering which story had actually been completed: the main one? A secondary character's? Or one far subtler, reconstructed from the interstices of the dialogue?

Regardless, the collector cards, as well as the candies offered by the twins Fred and George Weasley, held a powerful attraction for the treasure-hunter player and for the feeling of audacity that exploration awakens. The character

The Magic of Video Game Adaptation:
The Admirer Becomes the Caster in *Harry Potter and the Philosopher's Stone/Sorcerer's Stone*
César Alfonso Marino

stories guided the players into the deeper worldbuilding of Hogwarts, allowing them to share in its folklore and even discover many of the magical beings of the bestiary along with a brief explanation of their origin. This was the true story that unfolded through the collection of cards and the perseverance of the player who toured Hogwarts and its surroundings to complete the game.

The collector cards and other prizes justified the exploration dynamic of the game, because without the lure of accessing Hogwarts' secrets, would it make sense to walk its endless corridors? Or look behind every nook of furniture, behind every crack in the mirror or irregularity in the walls concealing a secret passage? This exploration was based on the need to solve the game but also to discover and understand more of the universe imagined by J. K. Rowling. In this way, exploring the endless corridors of the school became an attainable goal for the player, just as a puzzle became a bearable challenge. The test of dealing with a sometimes-frustrating search was rewarded with access to privileged content, revelations that would give even more life to the pre-existing universe known through the book and film.

Still, the original release looked less than imposing, which took away much expressive power from its medieval and labyrinthine architecture. Exploring Hogwarts in the console version (Warthog Games, 2003) seemed like a task within reach, an almost trivial challenge, since there was not much to show. This version was not intended to recreate as much of the magic of the film using the landscape, because it was hoped that the animated characters would get by on their own merits. The 2001 version for Windows and Mackintosh had been a rewarding experience, winning more than one smile among the fans who hoped to be Harry, because, in effect, the designers had managed to capture the essence of the characters and their emotional arc as they progressed towards discovering the secret of the philosopher's stone.

From PS One to PC

The readaptation of the PS One (PlayStation One) mechanism in 2001 played an important role in shaping the PC version of *Harry Potter and the Philosopher's/Sorcerer's Stone* because the combination of keyboard and mouse allowed for an unprecedented technical innovation: to use the mouse as if it were a wand.

The PS One version can be considered the imperfect sketch of a platform adventure with puzzles that try to faithfully recreate the spirit of the film but put more emphasis on a caricatural rather than realistic aesthetic. The characters' animations in this version are very fluid, and the mechanics highlight the intention for the player to interact with most of the objects that appear. In this way, Harry manoeuvres his wand to formulate a spell or jumps from one platform to another while his enemies multiply. In regular Hogwarts classes depicted in the game, to succeed in the lesson the player must submit to an intricate combination of buttons that resembles more a puzzle of memory than skill, a skill that is achieved in the PC game by allowing the player to imitate the movement of the wand with the mouse.

In this sense, the PC version aimed to enhance what was already working for the PS One version with a more concrete vision. The merit of this was not the exchange of one experience for another, but the discovery of another layer of experience that a video game adaptation of a book or film can provide. What had previously been thought of as an adventure platform game was now completed through an approach that broke with the linear narrative, that is, with the mere succession of events chained or arranged in chronological order, to allow the player to travel alone through the world of Hogwarts.

The team of developers behind the PC version realized that there was much more material to use and adapt to the game. The first version had been a rewarding experience, pleasing the fans who hoped to walk in Harry's footsteps, because, in effect, it managed to capture the essence of the characters and the emotional impact of the conflicting situations in which they were immersed while advancing in the discovery of the secret that would lead to the philosopher's stone. The real innovation sought by developers would come with the PC version and the recycling of a story that could be improved on a variety of different artistic and technical levels.

Consider, for example, what was gained in the graphics department. The textures of the different environments in the PC version were much more realistic and defined in their resolution than those of the PS One. While the PS One version limited the contours of the cartoon character to the player's horizon, the PC version looked to realism to summon an echo of the experience provided by the film, including interaction with a more realistic environment and a less caricature-like character, invoking the sensation of another dimension of space and topography through 3D graphics. This time, one could guide the player inside the very walls of Hogwarts. The player could experience how it feels to take a shortcut through a secret passage to attend a class, explore

The Magic of Video Game Adaptation:
The Admirer Becomes the Caster in *Harry Potter and*
the Philosopher's Stone/Sorcerer's Stone
César Alfonso Marino

Figure 1: Harry Potter and the Philosopher's Stone/ Sorcerer's Stone *on Xbox* (2003).

the forest or reach the cabin of Rubeus Hagrid. In this way, the creators had considered the distance of the earth and covered it in a more realistic way.

Back to the consoles

The developers of Electronic Arts were confident that they could further polish their work. In addition, the recent change of generation in the PlayStation – with the appearance of the PS2 (PlayStation 2) in 2000 and GameCube and Xbox in 2001, suggested the imminent evolution of the saga. But there was a problem: how would the story continue?

The first version of the game adaptation had landed on a console that was soon removed from the market, so the continuation of the series was interrupted. A decision had to be made and Electronics Arts did not hesitate: the new generations meant a restart of the saga. However, this time, Electronic Arts would only be responsible for distribution and would leave development in the hands of studios such as Amaze Entertainment, Argonaut Games and Eurocom.

The version of *Harry Potter and the Philosopher's Stone/Sorcerer's Stone* that appeared for PS2, GameCube and Xbox (developed by Warthog Games in 2003), began with Harry's first important choice: his magic wand, which led to an unusual exploration inside Ollivander's, an event not paralleled in the film. Master classes in which players tried to cast spells through emulating wand movements with the mouse were replaced with an unthinkable variant: adventures expanded far beyond the original story.

The formula, which was used for the first three video game instalments – *Harry Potter and the Philosopher's Stone/Sorcerer's Stone, Harry Potter and the Chamber of Secrets* (Electronic Arts, 2002) and *Harry Potter and the Prisoner of Azkaban* (Electronic Arts, 2004) – aimed to recycle all the best features of the first version of *Harry Potter and the Philosopher's Stone/Sorcerer's Stone* and apply everything that had been learned through its development. However, the fourth instalment was less popular: *Harry Potter and the Goblet of Fire* (Electronic Arts, 2005) made innovative changes, but the structure of unlockable levels did not coincide with a player's exploration, a condition that fans had demanded. It should not be surprising that, because developers listened to fans, *Harry Potter and the Order of the Phoenix* (Electronic Arts, 2007) is remembered as one of the most successful instalments of the video game franchise.

Harry Potter and the Goblet of Fire's appearance was destined to cross the choices previously imposed by the requirements of the consoles and chosen for the alternative PC version. The fourth instalment of the saga formed a synthesis that would last until last two instalments: *Harry Potter and the Deathly Hallows: Part 1* (Electronic Arts, 2010) and *Harry Potter and the Deathly Hallows: Part 2* (Electronic Arts, 2011). Thus, with the last five instalments, finally the PC and console versions had coincided, opening up new ground with adventures that omitted nothing. Everything was within the reach of the enthusiastic player: to learn, travel, explore and collect; to complete adventures and overcome obstacles in the mini-games. Harry Potter had fulfilled his mission; his foray into video games had been unlike anything seen before. In fact, he had created a path of his own with a seal of distinction.

An expanded universe
The concept of the expansion of the saga, understood as a prolongation of the universe that is known from the books and films, was developed by J. K. Rowling herself, who from the beginning was very interested in fans having the opportunity to explore the world of *Harry Potter* from different angles and locations. In the specific case of video games, this premise is corroborated by the licences granted to developers to play freely with different elements of the saga without feeling pressured to correlate exactly with the events that take place in the books and films. This explains why the first instalment of the game offered the 'Flipendo' spell, which had not yet appeared in the books or films.

However, if we think of this detail as part of the mechanics of the game, we can understand why there was a real need to introduce this spell. The framework of the platform game genre required a wide range of actions and, to a large extent, this was provided by the introduction of this small anachronism. It was not the only one, but much would have been lost had Harry not been granted the spell, allowing him to manipulate his environment, use a tricky duelling spell and access new areas of the map by activating magical switches from a distance.

The adaptation also had to be allowed certain licences to make the game playable. Several of the narrative aggregates, such as puzzles or improvised dialogues, broke completely with the official story. Nonetheless, the fascinating new disputes and confrontations, like duelling with Draco Malfoy, provided

The Magic of Video Game Adaptation:
The Admirer Becomes the Caster in *Harry Potter and the Philosopher's Stone/Sorcerer's Stone*
César Alfonso Marino

the player with unique experiences. Who could forget the battle with the magic firecrackers and the obstacles that had to be surmounted thanks to Little Draco's cunning? Moreover, these additions were well-regarded because the video game preserved the essential plotline and the conflict between good and evil that cemented it. In essence, the player could recognize his/her role because the experience was similar to that of the first book and film.

The PS One version, amended and polished for the PC, had discovered a formula as magical as those used in the potions of the Defence Against the Dark Arts classes, so the official video game saga gained more life with the continuous addition of small details. Not only did we end up knowing more about the *Harry Potter* universe through the stories told by the collector cards, but, for example, the malevolent genius of Draco ended up becoming more palpable, with suggestive dialogues as preludes to confrontations that had never taken place in the books or films. Instead, in the video game the developers found their *raison d'être* by stressing and modifying the original concept. In principle, we accepted the games because they were entertaining, but we also accepted them because we did not perceive any contradiction with what we had already seen in the book or film, and there were no arbitrary modifications that distorted our image of the character.

However, for the final step of this enriching transformation to take place, to really mature in the possibilities of the legacy of the saga, something more had to happen, and it did: J. K. Rowling became fully involved in the project, no longer as an assistant or consultant during the creation process, but as an active member of the script development team. The writer who had so captivated us with her imagination had come to realize that she could continue creating her incredible world through the video game saga. This collaboration gave real form to players' concept of an expanded universe.

Perspectives for the future
The recent release of *Harry Potter: Hogwarts Mystery* for iOS and Android smartphones and tablets (launched on 25 April 2018 by Warner Bros. Interactive Entertainment's new label Portkey Games), invites us to review previous contributions to the *Harry Potter* video game saga and to rethink how much the saga has matured since its first appearance in 2001. The innovative ideas of the official saga, such as using the wand to formulate a spell; attending Potions or Transfiguration; revelling in a mini-game while the main story is

Figure 2: Screenshot from
Hogwarts Mystery (2018).

put on hold and fighting an open magic duel, remain in this new video game. However, they have been incorporated with a new slogan that brings forth the undisputed gaze of the creator through the telling of a story that has not yet been told. As the trailer says, in Dumbledore's words: 'It is our choices, Harry, that show what we truly are, far more than our abilities' (Pottermore News Team, 2018). Jam City spent two years crafting the game's story and licensed the voices of Michael Gambon, Warwick Davis and Dame Maggie Smith. The music is reminiscent of the films', while the art really does feel immersive enough to take players into the Potterverse… though Rowling did not write the plot.

Art director David Nakayama shared a few thoughts with Valerie Estelle Frankel at *San Francisco Comic-Con* (9 June 2018) on why this new game is significant: 'The last time we had any kind of *Harry Potter* game was, y'know, back in the console days when they were sort of just recreating the events of the movies.' He added that the new material is the biggest draw:

> There's never been [a video game] that wasn't Harry's story. What's really cool about our game is […] It's totally fresh content, brand new stories in this environment. Oh, and I might have buried the lead in the fact that it's about you [the player].

Players can create a character, give him or her a name, unique appearance and House, and make choices based on whether to be friendly, courageous or wise.

In *Hogwarts Mystery*, we have the opportunity to create a character from scratch and live through his/her eyes the world of magic that Hogwarts presents, with the interspersed conflicts and mysteries that are woven through its corridors. The adventure that this video game proposes is plotted through

The Magic of Video Game Adaptation:
The Admirer Becomes the Caster in *Harry Potter and the Philosopher's Stone/Sorcerer's Stone*
César Alfonso Marino

the life of the ordinary student, the student who apparently does not stand out from the rest but has a story as valuable and significant as any other secondary character that has accompanied Harry.

Nakayama described glowing Internet praise focusing on how players 'feel like they're forming relationships with the characters in the game'. There's fanart, fanfic, cosplay and so on all around, and fan creation continues to inspire more innovation. The player character's new best friend Rowan Khanna is Indian... and can be male or female, allowing for the possibility of even greater diversity. Further, Nakayama said, returning characters 'that maybe weren't touched on all that deeply in the films or even in the books', like Bill and Charlie Weasley, Professor Kettleburn and even Scabbers, get more story. The story takes place when the latter were all at Hogwarts, before Harry arrives. These characters include fan favourites like Snape and Tonks, on whom fans are delighted to get new material.

Making such a game truly takes fandom to new levels, as Nakayama discovered:

> *I accepted the assignment to art-direct the game because I like* Harry Potter *very much. I've read the books, I've seen the movies, I enjoyed all of it. And so, when that was offered, I said 'Yeah, I'd like to do that.' But in working on it, and learning more and more about the universe, like, y'know, how deeply the set designers went to craft that world, like just Dumbledore's office alone [...] We had to study what was done in the films and recreate it in the games.*

In the interview, he went on to describe a single strange telescope contraption in Dumbledore's office, which can adjust the observatory and move it up to the astronomy classroom, and how much effort it must have cost the filmmakers to recreate it. The game's Hogwarts Castle is filled with such artfully crafted bits of fanlore. According to Nakayama, filmmakers themselves were surprised by how much the game added. Going deeper and deeper into the world makes game creators appreciate it more. As Nakayama concluded, 'I am more of a fan of *Potter* now than before I started'.

For all these reasons, *Hogwarts Mystery* represents not only the story that was not told, but also the imperfect original spin-off fiction that was never published but can now finally come to light. It has ignited a new spark and new possibilities for the player, who had previously been enthusiastic about the flashes of magic achieved through the mechanics of the first video game, but can now feel like his/her own character in his/her favourite saga, occupying a place in the House of his/her choice and duelling spiders with Hagrid and Charlie in the Forbidden Forest while discovering new secrets hidden there. That is the twist that the extended *Potter* creators now give the saga. The universe is ever-expanding, the universe that began to be reimagined and transformed when it skipped from the console to the PC and back again with greater impetus. ●

GO FURTHER

Online
'Watch the First Trailer for New Mobile Game *Harry Potter: Hogwarts Mystery*'
Pottermore News Team
Pottermore. 18 January 2018, https://www.pottermore.com/news/watch-the-new-trailer-for-new-mobile-game-harry-potter-hogwarts-mystery.

Interviews
Interview with David Nakayama
Valerie Estelle Frankel
San Francisco Comic-Con. 9 June 2018.

Video games
Harry Potter and the Philosopher's Stone/Sorcerer's Stone [Game Boy Advance, Game Boy Color, OS X, PC, PlayStation]
(Electronic Arts, 2001)

Harry Potter and the Chamber of Secrets [Game Boy Advance, Game Boy Color, GameCube, PC, PlayStation, PlayStation 2, Xbox]
(Electronic Arts, 2002)

Harry Potter and the Philosopher's Stone/Sorcerer's Stone [GameCube, PlayStation 2, Xbox]
(Electronic Arts, 2003)

The Magic of Video Game Adaptation:
The Admirer Becomes the Caster in *Harry Potter and*
the Philosopher's Stone/Sorcerer's Stone
César Alfonso Marino

Harry Potter and the Prisoner of Azkaban [Game Boy Advance, GameCube, PC, PlayStation 2, Xbox]
(Electronic Arts, 2004)

Harry Potter and the Goblet of Fire [Game Boy Advance, GameCube, PC, PlayStation 2, PlayStation Portable, Xbox]
(Electronic Arts, 2005)

Harry Potter and the Order of the Phoenix [Game Boy Advance, GameCube, Mac OS X, Nintendo DS, PC, PlayStation 2, PlayStation 3, PlayStation Portable, Wii, Xbox 360]
(Electronic Arts, 2007)

Harry Potter and the Half-Blood Prince [mobile, Nintendo DS, PC, PlayStation 2, PlayStation 3, PlayStation Portable, Wii, Xbox 360]
(Electronic Arts, 2009)

Harry Potter and the Deathly Hallows – Part 1 [mobile, Nintendo DS, PC, PlayStation 3, Wii, Xbox 360]
(Electronic Arts, 2010)

Harry Potter and the Deathly Hallows – Part 2 [mobile, Nintendo DS, PC, PlayStation 3, Wii, Xbox 360]
(Electronic Arts, 2011)

Harry Potter: Hogwarts Mystery [Android, iOS]
(Warner Bros. Interactive Entertainment, 2018)

'IT IS OUR CHOICES, HARRY, THAT SHOW WHAT WE TRULY ARE, FAR MORE THAN OUR ABILITIES'

ALBUS DUMBLEDORE
(HARRY POTTER AND THE CHAMBER OF SECRETS)

Fan Appreciation #2:
Justin Zagri (*Severus Snape and the Marauders*)
Lisa Gomez

Justin Zagri's headshot (2016).

Figure 1: The Greater Good
(2013).

Justin Zagri is an award-winning filmmaker who works on projects ranging from feature films to commercials and trailers to sizzle reels. His clients include names like Kelly Rowland of Destiny's Child, Kat Von D of LA Ink, Funny or Die, CBS and more. His work has been seen worldwide in theatres and on television and the Internet. His films have been featured in publications such as *Entertainment Weekly* and *Time*, and on websites such as BuzzFeed, MTV, Elite Daily, BBC, UNILAD and others.

Figure 1: The Greater Good (2013).

Lisa Gomez (LG): In 2013, you released a very popular and incredible *Harry Potter* fan film called *The Greater Good*, which chronicles the epic fight between Dumbledore and Grindelwald. Did the success and fan reception of that influence your decision to create *Severus Snape and the Marauders* [2016]?

Justin Zagri (JZ): It did! I realized that I might be able to make another one with higher production value as I had a growing fanbase!

LG: The *Harry Potter* fandom has been lucky to have several fan films and parodies written about it, but none have truly captured the world and complex thematic material as easily or as magically as *Snape and the Marauders*. The cast, crew, script, music and visual effects all seamlessly work together to produce a truly emotional and impactful film. All of that comes directly from the director's vision. How long have you been directing?

JZ: I have been directing for over a decade, but I'd say my work has gotten to a certain level of professionalism for the past five years.

LG: Every *Harry Potter* fan desperately craves a movie about Snape and the Marauders. Was there a specific moment that you can remember when you definitively made the choice to actually want to make this film?

JZ: I'm pretty sure it was after the success of *Greater Good* that went far beyond my expectations that I wanted to make another film. I realized I had a growing fanbase and they might help me make a movie with a real

Fan Appreciation #2
Justin Zagri

budget. *Greater Good* was all out-of-pocket, barely more than a couple of grand to make. I knew I could do better with a budget. So yeah, that's pretty much the moment I knew. I didn't know it was going to be about Snape and the Marauders yet, though. That wasn't until I did a poll asking the fans what they wanted. I got my answer, and we took it from there!

LG: How did you first encounter *Harry Potter*? Was it the books or movies or both?

JZ: I encountered *Harry Potter and the Sorcerer's Stone*, the book [Rowling, 1997], first, which I liked but didn't love (I love it now in retrospect), and got back into the books after seeing the first movie [Columbus, 2001]. I became hooked after *Harry Potter and the Goblet of Fire* [the book, Rowling, 2000].

LG: Who was your favourite character from the books?

JZ: Dumbledore! Most powerful wizard, charming funny, weird, mysterious and a genius, pulling all the strings in the background. I loved him more and more as the books progressed.

LG: The writing of *Snape and the Marauders* is really fantastic. Not only did you capture the character's distinct voices, but you made some incredibly emotional and poignant moments come to life, when Lily embraces Snape, for example. What made you want to focus on this specific moment of these characters' lives?

JZ: Once it was decided who the characters were, I went and read all the books again and paid close attention to the moments that were the most important for Snape, Lily, James, etc., and of course, Snape's worst memory comes to mind. It said so much about all those characters in a brief moment, and I quickly thought... they never settled the score. What if they did? From there it was about how each character would act in that final showdown and why.

LG: Something I find really interesting about the script is how it frames all of the characters. One could argue that Snape is the hero of this film, or Lily or even James. You've written these characters with strong points of views and yet you've kept all of your bias out. For example, James is exactly how he's described in the books (a sort of arrogant and bullying type) and yet he does learn at the end that he was wrong and when Lily lifts him up, you believe why she's with him. With Snape, you really feel for him when Lily embraces him, but you also feel like she's making the right choice by not being his friend because of the choices he's made in his life. The theme that I get is, we're all heroes and villains. When writing the script, did you keep this interesting and complex theme in mind?

JZ: One of the cool things about the film is everyone gets a moment of strength or weakness. The circumstances push everyone to their breaking points in certain ways, and we see how they react. James to me felt that seeing Snape [during the film's present time] meant more than it used to. He sees him now as dangerous and someone to keep away from Lily and his friends. His methods were pre-emptive and ill-advised as all of his friends kept saying, but he felt he was doing the right thing. The trick to any character is you need to write them as if they feel they are the centre of the story. It's the secret to ensemble picks (learned that from Joss Whedon) and like any main character, they see themselves as the hero. Or at least, certainly not as the villain. If you look at it from a character-arc point-of-view, who had the most to learn, it's James. So the movie is secretly about James. Followed second by Pettigrew because he learns just how far he's willing to go to keep himself safe. Snape's real apology (his sixth-year apology was half-hearted at best) was a way to show Snape at his weakest and most vulnerable. Lily is the only person he would ever be vulnerable around, so it was great exploring what he would be like, what kind of heart he has that he hides so much.

LG: Something I love about the way all of the characters are portrayed is that they all have a moment when they truly act like themselves so perfectly, especially in moments of crisis. James bullies Snape but you sense a genuine love for Lily from him and he ultimately wants to protect the world from dark wizards, no matter how ill his intentions are. Remus is loyal but level-headed, not thinking it's a good idea to fight Snape. Sirius, even with his devil-may-care attitude and charm, is fiercely protective of James, joining the fight without a second's hesitation. Peter is fickle and wants to join Snape as soon as the fight seems lost. Lily saves the day and is the moral centre for James and Snape. When you wrote the script, did you think you had to include at least one moment that really shows who these characters are or did these moments come about organically when writing the story?

Fan Appreciation #2
Justin Zagri

Figure 2: Severus Snape
and the Marauders *(2016).*

JZ: Kind of both. I write a first draft and just let myself type and see what happens based on how I know the characters. Then I read it and start rewriting based on things I know need to happen. I need there to be a moment of cowardice for Peter. I need to show Snape lose control. I need to show how Lily's mere presence tempers Snape and James. What I wanted to show as well was how these characters were maturing. They all had a greater level of wisdom and self-confidence compared to their fifth year. James doesn't provoke Snape just because he exists, anymore. He's doing it because he feels he has to. Sirius is for once a little hesitant to start any trouble, thinking about the consequences when he brings up Azkaban. Peter is far more comfortable in his own shell (at least for a while) and Snape actually tries to be reasonable with James... at first. So to me, once I picked the idea (theme, throughline, any of those) that the film would be about maturing and growing from teens to adults, the creative process became very clear and easy to write.

LG: What was the casting process like? Did you already have certain actors in mind or did you hold auditions?

JZ: Everyone was auditioned, with at least one callback. I have a strict rule that I don't cast friends unless they audition and fit the part. Once in a while I write a part knowing a friend fits it, but that friend would be a professional actor, anyways.

LG: Were there any moments in the audition when you knew exactly who you were going to cast? Did the actors have a mannerism or quirk that reminded you of the actors in the movies/the way these characters are written in the books or did you cast strictly on talent, relying on their talent to create these characters and not just an impersonation?

JZ: I was focusing on these characters based on the books, and in the movies only from a visual perspective. I wanted to build these characters for this story independent of what the movies did, as they were adaptations of the source material. I wanted to do my own thing, but I knew having similar visual cues as the official films would get more people on board. The nice thing about all the characters is they are much younger than their book/movie counterparts, so doing an impression of Alan Rickman, David Thewlis or Gary Oldman just wouldn't work. Kevin Allen, who played Sirius, expressed concern about that. I reassured him he was playing a very different character, pre-war, pre-Azkaban, fifteen years younger. Casting Snape took a while, but I knew Mick would work out when I saw his callback with Lily. The two looked like they could be best friends. I knew the Marauders on the first callback too, but within minutes, before they even started going through their lines. They were chumming so well, like they already had known each other for years. When I had them go through the scene, I told them the lines weren't as important, feel free to go off-book. The five-page scene went on for twenty minutes. Any extra direction I gave them was just to solidify my decision.

LG: The sets and locations look incredible and really authentic, like they really fit into the *Harry Potter* universe. How did you find those perfect locations?

JZ: The forest was a ranch in Ventura County not far from us, and the bar was in Eagle Rock, California. We found it through lots of Google searches and film location set research. The bar felt pretty much perfect, even with a hog's head! We hid the parts we didn't want anyone to see (the paintings have TVs behind them) and dressed it up just a bit. Combine that with good lighting, a fully dressed background cast (they practically dressed themselves, by the way) and magic happens! Actually, it's funny – when the DP (director of photography) was all set to get our first shot, he asked for a special filter. He put it over the lens, and suddenly it looked like a *Harry Potter* film. Crazy how that works...

LG: The visual effects are so incredible: it makes an already professional film seem that much more real. Given the impressive fight sequence in the middle of the film, did you know how to work out the visual effects before you shot it? Or did you shoot it the way you envisioned it in your head and then designed the visual effects from that?

JZ: It was a bit of both as well. I storyboarded the whole film and went over all the shots that involve visual effects with my VFX supervisor. He tells me what he needs me to do, and we go do them. In several shots we

Fan Appreciation #2
Justin Zagri

had these little LED balls of light placed throughout the scene to create a 3D space, so the VFX guys could use them to track any shot that moved so their jobs could be easier.

LG: The wand work during the fights in this film are even more specific and more defined than they were in the *Harry Potter* films, which I really appreciate and admire. What was it like coming up with the wand choreography? What were the difficulties in shooting fight sequences like this?

JZ: I worked with Kevin Allen [who plays Sirius Black] on choreography. Did you know he's a professional pirate? Anyways, he's very good at fight choreography, so I asked for his help putting together the fight scene. The 1 vs 1 and 2 vs 1 were fully choreographed, but it got a little simpler as it became 3 vs 1 and 4 vs 1. The goal was to show each character's distinct styles based on their personality and try to show the duel being dynamic and strategic with each character having their own strengths [that] contribute to the fight.

LG: Did you have a favourite moment in the film, a moment that came across exactly like you saw in your head when you wrote the script?

JZ: FiendFyre came out pretty amazing, but there is one little shot that I always envisioned that came out perfectly. It's basic and simple, but the shot composition and blocking make it look like it belongs in a still-life painting or something. The wide shot when the Marauders put their hands on James's back: James is facing Snape, and James offers his hand. I love everything about that shot, that moment.

LG: The actors all have wonderful and seamless chemistry with one another. Did the actors rehearse before they filmed their scenes? If so, what was the rehearsal process like?

JZ: There was a lot of rehearsal, which contributed to adding lines in the movie. The opening two minutes before James enquires as to why Peter looks broody is all improv. I let them come up with their own little story beforehand and just said, 'after the master shot, make sure you repeat the basics of that first moment when we shoot coverage.' Their chemistry and skill were good enough that I let them add a whole moment to their scene.

LG: When you premiered the film on YouTube, it was a quick and successful hit. The film caught on extremely quickly with the *Harry Potter* fandom, which led to a lot of exposure from extremely prominent websites including BuzzFeed and BBC America. How did it feel to receive all of that incredible attention after all of your hard work?

JZ: We worked hard to get it onto BuzzFeed, because we had a feeling everyone else would pick it up right after. It worked, but it was when *Entertainment Weekly* wrote an article that I realized how big it was really getting. It felt amazing, vindicating and exciting that my work is worthy of these publications. Now all I need is people with money to think the same thing and fund my next film!

LG: As of writing this interview, *Snape and the Marauders* has acquired over 4 million hits on YouTube. Congratulations. Clearly this film is beloved all over the world by millions of fans. What's next? Are you working on something new in the *Harry Potter* universe with this incredible cast?

JZ: We are! I am personally working on my first feature film, a sci-fi romance called *Transcend*. In the meantime, I am working on expanding the YouTube channel, and I am working with Mick Ignis on a twelve-part radio play called *The Great Wizarding War*, which takes place right after *Snape and the Marauders* and continues their story.

LG: How can fans of yours keep up to date with your incredible work?

JZ: They can go to the production company's website www.broad-strokesproductions.com and sign up for the e-mail list, or they can become part of our Patreon!

LG: For those aspiring to create fan content for *Harry Potter*, what piece of advice would you give?

JZ: Do it 'cause you love it, but do the very best you can to make every aspect as good as possible, especially the writing and casting. If you can't get a hold of money to start, do it anyways! Make the best out of what you have. ●

Fan Appreciation #2
Justin Zagri

~~~~~~~~~~~~~~~

GO FURTHER

Online
'Fan Film *Severus Snape and The Marauders* is the *Harry Potter* Prequel You've Been Waiting for'
Sarah Doran
Radio Times. 15 July 2015, https://www.radiotimes.com/news/2015-07-15/fan-film-severus-snape-and-the-marauders-is-the-harry-potter-prequel-youve-been-waiting-for/.

'Harry Potter Prequel: Fan-made Video Surfaces'
Dana Getz
Entertainment Weekly. 24 March 2016, https://ew.com/article/2016/03/24/fan-made-harry-potter-prequel/.

'Harry Potter Fan Film *Severus Snape and the Marauders* Actually Looks Pretty Awesome'
Claire Hodgson
Cosmopolitan. 22 July 2015, https://www.cosmopolitan.com/uk/entertainment/news/a37401/harry-potter-fan-film-snape-marauders.

Film/Television
The Greater Good, Justin Zagri, dir. (Burbank, CA: Broad Strokes, 2013).

Severus Snape and the Marauders, Justin Zagri, dir. (Burbank, CA: Broad Strokes, 2016).

'AFTER ALL THIS TIME?' 'ALWAYS'

SEVERUS SNAPE
(*HARRY POTTER AND THE DEATHLY HALLOWS*)

Chapter
05

The Wizarding World of *D&D*: The Art of Roleplaying in the Potterverse

S. Evan Kreider

→ J. K. Rowling has created a world so wondrous and compelling that many fans truly wish they could live there as wizards themselves. Unfortunately, the real world prevents that in any literal sense, but fans have found many substitutes, from playing video games to writing fanfiction. One particularly interesting avenue into Rowling's world is that of pen-and-paper roleplaying games, through which game masters can create their own stories set in the universe of *Harry Potter*, and players can create characters to adventure in those stories.

Figure 1: Dungeons & Dragons *(1974).*

Unfortunately, there is no official *Harry Potter* roleplaying game (RPG) at this time, but many fans have created their own hacks based on existing RPG systems. In fact, the popular RPG systems each emphasize very different aspects of the gaming experience, from battling monsters and evil wizards with powerful combat magics to the development of subtle interpersonal relationships and the drama they promote. Along the way, I also hope to show that RPG interpretations of an artistic franchise constitute a legitimate and parallel form of art themselves.

No discussion of roleplaying games can ignore the industry's 800-pound gorilla, *Dungeons & Dragons* (Tactical Studies Rules, Inc., 1974), so our own discussion might as well start there. *Dungeons & Dragons* (*D&D*) has been around since the 1970s in one edition or another, from the earliest days when it was presented as an add-on for fantasy-themed miniature warfare games, to the present day with the popular and successful fifth edition. There are many differences among the various versions of the rules, and many fans have their favourite (with criticism of other editions often quite spirited), but one thing that all versions share is an emphasis on the game part of 'roleplaying game'. That's not to say that players cannot engage in deeply immersive roleplaying of their characters, or that the dungeon master cannot tell epic tales with great drama and sophisticated themes. But the rules themselves have always focused on creating a gaming experience, with obstacles to overcome and challenges to face, and ways to chart success and failure relative to those obstacles and challenges. At first, this may not seem like the best approach to emulate fiction in general, much less *Harry Potter* in particular. Still, on further reflection, there are prominent aspects of the Potterverse that lend themselves well to the gamist approach.

One mechanism that *D&D* uses to measure progress is that of character levels. Levels represent a character's relative power in the game, and with increasing levels come increasing abilities, whether of magical power, martial prowess or other skills. In most iterations of *D&D*, player characters start at level one and move up as they gain experience until they reach the highest levels, at which point many campaigns conclude, and a new game, with new

The Wizarding World of *D&D*:
The Art of Roleplaying in the Potterverse
S. Evan Kreider

level 1 characters, begins. Levels seem especially suited to the Potterverse's emphasis on academia: each level could constitute a grade, or perhaps even a term. What constitutes a high level varies depending on the edition of *D&D*, but certainly two levels per year would bring Harry and his classmates to a fairly high proficiency of wizarding by the time of the events of the final books, though with room to grow as they continue after their student years, perhaps even becoming faculty themselves.

Another mechanic, and one related to levels that fits well with the series, is that of experience points. These are earned by overcoming various challenges: accumulating them allows a character to level up. In older editions, experience points were awarded for defeating monsters and finding treasure, very much linking it to the 'dungeon crawling' style of the game at the time. Later editions developed other reward systems, including the use of non-combat skills and abilities, achieving larger adventure goals, roleplaying and so forth. Rowling's novels are filled with all sorts of opportunities for Harry and friends, from the 'dungeon crawling' style of monsters and treasure seen in the Forbidden Corridor or Shrieking Shack, to the more common classes and extracurricular activities. For example, the students could be awarded experience points for passing tests in class, as well as a larger goal-completion experience award for passing each class. Another excellent opportunity to award experience points could be found in playing Quidditch: each goal earned or prevented could award experience points, with the greatest number of points awarded for – of course – catching the Golden Snitch. House points too could contribute. Earning experience points for school activities dovetails nicely with earning levels as school progresses, since in gaming terms, one contributes to the other.

One major *D&D* mechanic more difficult to reconcile with the Potterverse is that of 'character classes'. A class is, more or less, a profession; it represents the character's primary training and grants them the class's associated abilities and powers. For example, the early editions of *D&D* had a fighter class who was the best (relative to level) in combat; a magic-user (later called 'wizard') who was the primary spell-casting class; and so forth. Choosing classes to represent the various characters in the novels, or to play characters who would fit in naturally with them, could be tricky: there would be few fighters or thieves in comparison with the obvious wizards, for example. The latter case is especially problematic, since it would be difficult to customize or to distinguish among many characters: if everyone's a wizard, then there isn't much difference in abilities. Later editions mitigate this problem to some extent, since there are more spell-casting classes (wizards, sorcerers, warlocks, druids, bards, etc.), all of whom are spell-casters, but with some different class-based abilities and associated spell lists. Some of these classes also allow for specialization in particular kinds of spells even within their class's spell list; for example, a wizard might specialize in illusion spells. Even these editions will probably under-utilize some other classes, but as long as there are different kinds of spell-casting classes and spells from which to choose, their absence probably wouldn't be noticed or missed that much.

On the topic of spells, here once again *D&D* might not be as good a fit. The spell-casting system in earlier editions is typically referred to by gamers as 'Vancian' – that is, inspired by the fiction of Jack Vance, especially his *Tales of the Dying Earth* series (1950–84). In this system, a magic-user has a spell-book containing the spells to which he has access, but he can only memorize a certain number of spells at any one time. Once he casts a memorized spell, it disappears from his mind, and he cannot cast it again until he has had a period of rest and a chance to rememorize it. (Divine spell-casters such as clerics work largely in the same way, minus the spellbook – they always have access to any spell available to their level, apparently by way of their patron deity's grace and inspiration.) The upside is that a memorized spell can always be cast success-fully (though the target may have a chance to resist certain effects), so long as the caster has the appropriate components available: verbal (the magic words), somatic (the appropriate gestures) and material (various required ingredients). Also, the magic-user does not need a wand to cast spells, though magic wands do exist in the worlds of *D&D*, with other uses. Obviously, there's quite a bit about this that doesn't map onto the Potterverse wizards very well. For example, once a wizard knows a spell, s/he can cast it repeatedly without rememori-zation, and there is a chance to fail the spell, depending on how skilled at it s/he is. For another example, s/he does typically require his/her wand to cast, and far fewer of his/her spells require material components. Some later editions of *D&D* help a bit here, by assigning spell slots that can be spent on any memo-rized spell (which allows more repeated casting of the same spell); they have rules for creating focusing devices such as wands that can be used to improve spell-casting in general, and they also reduce the number of spells requiring material components; however, that's not quite the same.

One last defining aspect of *D&D* rules is that of character race. In most

The Wizarding World of *D&D*:
The Art of Roleplaying in the Potterverse
S. Evan Kreider

D&D settings, race represents the species of the character, such as dwarf or elf, and a character must pair a class with a class; for example, one could be a dwarf fighter or an elf wizard. The core books of most *D&D* editions included the traditional (some call them 'Tolkienesque') races: dwarf, elf, halfling (i.e. hobbit), human and sometimes gnome, half-elf and half-orc. For a radically different line-up, additional setting handbooks were required to detail other races for player characters. It's not clear how suitable *D&D* is right out of the box for *Harry Potter*. Though some of these races are present, Rowling redesigned most to be less Tolkienesque, as she takes her house elves from English folklore and omits the generic hobbits. Furthermore, the main characters – presumably the ones being run by the players – are primarily human, with other races probably relegated to non-player characters, controlled by the dungeon master to serve as antagonists, sidekicks and the like. On this point, Potterverse gamers seem to have two options: they can either stick to the human races in the core books (and let the dungeon master improvise a bit for non-player characters), or they can make their own mechanics for these other races, especially if they desire to use them for player characters.

It is precisely all this 'gamism' that supports the conclusion that *D&D*-style RPG interpretations of Rowling's world should be taken seriously as a form of art parallel with the novels themselves. According to some very important philosophers, art and aesthetics involve a kind of play. For example, Immanuel Kant, perhaps one of the most important modern aestheticians, argues that we ought to analyse aesthetic beauty, both in the natural world and the arts, less in terms of the objects themselves, and more in terms of our responses to those objects. Specifically, beauty lies not in those objects so much as in the pleasure that we experience in reaction to them. This pleasure arises from what Kant refers to as the 'free play' between our understanding and imagination. According to Kant, these objects do prompt our rational understanding, but not by way of fully realized and objective concepts that are involved in purely intellectual pursuits such as philosophy and science. Instead, they engage our understanding through a kind of thinking without such concepts, wherein we contemplate various formal features of the aesthetic objects without trying to capture them in a fully intellectual way, and thus also engage the imagination. This interplay between our understanding and imagination is literally an inter-play – emphasis on 'play' – that we find pleasurable. This is arguably very much the same sort of pleasure or fun that one experiences from gaming in a fictional world, rather than merely reading about it.

Hans-Georg Gadamer is another important philosopher who emphasizes the play aspect of art. To say that art is play is not to trivialize it, but to show its interactive aspects: for Gadamer, art is not merely an object, but something with which the audience interacts, even if in the role of spectator. An obvious example is a live-music performance. As the musicians play, the audience listens, hums along, taps their feet, applauds between songs and so forth. In this way, they are brought into the work of art, which is not merely an expression of the artist, but an opportunity to experience and reflect. Through this, the audience derives a kind of aesthetic satisfaction not unlike that of Kant's pleasurable free play between understanding and imagination. This also means that each audience member brings something of themselves to the work of art. An obvious comparison is that of reading a book, in the sense that each reader has his/her own interpretation. That's not to say that every interpretation is equally correct – an interpretation must be based on the text at least – but it does mean that there can be more than one 'right' reading, in the context of the reader's own feelings, experiences and so forth. To call this interaction with art a type of play is far from trivializing it; rather, it means that the audience is just as important as the art and the artist, all of which must interact. With this in mind, it seems that an RPG approach to *Harry Potter*'s world contributes even more, as the players can interact much more fully with the world by playing in it rather than simply reading about it.

Of course, not all roleplaying games do things the way that *Dungeons & Dragons* does; in fact, many were created precisely to offer alternatives to *D&D*'s various 'gamist' approaches. One notable example is *RuneQuest* (Chaosium, 1978), one of *D&D*'s early competitors, whose rules were eventually adapted into the company's house system for other games (most notably, *Call of Cthulhu* [1981]). This system, eventually called the basic roleplaying (BRP) system, was in turn taken up by other games such as *Legend* (Mongoose Publishing, 2014) and *OpenQuest* (D101, 2015). The fundamental approach of BRP, compared to *D&D*, is far less about gamism, and much more about creating a simulation of a fictional world, providing consistent and coherent rules through which the player characters can feel a sort of realism. It's important to understand that this is not that of merely mimicking the real world (after all, the setting may contain magic and monsters), but rather, of creating a sense of verisimilitude, so that the setting feels real to the players once they buy into the setting's assumptions. With

The Wizarding World of *D&D*:
The Art of Roleplaying in the Potterverse
S. Evan Kreider

this approach, players tend to be less interested in self-conscious gaming and more in immersing themselves into an alternate reality.

One way that the BRP family of games typically does this is by eliminating character classes, which on the simulationist view are overly artificial and constraining. Instead, BRP characters typically have a detailed and diverse array of skills, each of which covers not only general areas of ability (e.g. combat, magic, communication), but specific skills within each area (e.g. specific weapon types, unarmed attacks, dodging and parrying). Some BRP games do still incorporate professions to reflect a character's focused training, but even these are typically handled as a set of points that can be put into specific skill categories, while still allowing each character to develop additional general skills. Ultimately, though, no character is completely disallowed any skill (unless a particular iteration of BRP goes out of its way to offer that limit for some reason), so one's wizard character may still be handy with a sword, or one's warrior character may still have a few spells available.

This skill-based approach is especially good for simulating the magic of the Potterverse. For one, each spell can be its own skill, mimicking the importance of mastering spells in the fiction. Further, each skill has a rating that measures how good the character is with it, including whether the character succeeds in casting the spell each time. This reflects the various fictional character's personal aptitudes. For example, Ron struggles a great deal with his spell-casting compared to Harry or Hermione, at least until the very last books, in which he seems finally to catch up with his friends; his 'late-bloomer' approach to spell-casting could easily be reflected by lower skill ratings early on. In addition, skills improve in BRP with each successful use, with the opportunity of making an improvement roll. However, the better one gets at a skill, the harder it is to improve, reflecting the learning curve. Since Harry and Hermione are more successful early on, it makes sense that they would have more improvement rolls then; however, as they top out, Ron has more of an opportunity to catch up. The skill-system approach to magic also works nicely with magic specialization in the Potterverse since various types of skills can be grouped. For example, there is combat magic, which maps onto the 'Defence Against the Dark Arts' training that the young wizards receive. Other types of magic fit into various curricula, such as alchemy and divination, which allows for further specialization and individuation, so that not everyone is 'just a wizard'.

In addition to BRP's approach to magic, there is also a very different ap-

proach to combat and other physical dangers, reflecting the more simulationist and less gamist approach, whereas *D&D*'s gamist approach includes
mechanics such as armour class (likelihood of evading blows) and hit points
(potential damage before death or incapacitation). In *D&D*, wearing armour
unrealistically raises one's armour class (since heavy armour doesn't increase
dexterity). On BRP's more simulationist approach, armour functions as dam-
age-reduction to address just this issue. In *D&D*, hit points increase with each
level, so that a level 1 character might die from one good sword hit, but a level
10 character might survive several such hits from the same weapon. In BRP,
to reflect a more realistic and intuitive approach, hit points are typically set
throughout the character's development, perhaps improving slightly if some
associated attributes (e.g. constitution or size) increase, but giving dodging
and parrying higher priority. The BRP approach is arguably a better fit for ad-
venturing in the Potterverse, as it makes combat more dangerous, and not
much less so any later in one's career, and is therefore something to be avoided if possible, which Harry and his friends do. This in turn better reflects the
kinds of stories Rowling tells, since combat makes up a comparatively small
part of the narrative, and the characters remain vulnerable, with some like
Hedwig and Fred dying in the final volume.

The simulation approach that roleplaying games such as BRP take is a perfect example of a philosophical view of the arts known as *mimesis*, roughly
translated as 'imitation' or 'representation'. According to mimetic theories, the
arts create a virtual version of the world and objects in it. One of the earliest
and most famous philosophers to put forward a version of this theory is Plato,
although in his view, mimesis was mostly undesirable, with all of the negative
connotations of the word 'imitation': art involves fakery and illusion, not truth
and reality, and ought to be avoided in favour of philosophy (naturally). However, other mimetic theorists have a more positive spin. One more recent (and
also very important) philosopher, Suzanne Langer, argues that the arts create
something virtual that allows us to contemplate human experience and emotions in an even more sophisticated and philosophical way than life itself is often able to present. Various dramatic arts such as literature, theatre and film
create a virtual world for the viewer or reader to experience. In this way, simula-
tionist-learning RPGs certainly meet the definitions of art, creating as they do
their various imaginary settings, and they may do so even better than other art
forms, as they once again allow the players a more active engagement with the

The Wizarding World of *D&D*:
The Art of Roleplaying in the Potterverse
S. Evan Kreider

virtual world. In this way, RPGs such as BRP seem at least as virtual as the arts, if not more so, and thus have a claim as a legitimate form of art.

Figure 2: Fate Accelerated *(2013).*

Of course, not every player wants this approach to gaming in Harry's world. Though RPGs/BRPs are good at good at creating an imaginary world that one can inhabit, some players might feel that its emphasis on verisimilitude interferes with allowing them to fulfil their goals in their imaginary worlds – not to live a virtual life, but to tell stories and create dramatic narratives. To that end, several games have been developed over the years under the rubric of 'fiction, not physics'; that is, the rules should worry less about internal consistency according to the worlds' virtual laws of nature (as it were), and more about emulating fiction, with its emphasis on character, plot, theme and the like. One of the most notable examples is *Fate* (Evil Hat, 2003). Like the BRP family, *Fate.* has many variations and applications, but one of the core versions, *Fate Accelerated Edition* (*FAE*) (Evil Hat, 2014), is particularly apt for collaborative storytelling.

One particularly interesting thing about *FAE* is that it eschews traditional character skills in favour of other mechanics such as approaches and aspects. Approaches are closest to traditional skills, in that they are given ratings that a player adds to his dice roll to see if his/her character has succeeded at something; they include Careful, Clever, Flashy, Forceful, Quick and Sneaky. It's tempting to think of approaches as mere skill bundles, and they can be used that way sometimes; however, they are primarily meant to represent the personality and style of the character, and as such, each approach works for a number of actions, as long as it makes some sort of dramatic sense. For example, Forceful could be used to punch someone in the face (normally handled by a combat skill), interrogate a suspect 'bad-cop' style (normally handled by a communication skill) or blast someone with a powerful attack spell (normally a magic skill). Aspects, on the other hand, are phrases or short sentences that pick out more specific and dramatically important features of the character. The 'high concept' aspect summarizes the core role of the character in the story, perhaps reflecting his/her profession, specialization and/or background. The 'trouble' aspect reflects something about the character that tends to make his/her life difficult and creates dramatic conflict, such as a mysterious past or a mortal enemy. Other aspects are used simply to round out the character in almost any way the player can imagine.

The most important thing about these mechanics is that they contribute to storytelling, both during the character-creation process, as well as during play. Aspects are particularly valuable in this regard, since they imply something about not only the character, but also the gaming world itself. For example, if someone chooses the high concept of 'Half-Blood Wizard Prodigy', she is telling us not only that magic exists, but that not everyone can cast magic, and that there is a presumed connection between heritage and magical ability, which she herself challenges by having exceptional ability despite not being of pure blood. For another example, if someone chooses 'Hogwarts Divination Professor', she has established that there is a school called 'Hogwarts' where wizarding is taught, and that one important branch of magic taught there is divination. For one last example, if someone chooses 'The Boy Who Lived', he is telling us that he has a nemesis who bears him ill will from childhood, and is likely to resurface to cause him even more problems. Like aspects, approaches also contribute to the storytelling, especially through in-character play. Each character has one approach in which s/he is particularly strong, and each player is encouraged to use that approach, so long as it makes dramatic sense. Combat is an excellent example. Forceful is the most obvious approach, requiring little more than swinging a fist; Malfoy's gang members, such as Crabbe, would probably favour this approach. However, the rules absolutely allow for other approaches so long as the player gives a dramatic justification: one might make a Flashy attack with pyrotechnic magics, or a Quick attack with the help of one's racing broomstick. In any case, it's less about trying to game the system to overcome the challenge, as the *D&D*-style gamist might prefer, and more about what makes for an interesting narration that tells us something about one's character type.

Another definitive mechanic here is Fate Points, a kind of currency that players can spend for various effects, most of which are designed to promote the story's dramatic features. Fate Points can declare a minor story detail. For example, imagine the wizarding students were roused in the middle of the night and dragged off for some misadventure without the opportunity to prepare or even change into street clothes. Once confronted with a problem for which magic might be especially handy, a player might spend a Fate Point to

The Wizarding World of *D&D*:
The Art of Roleplaying in the Potterverse
S. Evan Kreider

declare that his/her character has brought his/her wand with him/her, despite the lack of obvious opportunity to have done so, just so long as s/he can explain why in a dramatically interesting way. ('Hey, she sleeps with it under her pillow!' she might declare.) More importantly, players may spend Fate Points to invoke or compel aspects – that is, to gain an advantage or cause a problem – either for his/her own character or that of another. This also allows the player to contribute to the story by deciding when the character's aspects will be dramatically interesting enough to have a mechanical effect on the gameplay. To this end, double-edged aspects – ones that can easily be used for good or bad effect – are particularly good at contributing to the story to promote the twists and turns of plot and fortune. For example, 'The Boy Who Lived' aspect might be invoked to help Harry divine Voldemort's plans, or it might be compelled against him to allow Voldemort to do the same to Harry. In these ways, Fate Points are there not to win the game, or simulate reality, but for dramatic effect.

With its emphasis on collaborative storytelling, *Fate* obviously has even more parallels with the dramatic arts than other RPGs, and as such, already has an obvious case to qualify as an art form itself. Aristotle's analysis of dramatic theatre (particularly tragedies) in *Poetics* is especially helpful in explaining why. According to Aristotle, good drama is more than a collection of random events – which one might find in more gamist or simulationist approaches to RPGs – but a coherent and unified series of events that create an overall plot and story structure, which in turn reveal the personalities (especially the virtues and flaws) of the characters and allow the audience to learn lessons about human life, as well as to experience a catharsis of important human emotions such as pity and fear. It's easy to see how *Fate*'s mechanics allow the players to do all these things, giving it as much claim to art as a theatrical play or a novel. The difference, though, is that rather than serving merely as author or audience, Fate's gaming experience allows the players to serve in both roles, as active participant in the co-creation of the aesthetic reality.

As we have seen, there is more than one way to approach gaming in the Potterverse, and more than one game to help us do so. So, which is the best way? Whatever way you like, of course! Having said that, the author would be remiss if he didn't recommend a few of his own favourites for each style. For a gamist approach, it's easy to suggest the current fifth edition of *Dungeons & Dragons* (Wizards of the Coast, 2014), not only because it is well-supported and very popular, but also because it brings together decades of experience in creating an engaging gamist experience; however, those who are interested in exploring *D&D*'s roots could try a 'retroclone' such as *Labyrinth Lord* (Goblinoid Games, 2007), which attempts to replicate early editions of *D&D* while presenting the rules in a clearer and more concise package. For those interested in trying out a simulationist approach with a member of the BRP family, *OpenQuest* serves as a free and streamlined option, while those interested in a heftier BRP ruleset would be well-advised to check out Design Mechanism's *Mythras* (2016) and its various supplements. Finally, those looking for a narrative approach can't go wrong with *Fate Accelerated Edition*, especially if they want to create their own version of the Potterverse; moreover, *Dresden Files Accelerated* (Evil Hat, 2017) provides a specific implementation of the *Fate* rules designed around the *Dresden Files* universe, which could be mined for magic systems and various supernatural character types. Of course, there is no one true way; it all depends on what kind of experience the players desire. What unites all of these is a genuine desire to do justice to the world of *Harry Potter*, and an opportunity to co-create something that pays respect to Rowling's art, while also creating something of aesthetic value itself, and that is what art is all about. ●

~~~~~~~~~~~

GO FURTHER

Games
Dungeons & Dragons
(Lake Geneva, WI: Tactical Studies Rules, Inc., 1974), http://dnd.wizards.com.

RuneQuest
(Ann Arbor, MI: Chaosium, 1978)

Call of Cthulhu
(Ann Arbor, MI: Chaosium, 1981)

Fate
(USA: Evil Hat, 2003), https://fate-srd.com.

The Wizarding World of *D&D*:
The Art of Roleplaying in the Potterverse
S. Evan Kreider

Labyrinth Lord
(Appleton, WI: Goblinoid Games, 2007), http://goblinoidgames.com/index.php/downloads.

Dungeons & Dragons
(Renton, WA: Wizards of the Coast, 2014)

Fate Accelerated Edition (FAE)
(USA: Evil Hat, 2014), https://www.evilhat.com/home/fae.

Legend
(Swindon: Mongoose Publishing, 2014).

OpenQuest
(Manchester: D101, 2015), http://d101games.com/openquest.

Mythras
(Grafton, ON: Design Mechanism, 2016), http://thedesignmechanism.com.

Dresden Files Accelerated
(USA: Evil Hat, 2017), https://www.evilhat.com/home/dresden-files-accelerated.

Online
'Witchcraft & Wizardry, a *Fate Accelerated Edition* Harry Potter game (WIP)'
Qwo
Reddit. 10 May 2017, https://www.reddit.com/r/rpg/comments/6abamn/witchcraft_wizardry_a_fate_accelerated_edition.

'Basic Rules for *Dungeons & Dragons*.' Dungeons & Dragons, 6 October 2018, http://dnd.wizards.com/articles/features/basicrules.

'Make Your *DnD* Campaign Truly Magical by Accio-ing These Harry Potter Character Sheets.' Geek & Sundry, 21 January 2016, https://geekandsundry.com/harry-potter-character-sheets-to-make-your-dnd-campaign-truly-magical.

'*OpenQuest* System Reference Document.' D101 Games, http://d101games.com/open-quest/openquest-developers-kit.

Part 3
Critical World

Chapter
06

Tommy Taylor Reveals Harry's True Power: Stories and Fans Can Reshape Our World

Joel Hawkes

→ Mike Carey and Peter Gross's comic book series *The Unwritten* (2009-15) follows the adventures of Tom Taylor – son of author Wilson Taylor who has written a series of fantasy novels about a boy wizard with the same name as his son.

Figure 1: Cover art for The Unwritten by Yuko Shimizu (2013).

The fictional brown-haired, bespectacled Tommy attends wizarding school, and, accompanied by two friends, Sue Sparrow and Peter Price, he must repeatedly battle his nemesis Count Ambrosio, an immortal vampire responsible for the death of Tommy's parents when he was a baby. The resemblance to *Harry Potter* is intentional. Carey and Gross's series might be read, on one level, as *Potter* fanfiction, but as Carey explains, while *Potter* is clearly a shaping influence, it was not the starting point of the series; rather, as the comic developed and 'became about celebrity and the sort of viral spread of ideas in popular culture [...] [t]he character of the boy-wizard seemed to be tailor made' (cited by Hallett). *The Unwritten* takes inspiration, then, from the *Potter* (fan) phenomenon to illustrate how stories can transform our world, culturally and, indeed, physically. At the beginning of *The Unwritten* comic series, the 'real' Tom, speaking at a Tommy Taylor convention about his fictional counterpart, is revealed to be the Tommy Taylor of the novels ('Tommy Taylor and the Bogus Identity', [2010]): fiction and 'reality' collide as Tom takes on the powers of the boy wizard and becomes a saviour figure worshipped around the world. Through his magical connection to storytelling, Tom/Tommy jumps between physical landscapes and fictional ones (Taylor's novels, *Moby-Dick* [Melville, 1851], *Frankenstein* [Shelley, 1823], etc.), battling a dark cabal who seek to control the world through their stories. This fantastical landscape makes readers conscious of the ability of stories to shape the world around us. It is a celebration of storytelling.

Inspired by *The Unwritten* as a kind of *Potter* fanfiction, fans can finally see the power of the Potterverse and especially its devotees to transform the world around us. From imagined and 'real' sites in the *Potter* novels and films, to the blurring of these through fan 'pilgrimage', the *Potter* phenomenon has remapped and reshaped locations across Britain, and reminds us how, like Tom Taylor, we exist between the physical world and the written landscapes of our favourite stories.

Tommy Taylor Reveals Harry's True Power:
Stories and Fans Can Reshape Our World
Joel Hawkes

Stories are who we are

The Unwritten emphasizes the importance of storytelling in the *construction* of the self and society by referencing *Harry Potter*, one of the most successful and influential stories of the early twenty-first century. Still, the comic acknowledges that such a tale does not stand alone but gains its power from a tradition of storytelling. In *The Unwritten*, Wilson Taylor writes fourteen novels about a boy wizard, Tommy Taylor, setting loose a powerful story in the world, to combat a group that have long controlled the world through their own storytelling. We see the cabal task writers, through history, manipulate stories: one member tells Rudyard Kipling, 'Empire and Sacrifice. You supply the words and the tune' ('Tommy Taylor and the Bogus Identity'). Kipling's words rally people to the cause of the British Empire – words that instil belief and help the Empire grow. As the cabal shifts its attention to the United States of America, it employs Samuel Clemens (Mark Twain) to help establish the stories of a new regime ('Tommy Taylor and the Bogus Identity'). The comic explores how stories not only change our understanding of the world but the world itself. The right story can help birth an empire, send thousands to war, even create a new religion.

The story of Tommy, the boy wizard, is powerful because it draws from archetypal traditions of storytelling, just like *Harry Potter*. In a standalone tale, *The Unwritten: Tommy Taylor and the Ship That Sank Twice* (2013), Carey and Gross provide a version of the first Tommy Taylor novel, crosscut with Wilson's Taylor's struggle to write the book as a modern myth. Early attempts draw from familiar narratives – Superman as a baby sent into space to escape a dying planet or characters battling Egyptian gods. The writer is 'playing variants on the templates that are already there: Narnia, *Lord of the Rings*, Superman, and all their bastard offspring' (*The Unwritten: Tommy Taylor and the Ship That Sank Twice*). As Tom admits at a convention panel, in the opening pages of the series, yes, Tommy Taylor does have 'similarities with *Harry Potter*. Books of Magic. *The Worst Witch*' ('Tommy Taylor and the Bogus Identity'). *Potter* is of course inspired by these other sources as well – that's part of their point. Harry Potter is also a powerful archetypal figure who taps into traditions of storytelling of the mythic questing hero as outlined by Joseph Campbell in *The Hero with a Thousand Faces* (1949), while the orphan boy, with a special heritage, great power and a fate to be fulfilled is a timeless and much used archetype and narrative. In *The Unwritten: Tommy Taylor and the Ship That Sank Twice,*

Wilson looks to tap into the power of such a figure, to create an archetype so powerful 'that he works backwards and erases his own precursors'. Arguably *Harry Potter* is – for the present moment, at least – this archetype, drawing from foundational stories and myths of European and American society, and traditions of fantasy writing, in a way becoming part of society's cultural narrative. He is the archetypal hero. Everyone knows the story of Harry Potter, right?

The power of Harry to effect change in the world comes then not from the story but through the reception of the story – through, in a sense, belief. Something of Potter's great cultural impact is due to his position as a saviour figure, but this is only the beginning. As the 'boy who lived', and in the final book/film the boy who dies and rises from the dead, we are reminded of the Christian story of Christ but also of Christ's predecessors, the dying and rising God/King – Osiris, Attis or Adonis. Prometheus, too, suffers for the redemption of humankind. Carey and Gross explore the power of the saviour embodied in Tom/Tommy – he is also a figure who dies and rises again. This saviour has dominated storytelling across the world for centuries. An archetype carries great meaning and influence, but it is belief that truly empowers him. In *The Unwritten*, Tom can channel magical powers from the novels and his fictional counterpart because many readers and fans around the world believe in the stories – they love and read them. Belief and practise give the tales, and Tom, power. The objection to *Harry Potter* by some Christian groups in the United States speaks to this – Potter is almost a challenge to another saviour figure's pre-eminent cultural position. Indeed, Iver Neumann suggests that *Potter* is part of an emergence in the West of a new type of religion that blends traditional religious practices and cultural consumption to produce more individual religious experiences. *Potter* as a religion? That really would change the world. The film adaptations, the extreme marketing and branding build the power of the *Potter* stories, but it is the fans (the 'believers') that have the most impact. Child readers and viewers have grown into teenage fans; now thousands gather at conventions and take part in cosplay events. Even as you sit alone to read a *Potter* book, there are likely thousands of people around the world doing the same. Are these events and gatherings and readings like a religious practice?

In *The Unwritten*, Tom's companion, Richard Savoy (the real-world version of Tommy Taylor's wizard best friend, Peter Price) runs a website devoted to

Tommy Taylor Reveals Harry's True Power:
Stories and Fans Can Reshape Our World
Joel Hawkes

updates on Tom/Tommy. These postings and extracts from other fansites, blogs and chat rooms are interspersed through the comics to show the effect of the boy wizard's adventures on the world. When Tom needs to draw power from the story, Savoy posts requests online to fans: read the books out loud, recite your favourite passages, act out scenes, type out your own fan stories, and '[i]f you're religious, pray for him' ('Tommy Taylor and the War of Words', [2012]). Tom taps into the power generated by these acts. The comic shows how great stories live through their readers. The tales become part of a communal experience, what Carl Jung called the collective unconscious – what Tom Taylor calls the: 'Fictional Unconscious. The minds of all the millions of people who read' ('Leviathan' [2011]). It is Tom Riddle (Voldemort), in *Harry Potter and the Chamber of Secrets* (Rowling, 1998), who draws attention to what a 'silly little book can do'. This aspect of Tom's stories reveals the power of the *Potter* phenomenon far beyond its popularity: like Tom does literally, *Harry Potter* has become a channel for fans' imagination leading to fannish adventures and transformations of their world. Through individual and group readings, online postings, conventions and gatherings, all inspired by a book, *Harry Potter* has become one of the great archetypes of a transcultural consciousness, with the ability to reshape our world.

Storytelling as a spatial phenomenon

An important part of *Potter*'s influence, like that of any novel, is its ability to transform our sense of space. Stories occur in places: characters often exist in a world not unlike ours – they move through streets, inhabit houses and travel via different modes of transport. The landscape of the *Potter* stories is closely aligned with the everyday spaces of Britain – and something of the appeal and relatability of *Potter* might be located in this similarity. We recognize a Scottish landscape as we near Hogwarts and acknowledge London, especially named locations like King's Cross train station in the city. In a study of teenagers who grew up with *Harry Potter*, Ranjana Das found that interviewees remembered and related to the books and films through 'references to the real': red London buses and King's Cross, school 'Houses' and the real (not magical) train of the Hogwarts Express. The Potterverse is in some ways already part of our 'reality'. Yet, at the same time, the suburbia in which Harry grows up, in the Dursley's home, 4 Privet Drive, of Little Whinging, Surrey, is all too familiar to many of us. As a location of dreary oppression and forced conformity, the home epitomizes the homogenized streets and boxed houses of the ubiquitous British suburb. Readers see something of their own (dreary) everyday life and its spatial context and glimpse their own longing for release from such a world. The fantasy puts magic into our Muggle lives, but as with all good fantasy it also reflects on relevant issues such as struggles to fit in at school; conflicts of sex, race (see Ostry) and class (see Park); and explores the various myths and stories of British history and identity. The novels are, in many ways, place- and culture-specific – set in Britain, pondering British issues, even fuelling the sense of nostalgia for something older and better and historical ('magic?'). Nostalgia is a powerful cultural force in Britain at the beginning of the twenty-first century. The *Potter* landscape, then, reflects our own milieu.

This mapping of Britain through seven novels doesn't just tap into the British zeitgeist, reflecting physical, cultural and political landscapes; it also transforms them. A member of the cabal in *The Unwritten* proclaims that '[s]tory is a property of space' ('Tommy Taylor and the War of Words'). Like many tales before it, *Harry Potter*'s stories have imbued physical location. *Potter* is mapped onto Britain. We begin to associate certain real locations with the stories. King's Cross station in London is one important real-world site, home to Platform 9 ¾ in the stories, from where the Hogwarts Express departs. Other locations have taken on *Potter* significance, not from the novels but rather the films: Tower Bridge and Westminster see the flight of the Order of the Phoenix in the fifth film, *Harry Potter and the Order of the Phoenix* (Yates, 2007); we see the Knight Bus squeeze between two double-deckers on Lambeth Bridge in *Harry Potter and the Prisoner of Azkaban* (Cuarón, 2004); and the Millennium Bridge is attacked by Death Eaters in *Harry Potter and the Half-Blood Prince* (Yates, 2009). Many more real sites are used as settings for imaginary locations. An optician's shop in Leadenhall Market becomes the Leaky Cauldron – the entrance to Diagon Alley – which is also filmed in Leadenhall Market in *Harry Potter and the Philosopher's Stone/Sorcerer's Stone* (Columbus, 2001). The exterior of Australia House doubles as Gringotts's Bank and Great Scotland Yard becomes the visitors' entrance to the Ministry of Magic. Outside of London, Alnwick Castle is used for Hogwarts, though Hogwarts is also filmed at various locations at Oxford University. Most spectacularly, Duke Humphrey's Library, in Oxford's Bodleian Library, doubles as Hogwarts's Library. Finally, the now-iconic Glenfinnan Viaduct in Scotland is

Tommy Taylor Reveals Harry's True Power:
Stories and Fans Can Reshape Our World
Joel Hawkes

the track over which Harry and Ron fly the Weasleys' car in *Harry Potter and the Chamber of Secrets* (Columbus, 2002). The films, more than the books, map the Potterverse onto 'real' locations.

Harry Potter does what many stories have done before – it attaches itself to place. Physical sites become better known because of their literary and film associations; they take on narrative, become loaded with meaning. James Cateridge uses the concept of 'deep mapping' to read the influence of *Potter* on Oxford – the films helping to create a layered map constructed of the many tales that are associated with a location, and accessible to the knowing visitor, who uses 'movie maps, guides and online cartography to enable a seductive fantasy of *embodiment*, a means to temporarily inhabit a fictional hero by entering their world' (original emphasis). He goes on to recognize that this 'fantasy space is not quite the real Oxford'. But, of course, the fantasy world of *Potter* does manifest in, and rely upon, the real Oxford milieu. Sites significant to fictional storytelling can then be mapped and located in the 'real', physical, world.

The Unwritten explores this power of mapping. Tommy is left a copy of the 1507 Waldseemüller map of the world – the first map to use the name America – 'a vision of the world that actually changed the world' ('Inside Man' [2010]); on it, Post-it Notes identify places, authors and books – key locations of storytelling, like the Villa Diodati, in Switzerland, the house where Mary Shelley created *Frankenstein* (and where Wilson Taylor chooses to write the Tommy novels ['Tommy Taylor and the Bogus Identity']), or Pittsfield, Massachusetts, where Herman Melville wrote *Moby-Dick*. To be able to tap into the power of storytelling, Tom's father teaches him maps of literary locations: passing the Senate House in London, Tom identifies the building as the Ministry of Truth from George Orwell's *1984* (1949) – Orwell worked here and took inspiration from this building ('Tommy Taylor and the Bogus Identity'). He goes on to point out 221B Baker Street, which 'didn't actually exist when Conan Doyle wrote' Sherlock Holmes, and acknowledges the Foundling Hospital at Coram Fields ('Tommy Taylor and the Bogus Identity'), where Dickens found inspiration for *Oliver Twist* (1837–39), and where Tattycoram of *Little Dorrit* (1855–57) grows up. Walking through London, Tom identifies a house in Bloomsbury where Virginia Woolf lived and 32 Windsor Gardens, where Paddington lived with the Brown family ('Dead Man's Knock' [2011]). There's a nod to *Potter*, too, when a cardboard cut-out of Tommy Taylor, advertising the release of a new Tommy

Figure 2: An owl visits the
King's Cross platform. King's
Cross, London (2014).

novel, is seen on Platform 9 of King's Cross ('Dead Man's Knock'). Fictional
and physical locations, from the book and where the authors were known to
have lived or written, blur on the map as they do in the minds of fans. Tommy,
by channelling his belief in his fictional counterpart and his increasing belief
that he is Tommy the wizard made manifest, is able to slip between written and
physical worlds and conjure characters from books onto the streets. It is the
colliding of literary and physical spaces that allows this to happen – everything
happens in the available space. The comic examines the power of fans' belief
and its influence on the real world. In a sense, fans visiting sites to see the locations of the *Potter* films, and sites from the books, cross over into the realms
of the stories – an imaginative crossing that can transform physical space.

The belief of fans can rewrite space

In following the *Potter* books and films like 'maps', fans set out into the physical landscape and transform it. This is nothing new, but *Potter* is perhaps the
most dominant presence in London today. Fan trips to *Potter* sites can be read
as acts of pilgrimage – and this physical presence has a real impact on the
landscape. As Dean MacCannell explains in his study of tourism, such visits
allow one to connect 'one's own marker to a sight already marked by others',
thereby reaffirming its worth through participation in a 'collective ritual'. The
books and films make the connection to a physical location, and then visitor
after visitor cements that location and its *Potter* significance. This is a practice of place, usefully understood through Michel de Certeau's influential
The Practice of Everyday Life (1988). De Certeau conflates text and physical

Tommy Taylor Reveals Harry's True Power:
Stories and Fans Can Reshape Our World
Joel Hawkes

space, suggesting that a reader reading a book 'slips into the author's place' and that just as the urban-planned street is 'transformed into a space by walkers', the written place is transformed into space (is practised) by the reader as s/he reads. A mapped place is opened up as we move through it (reading or 'walking'). And, we can, of course, read a physical street as well. We read onto it memories of events there, connecting it in our minds to other places we have been, or, we can read onto the street the stories and places of *Harry Potter*. Reading *Potter* onto London is such a popular pastime that numerous companies do walking or bus tours of '*Potter*' sites. A number of websites help you plan your own *Potter* tour. Sites like King's Cross are practised (read and walked) by so many people that they become a *Potter* location in the popular imagination. Everyone knows a young wizard travelling to Hogwarts needs to leave from this station.

This double movement of fans (reading and 'walking' – or, perhaps, flying a broomstick) doesn't just help invest meaning in place; it can change the popular imaginary of place and alter it physically. Here it is useful to jump, like Tommy Taylor, into another literary text to illustrate the power of writer and fans: one of the most successful British writers in transforming a landscape is Thomas Hardy, the nineteenth-century novelist, whose literary creation of Wessex reshaped south-west England and England itself. In his novels, he renames the south-west counties Wessex – drawing from the older Wessex name of the Anglo-Saxon Kingdom, whose ruler Alfred is seen to have overseen the emergence of England as a nation. The historical and mythical associations are a heady mix, while his novels present a rural world being transformed by the modernity (trains, machinery, etc.) of the nineteenth century. The novels not only tap into the popular imaginary of England as a rural idyll, but also help establish it. So popular were the novels that a tourism industry grew up around them at the beginning of the twentieth century, with guide books aligning fictional place names with the real locations that inspired them. Today you can go and visit Hardy's home in Dorset – the heart of his fictional Wessex – but you can also walk around the locations inhabited by his fictional characters. Companies, including utility services, take on the Wessex name. Even though no such region officially exists, you can visit it. Not everyone has read a Hardy novel, but most can point you in the direction of Wessex, and they know it is a rural landscape, and know that, well, that's what England's like. The myth of England, the idea of England, is transformed.

Potter is well on the way to reshaping Britain in a similar way: Britain is the country of *Harry Potter*, as the prime minister of the United Kingdom (played by Hugh Grant) in *Love Actually* (Curtis, 2003), exclaims in celebration of the nation. Just as tourists in pursuit of Hardy changed a landscape, so *Potter* fans have a bodily impact on space. Their presence changes meanings and even names, but also physical space. Fans eager to see the Glenfinnan Viaduct in Scotland have risked their lives trespassing on the lines ('*Harry Potter* Fans Warned after Near Misses on Glenfinnan Viaduct' [2017]); parents with children have been spotted walking the viaduct on foot ('Couple and Child Seen Running on *Harry Potter* Railway' [2015]). News agencies report the stories and the *Potter* associations of the site, while increased security around the track shows the impact of fans on the physical locale. Visitors to *Potter* sites, from Oxford to London, like Leadenhall Market, bring people and money into communities – space is adapted to manage numbers, while shops begin to offer *Potter* products. The BBC reported in 2016 – citing a London School of Economics professor – that the franchise was worth £4 billion to London alone ('*Harry Potter*'s Magical Effect "Worth £4bn to London"'). The '*Harry Potter* effect' was also credited with the rise of boarding school enrolments in the United Kingdom 2000–03, as Garner writes: children wanted to go to boarding school like Harry, Hermione and Ron. Academic *Potter* events, like the first British *Potter* conference at the University of St Andrews in 2012, *A Brand of Fictional Magic: Reading Harry Potter as Literature*, discussed the books as 'serious' literature, bringing people together from across the country. More common still are fan events like *Harry Potter*-themed dances or Halloween parties. Fan conventions like *DiagCon* in Manchester (2018), or the more established *LeakyCon* (in Texas in 2018) continue to mobilize thousands of fans to celebrate all things Harry. There is, then, a physical presence of fans practising space, adding *Potter* 'markers' to locations, changing the physical spaces we inhabit – and not just in Britain. *Fantastic Beasts and Where to Find Them* (book: Rowling, 2001; film: Yates, 2016) begins with a reimagining of New York; Chestnut Hill College in Philadelphia holds an annual conference for high school scholarship called *Wands and Wizards*, formerly the *Harry Potter Festival*; while *Teen Vogue* reported *Harry Potter*-themed signs at the recent anti-gun protests in the United States. Their inspiration was found in Hogwarts students' resistance to Death Eaters, whom many equated with the NRA, De Elizabeth notes. As Carey and Gross are keen to point out in *The*

Tommy Taylor Reveals Harry's True Power:
Stories and Fans Can Reshape Our World
Joel Hawkes

Unwritten, the right story in the right place at the right time can shape a nation or change the world order itself. *Potter* in various ways is mobilized on our streets, in convention centres, in schools (where it is used to teach), at protests and even in our heads in our day-to-day meanderings.

This ability of fans and the *Potter* phenomenon to reshape space around us is, perhaps, most particularly manifested at King's Cross station in London. A recent meeting of fans there helped keep *Potter*'s presence alive. Thousands turned up (including actor Warwick Davis, who plays Professor Flitwick in the films) on the 1st of September, 2017, the date in the final novel when Harry's son, Albus Severus Potter, first boards the Hogwarts Express. Fans – dressed as *Potter* characters or in the colours of the Hogwarts Houses – celebrated on Platform 9 and around the station, many taking photographs in front of the sign for Platform 9 ¾ that has long been part of the station – positioned above a luggage trolley, with a bird cage on top, which appears to be disappearing through a solid brick wall. This very physical manifestation of *Potter* at the station reveals how the station begins to exist on a continuum of everyday life/literature/film. The BBC's Daniel Rosney reports one fan at the event, who explains: 'It's such a sense of community I'm really glad to be here and it's this whole place which makes me feel like I belong there.' Fans and place meet – a sense of belief and belonging come together through place – at a King's Cross platform and in front of the beautiful red Victorian Gothic architecture of St Pancras International next door. Just inside King's Cross, fans purchase merchandise at the Harry Potter Shop at Platform 9 ¾, from Dobby plushes, copies of the Marauders Map, Gryffindor Quidditch sweaters and wands, to chocolate frogs and Every Flavour Beans. The frogs might not jump, and the beans don't come in bogey flavour, but the reality between page and place blurs just a little more. The famous lines from the Kevin Costner film, *Field of Dreams* (Robinson, 1989), went, '[i]f you build it, they will come' (with a little nod here to the Mandela Effect). We might now reverse this: if you come, they will build it. *Potter* fans are remapping and reshaping the streets and locales of London – a kind of magical act in itself.

The commitment and continued excitement of fans engenders place with *Potter* meaning; encourages a plethora of stores to sell *Potter* wares; sees tour companies plan *Potter* tours; and has others organize conventions and conferences that discuss and celebrate the boy wizard and his world – which is, of course, in a sense, our world, too, for his story exists here. And it is our stories that make us who we are, that build and unite communities. It is our stories that we move in and out of every day as we recall past events, chat about the latest movie, reminisce with a friend, read novels, then read the street as we walk to school or work. These stories don't just make us; they remake the world – they exist in space, just as we do. Therefore, they determine how we move through those spaces, physical, cultural, social, imaginative, political. Space is a useful and adaptable metaphor to understand the construction and practice of our world. And '*Potter* space' seems particularly adaptable, ubiquitous and lasting. It is 'rewriting' so much, and, in a sense, fans take it with them wherever they go. ●

GO FURTHER

Books
The Irresistible Rise of Harry Potter
Andrew Blake
(New York: Verso, 2002)

The Unwritten: Tommy Taylor and the Ship That Sank Twice
Mike Carey and Peter Gross
(Burbank, CA: DC Comics, 2013)

The Practice of Everyday Life
Michel de Certeau (trans. Steven Rendall)
(Berkeley, CA: Blackwell Publishing, 1988)

The Tourist: A New Theory of the Leisure Class
Dean MacCannell
(London: Macmillan, 1976)

Comic books
'Tommy Taylor and the Bogus Identity'
Mike Carey and Peter Gross
The Unwritten 1 (New York: Vertigo, 2010)

Tommy Taylor Reveals Harry's True Power:
Stories and Fans Can Reshape Our World
Joel Hawkes

'Inside Man'
Mike Carey and Peter Gross
The Unwritten 2 (New York: Vertigo, 2010)

'Dead Man's Knock'
Mike Carey and Peter Gross
The Unwritten 3 (New York: Vertigo, 2011)

'Leviathan'
Mike Carey and Peter Gross
The Unwritten 4 (New York: Vertigo, 2011)

'On to Genesis'
Mike Carey, Peter Gross and Vince Locke
The Unwritten 5 (New York: Vertigo, 2012)

'Tommy Taylor and the War of Words'
Mike Carey and Peter Gross
The Unwritten 6 (New York: Vertigo, 2012)

Extracts/Essays/Articles
'Deep Mapping and Screen Tourism: The Oxford of *Harry Potter* and *Inspector Morse*'
James Cateridge
In *Humanities* 4 (2015), pp. 320-33.

'"I've Walked This Street": Readings Of "Reality" In British Young People's Reception of *Harry Potter*'
Ranjana Das
In *Journal of Children and Media*, 10:3 (2016), pp. 341-54.

'Roles of Films and Television Dramas in International Tourism: The Case of Japanese Tourists to the UK'
Chieko Iwashita
In *Journal of Travel & Tourism Marketing*, 24 (2008), pp. 139-51.

'Pop Goes Religion: Harry Potter Meets Clifford Geertz'
Iver Neumann
In *European Journal of Cultural Studies*, 9 (2006), pp. 81–100.

'Accepting Mudbloods: The Ambivalent Social Vision of JK Rowling's Fairy Tales'
Elaine Ostry
In G. Anatole (ed.). *Reading* Harry Potter: *Critical Essays* (Westport, CT: Praeger Publishers, 2003), pp. 89–102.

'Class and Socio-Economic Identity in Potter's England'
Julia Park
In G. Anatole (ed.). *Reading* Harry Potter: *Critical Essays* (Westport, CT: Praeger Publishers, 2003), pp. 179–90.

Online
'Best *Harry Potter* Signs at the March for Our Lives'
De Elizabeth
Teen Vogue. 25 March 2018, https://www.teenvogue.com/story/best-harry-potter-signs-march-for-our-lives.

'Boarding Schools Miss Their *Harry Potter* Magic'
Richard Garner
The Independent. 28 April 2004, https://www.independent.co.uk/news/education/education-news/boarding-schools-miss-their-harry-potter-magic-58153.html.

'Q&A with *The Unwritten*'s Mike Carey'
Alison Hallett
Portland Mercury. 1 July 2010, https://www.portlandmercury.com/BlogtownPDX/archives/2010/01/07/an-qanda-with-the-unwrittens-mike-carey.

'Muggles Turn Up at Platform 9 ¾ to Wish Albus Severus Potter Well'
Daniel Rosney
BBC News. 1 September 2017, http://www.bbc.co.uk/newsbeat/article/41121105/muggles-turn-up-at-platform-9-34-to-wish-albus-severus-potter-well.

Tommy Taylor Reveals Harry's True Power:
Stories and Fans Can Reshape Our World
Joel Hawkes

'Couple and Child Seen Running on *Harry Potter* Railway.' BBC News, 7 October 2015, http://www.bbc.com/news/uk-scotland-highlands-islands-34466008.

'*Harry Potter* Fans Warned after Near Misses on Glenfinnan Viaduct.' BBC News, 19 May 2017, http://www.bbc.com/news/uk-scotland-highlands-islands-39976271.

'*Harry Potter*'s Magical Effect "Worth £4bn to London".' BBC News, 28 September 2016, http://www.bbc.com/news/av/uk-england-london-37501694/harry-potter-s-magical-effect-worth-4bn-to-london.

Film/Television
Field of Dreams, Phil Alden Robinson, dir. (USA: Universal Pictures, 1989).

Harry Potter and the Philosopher's Stone/Sorcerer's Stone, Chris Columbus, dir. (USA: Warner Bros, 2001).

Harry Potter and the Chamber of Secrets, Chris Columbus, dir. (USA: Warner Bros, 2002).

Harry Potter and the Prisoner of Azkaban, Alfonso Cuarón, dir. (USA: Warner Bros, 2004).

Harry Potter and the Order of the Phoenix, David Yates, dir. (USA: Warner Bros, 2007).

Harry Potter and the Half-Blood Prince, David Yates, dir. (USA: Warner Bros, 2009).

'OF COURSE IT IS HAPPENING INSIDE YOUR HEAD, HARRY, BUT WHY ON EARTH SHOULD THAT MEAN THAT IT IS NOT REAL?'

ALBUS DUMBLEDORE
(HARRY POTTER AND THE DEATHLY HALLOWS)

Fan Appreciation #3:
Matt Maggiacomo
(executive director, HP Alliance)
Valerie Estelle Frankel

Matt Maggiacomo's Twitter profile (2015).

Matt joined the Harry Potter Alliance (HP Alliance/HPA) in 2007 as a founding member of its Board of Directors – around the same time he quit his day job to become a full-time wizard rocker. He spent the next five years touring the United States and Canada as the Whomping Willows and used his fringe Internet stardom to raise money for the HPA and promote its chapters programme. In July 2013, Matt left the HPA's Board and accepted a job as the organization's first chapters director. After presiding over the programme's expansion into six continents and facilitating the creation of Granger Leadership Academy, Matt became the HPA's third executive director in January 2015. Matt enjoys being a Dad in Plaid, cat lady, amateur gardener and unofficial Providence tour guide in his spare time.

Valerie Estelle Frankel (VEF): How long have you personally been a *Potter* fan? I know you're in the Whomping Willows – which cons do you attend? And how would you say the fandom's been doing lately?

Matt Maggiacomo (MM): I've been a fan since 2001, when my ex-girlfriend convinced me to read *Harry Potter and the Sorcerer's Stone* [Rowling, 1997] in advance of the movie release. I've attended and performed at every *LeakyCon* since the first one in 2009, and every *MISTI-Con* as well. I've also attended and performed at *Phoenix Rising*, *Prophecy*, *Terminus*, *Azkatraz* and *Infinitus* [two tracks of *Harry Potter*-focused conventions sponsored by HP Education Fanon, Inc. and by the educational group Narrate Conferences], plus a number of smaller cons and festivals with a wizard rock component.

VEF: So how did being *Potter* fans translate to charity, in your opinion? Is there a tie-in with the music? And do you see other fan groups approaching what you all are accomplishing?

MM: The *Harry Potter* books aren't shy about promoting a worldview that includes equality, social justice, participatory citizenship and intergenerational mentorship, and those qualities are reflected in core *Harry Potter* fandom. For example, within the wizard rock community, we saw a handful of experienced musicians helping dozens of younger songwriters learn how to record, release and promote their music, and most bands had some kind of charitable element worked into their financial model. One band dedicated their fundraising to the genocide in Darfur, another to

Fan Appreciation #3
Matt Maggiacomo

marriage equality, many others to women's rights and gender equity. And when you asked a band why they were advocating for a particular issue, their answer was something along the lines of, 'Isn't that what wizard rock bands do?' Charity and advocacy are natural fits for folks who see themselves as living out the values of the *Harry Potter* series. I believe the *Star Trek* fandom is the only other fan community with this type of widespread social activism. Many newer fandoms are active, but the focus tends to be on improving representation in various iterations of their favourite story – which is great, but the goals are more limited in scope.

VEF: I believe you all started by teaming up with stars, like wizard rock bands. Can you recall a particularly cool event?

MM: Yes! The HPA has turned to celebrities many times to amplify our work. In 2010, we partnered with John Green and actors from shows like *Heroes* [2006–10], *True Blood* [2008–14], *Lost* [2004–10], *Firefly* [2002–03] and *The Wire* [2002–08] to raise $123,000 for Partners in Health, for use in their disaster relief efforts in Haiti. The project was assembled in a matter of a few days, with HPA staffers working around the clock to put together a crowdfunder, design a website, organize a livestream telethon and confirm celebrity appearances. It was a wild experience and showed the true power of a united and connected fandom.

VEF: Do you think Harry himself would join your team? Or Hermione? What about J. K. Rowling?

MM: Hermione would've come up with the idea and built it from the ground up, and then she would've talked Harry into starting a chapter. J. K. Rowling has publicly endorsed our work, but her advocacy efforts are focused on her awesome organization, Lumos.

VEF: Is there a mission statement? How do you choose your causes?

MM: Mission statement: the Harry Potter Alliance turns fans into heroes. We're changing the world by making activism accessible through the power of story.

We've developed an issue platform and we are committed to forwarding these issues in any way we can: education and libraries, gender equity, LGBTQ+ equality, media reform, racial justice, climate change and youth

Figure 1: The HPA
ScarBurrow, University
of Toronto Scarborough
executive team: Amreen
Popatiya, Hifza Buhari,
Natasha Seeram, Shagun
Kanwar, Agarsh Satheesh
and Strahinja
Govorcinovic (2017).

advocacy. We have a team of researchers who keep us updated on developments relevant to these issues, and we use that research (and input from our various strategic partners) to determine opportunities for action and engagement.

VEF: The campaign that really struck me, roundabout book seven, was your battling the Horcruxes like the Starvation Wages Horcrux and bullying and depression Horcruxes and so forth. How about you?

MM: It's really hard to choose; the one single thing I'm most proud of is how each of our campaign victories has been a community effort. It may not always be apparent from the outside, but our biggest campaigns have all been organized and implemented by staff and volunteers, with many creative and committed people offering strategic and logistical input. Furthermore, we've cultivated ladders of advancement within our organization and programmes, allowing many volunteers to grow in leadership and responsibility. Currently, all but one of our employees started out as volunteers on some level. Our director of leadership and education started out as a chapter member in Arizona, and now she runs the programme that initially got her interested in the HPA. That type of dynamic is really special.

VEF: And the Granger Leadership Academy helps with that, doesn't it? Can you tell us more?

Fan Appreciation #3
Matt Maggiacomo

Figure 2: HPA ScarBurrow
co-presidents Natasha
Seeram and Shagun
Kanwa (2017).

MM: It's a three-day event featuring in-depth training workshops, group projects and real-world activism, plus a variety of keynotes and presenters who help expand attendees' perspectives on leadership. In many ways, it's meant to be a culminating experience for folks who've participated in our programmes and campaigns. Our goal is to send 200 activists out into the world feeling more confident in their ability to organize change and make a real difference.

VEF: How big is the Harry Potter Alliance now? Where do you find most of your new members? And what does it take to set up a chapter?

MM: I'm just going to answer the first two questions, as the third question is answered on our website [http://thehpalliance.org/chapters]. The Harry Potter Alliance has 225 chapters across six continents, in 40 countries worldwide. Our central organization has five employees and over 90 volunteers. We have over 80,000 active members, and nearly 15,000 of them are donors. Currently most of our new members find us via social media, at major conferences like the American Library Association's annual conference, and on high school and college campuses where there are active chapters.

VEF: What have you been doing lately?

MM: Currently, we're finishing up our ninth annual Accio Books campaign! We're working with the Boys and Girls Clubs of Puerto Rico [recently devastated in a hurricane] to create four new lending libraries at Clubs across the island.

VEF: Do you crossover with other fandoms or mostly stick to *Potter*? What about other charities? Political groups?

MM: Currently, our closest partners are the American Library Association, Fight for the Future, Public Knowledge, Define American and She's the First. We explore other fandoms through our Fandom Forward toolkit series [https://www.thehpalliance.org/fandomforward]. In the past, we've organized major campaigns using the Hunger Games series as a framework.

VEF: Do you see things changing now that the books and movies are out? For that matter, has there been a post-2016 boom, with *Cursed Child* [Rowling, Thorne and Tiffany] and *Fantastic Beasts* [Yates, dir.] reviving the franchise?

MM: I think the post-2016 boom has more to do with the results of the US election in 2016 [which elected President Donald Trump, to many progressive fans' dismay], to be honest. We've seen a renewed spirit of participation and an influx of people interested in tapping into our programmes and partnering with us on educational resources. We've also seen a burst of more traditional organizations getting interested in using popular culture as a framework and vehicle for their own work, and they have called upon us as the elder statespeople of this unique model.

VEF: Where would you like the HPA to go next?

MM: Hogwarts! In all seriousness, I would love to expand our budget so we can bring on more staff, take on bigger projects and grow our programmes so that millions of people find inspiration in their favourite stories to be civically engaged.

VEF: Any advice for fans of other franchises who'd like to make a difference?

MM: Don't be afraid of angering the creators of your favourite series. Get organized and feel free to use our toolkits as a resource!

VEF: And finally, how can *Potter* fans get involved now?

MM: Just follow these links:

- Join our mailing list (https://www.thehpalliance.org/join)
- Volunteer for the HPA (https://www.thehpalliance.org/volunteer)
- Start or join a chapter (https://www.thehpalliance.org/chapters)
- Donate to the cause (https://www.thehpalliance.org/donate)
- Join our nerdy book club (https://www.thehpalliance.org/apparatinglibrary)

Fan Appreciation #3
Matt Maggiacomo

- Attend Granger Leadership Academy (http://grangerleadershipacademy.com/)
- Check out our Wizard Activist School (https://www.thehpalliance.org/wizardactivistschool)

VEF: Wow! Clearly those seeking a *Potter*-charity crossover have all they need to get started. Thanks so much. ●

~~~~~~~~~~~~~~

GO FURTHER

Websites
Granger Leadership Academy, http://grangerleadershipacademy.com
The Harry Potter Alliance, https://www.thehpalliance.org

'DIFFERENCES OF HABIT AND LANGUAGE ARE NOTHING AT ALL IF OUR AIMS ARE IDENTICAL AND OUR HEARTS ARE OPEN'

ALBUS DUMBLEDORE
(HARRY POTTER AND THE GOBLET OF FIRE)

Chapter
07

Buffy, Hamilton and Jon Snow Go to Hogwarts: Literary Affordance and the Hogwarts Houses as Interpretative Framework and Rhetorical Tool

Jessica Hautsch

→ Is *Game of Thrones*'s Daenerys Targaryen Gryffindor, Hufflepuff or Slytherin? Should Angel and Spike, the vampires of *Buffy the Vampire Slayer*, be Sorted based on their vampiric or human traits? And what the heck would the Sorting Hat do with Lin-Manuel Miranda's Alexander Hamilton?

Questions like these are raised in YouTube videos and on Reddit threads and Tumblr blogs as online interfandom communities use the Hogwarts Houses from J. K. Rowling's *Harry Potter* series (1997–2007) to discuss and interpret characters, emphasizing the series' continuing relevance as it interacts with other popular fandoms. Gryffindor, Slytherin, Ravenclaw and Hufflepuff become a metric by which characters from novels, films, television shows and musicals are analysed, categorized and assessed.

As part of our education, we learn not only how to read texts but how to talk about them. James D. Marshall, Peter Smagorinsky and Michael W. Smith have noted that in school we are taught 'the conventional ways of talking about literature: the language, questions, and responses that are thought to be appropriate in given contexts and those that are thought to be less so'. However, as Henry Jenkins argues, fans are 'rogue readers', disrupting some of these discursive conventions. While fans employ many academic skills, like close reading, attention to diction, analysing characterization, parsing gestures and facial expressions and determining themes – in short, the interpretative conventions of academia – fan discourse deviates from academic norms (see *Textual Poachers* [1992]; 'Canon vs. "Fanon"'; and 'Canon, Fantext, and Creativity'). Fans have developed their own rhetorical frameworks and discursive genres for communicating their interpretations.

The use of *Harry Potter*'s Hogwarts Houses as a rhetorical and interpretative tool represents one of the alternative frameworks developed by the 'rogue readers' of multifandom communities. Peter Khost's theory of literary affordance, which examines how we make rhetorical uses of literary texts, reveals that in recent years, fans have made an affordance of the Hogwarts Houses as an interpretive framework to analyse and a discursive tool to discuss characters from other popular and classic texts. This interpretative lens allows fans on forums, Tumblr, YouTube and Reddit to explore, analyse and debate characters and their motivations. Disagreements about which Houses characters should be Sorted into often display competing views of characters, as well as fans' affective responses to them. However, fans' interpretations and (mis)understandings of the Houses themselves, especially Hufflepuff and Slytherin, also affect the efficacy of the affordance and the analysis it facilitates.

Buffy, Hamilton and Jon Snow Go to Hogwarts:
Literary Affordance and the Hogwarts Houses as Interpretative
Framework and Rhetorical Tool
Jessica Hautsch

The Houses

The Hogwarts Houses are first introduced in *Harry Potter and the Philosopher's Stone/Sorcerer's Stone* (Rowling, 1997). When Harry and the other first-year students arrive at Hogwarts, they are Sorted into the Houses, each associated with different character traits and values. The sentient Sorting Hat, which is enchanted to see into the psychology of the wearer, explains the ethos of each House: Gryffindors are 'brave at heart', full of 'daring nerve, and chivalry'; Hufflepuffs are 'just and loyal' and hardworking; Ravenclaws are 'wise' and curious, concerned with 'wit and learning' and Slytherins are 'cunning folks', whose ambition results in a kind of Machiavellian ruthlessness.

Within the *Harry Potter* series, the presence of the Houses is not unproblematic. Slytherin is initially stereotyped as the 'evil House'. In *Philosopher's Stone/Sorcerer's Stone*, Hagrid tells Harry, '[t]here's not a single witch or wizard who went bad who wasn't in Slytherin,' which is demonstrably untrue in the novels: Quirinus Quirrell was Ravenclaw and Peter Pettigrew was Gryffindor and they both broke bad. But the depiction of the Slytherin students, most notably Draco Malfoy and his minions Vincent Crabbe and Gregory Goyle, seems to reaffirm Hagrid's prejudice, instilling it in the reader. It is only after the Battle of Hogwarts and the actions of Horace Slughorn and Severus Snape that public and reader perception of Slytherin begins to change. Hagrid also, more delicately, disparages Hufflepuffs, telling Harry in *Philosopher's Stone/Sorcerer's Stone*, 'everyone says Hufflepuff are a loto' duffers, but –'. Comedy troops like the Second City (2011) have played with this stereotype, mocking the House, although Hufflepuff does have its adamant defenders, notably Rowling herself, as revealed by SnitchSeeker.com. Likewise, many critics, including Amanda Hunziker and Andrew P. Mills, have noted the exclusionary nature of the Houses and the ways in which they promote division, rather than unity, among the students. This tribalism also helps to enforce stereotypes; for example, we see Slytherin's antagonism largely from the perspective of our Gryffindor protagonists.

However, despite these somewhat problematic elements, the *Harry Potter* fan community has embraced the Hogwarts Houses as an emblem of their fandom and rush to discuss them online. In an ethnographic exploration of the wizard rock subset of the *Harry Potter* fandom, Kelli M. Rohlman notes that 'members tend to associate themselves with these houses' and conventions often include a 'Sorting Ceremony', underlining the importance of identifying with a House. This focus on the Hogwarts Houses can be generalized to the larger *Harry Potter* fan community. In fact, one of the first things a new member of Pottermore, a sanctioned fansite created by J. K. Rowling and the self-proclaimed official 'digital heart of the wizarding world', is prompted to do is to take a quiz determining the user's House. This identification is a way for fans to assert membership not only of the House, but to the fandom – knowing your House is a marker of belonging to the *Harry Potter* fan community.

In 2016, preparing for the release of *Fantastic Beasts and Where to Find Them* (Yates, dir.), Rowling added an additional Sorting ceremony for the American wizarding school Ilvermorny, introducing the American school's Houses: Wampus, Horned Serpent, Pukwudie and Thunderbird. However, these new Houses do not seem to have had the same resonance within the fan community. A 2018 Google Trends analysis shows that while searches for 'Ilvermorny Houses' eclipsed searches for 'Hogwarts Houses' in June and July of 2016, corresponding with their announcement, searches since the November 2016 release of *Fantastic Beasts* have dropped precipitously. This search trend suggests that fans were relatively underwhelmed by and uninterested in these Houses. It is possible that Hogwarts Houses were already established within the discursive community of the *Harry Potter* fandom and there was no need to supplement or replace them. Or, as Katharine Trendacosta suggests, part of the reason why the American Houses didn't catch on was because 'two of those names are – regardless of their real, and fascinating, origins – hard to say out loud without a little bit of humor. It's like giving Ilvermorny two Hufflepuffs'. She and Samantha Gross, a self-identified fan, are also critical of the way in which the Houses appropriate American Indian mythology. As Gross explains, the way in which Rowling interprets and uses the 'folklore creatures' that the Houses take their names from 'is lacking in accuracy, respect and proper understanding'. The cultural appropriation controversy that surrounds these Houses might be contributing to why they are not more widely embraced in the fandom nor used as an interpretive framework in the way that the Hogwarts Houses are.

Literary affordance
Harry Potter fans, then, use the Hogwarts (unlike the rarely-invoked Ilvermorny) Houses to reinforce their individual and communal identity. If I assert that I'm Ravenclaw, I am using the novels to say something about both myself

Buffy, Hamilton and Jon Snow Go to Hogwarts:
Literary Affordance and the Hogwarts Houses as Interpretative
Framework and Rhetorical Tool
Jessica Hautsch

and my fandom. In short, I am making a literary affordance of the *Harry Potter* novels. But before we get into defining 'literary affordance', first an explanation of what we mean by the term 'affordance'. James J. Gibson and Anthony Chemero have theorized the ways in which animals interact with and use their environment, the ways in which they make affordances of it. According to Gibson, affordances exist within the environment and emerge in conjunction with the animal's needs and abilities. For example, the conventional affordance of a broom is to sweep the floor, but I can also use it to clear away cobwebs from my ceiling or knock something down from a high shelf. I might make an affordance of it to shoo away my cat who has decided to chase one of the dust bunnies I've just swept up. And if I'm invited to play a game of Quidditch, I might use my broom for that as well. These affordances also depend on my innate abilities, unlike my cat, whose small size and lack of opposable thumbs means that she could not use the broom in the same ways.

By combining Gibson's and Chemero's work on affordances with reader-response literary criticism (see *The Reader, the Text, the Poem* [1978] and *Is There a Text in This Class?* [1980]), Peter H. Khost develops his theory of how readers and writers interact with and use texts. Khost defines literary affordance as 'uses readers make of features of literary texts through rhetorical application of them to unrelated situations'. These uses are often affordances that the original author did not intend or even anticipate, yet readers apply them to 'the[ir] lived experience'. These affordances of the text, like the affordance of the broom, emerge through the reader's interaction with the text and in response to a specific rhetorical context. For example, Courtney Ellefson's description of how the '*Harry Potter* books saved [her] life' makes a literary affordance. Ellefson writes,

> *Looking back I see these books as an analogy for depression: you cannot face it just once and have it be gone. Depression rears its ugly head again and again in your life and you have to fight it again and again. Depression is not an easy thing to get rid of, much like Voldemort.*

Although other readers, and Rowling herself, might not see Voldemort as analogous for depression, Ellefson perceived that she could make an affordance of the *Harry Potter* novels to think and write about her experiences with it.

Through their active and creative engagement with the novels, fans also

Figure 1: princessbilbo and UnrenderedCosplays. 'Gwenpool and Deadpool' at Stan Lee's LA Comic Con 2016.

make a literary affordance of *Harry Potter*, using the Hogwarts Houses as a discursive framework to analyse characters from different popular and literary texts and to communicate that. In her report on the 'Sorting *Hamilton*' at the *Leviosa Convention* (2016), Lorrie Kim notes that the panel began with a discussion of why fans use *Harry Potter* to talk about other texts: 'Why do we Sort in fandoms that are not HP? We talked about how useful the Sorting model is for understanding characters and real people'. Kim's comments reveal fans' awareness that they view the Hogwarts Houses as a 'useful' interpretative lens and rhetorical shorthand. In this tradition, interfandom communities make particular use of the Hogwarts Houses to analyse and discuss characters from *Buffy the Vampire Slayer* (1997–2003), *Game of Thrones* (books: Martin, 1996–ongoing; TV series: 2011–ongoing) and *Hamilton* (2015), though Tumblr blogs and forum posts Sort characters from many more fandoms, such as the *Lord of the Rings*, *Pride and Prejudice*, the Marvel Cinematic Universe, the *Great Gatsby*, *Doctor Who* and *Hamlet*.

Generally, literary affordances are not concerned with explaining the text, except for how it relates to the affordance; instead, they use the text rhetorically to explain a concept, persuade an audience or make a point. Khost asserts that 'whereas an interpretation is a textual response that is *about* the text, a literary affordance is a response to something else *through* a text' (original emphasis). The affordance of the Hogwarts Houses is not *about* the *Harry Potter* novels but rather about viewing other texts *through* them. As Kim writes, fans' use of the Hogwarts Houses allows them to 'view other stories through a Potterverse lens!' However, it is worth noting that sometimes the

Buffy, Hamilton and Jon Snow Go to Hogwarts:
Literary Affordance and the Hogwarts Houses as Interpretative
Framework and Rhetorical Tool
Jessica Hautsch

way in which a text is used depends on the reader's interpretation, as Khost notes. In this case, fans' interpretations of the Houses and their primary values and traits determine how the Houses are used.

Differing interpretations

Differing interpretations of the Hogwarts Houses have resulted in debates about their nature and the implications of those differences for Sorting. For example, in a number of analyses, other franchises' fans point to characters' loyalty as evidence that they belong in Gryffindor. In the fanfiction 'Better Be... Gryffindor' (2016) by ThePsychoticQueen, the ambiguously trustworthy vampire Spike cites Buffy the Vampire Slayer's 'unwavering loyalty' as the primary reason that she should be in red and gold. When Buffy insists that Spike too is Gryffindor, she supports her claims by saying, '[b]ut you're also brave. And loyal. You definitely have the qualities of a Gryffindor'. Other posts' analyses make similar arguments: Tumblr user Apprenticebard argues that little sister Dawn's loyalty suggests Gryffindor as her secondary House (Ravenclaw is her primary), and Mari on the Slayerettes boards posits, 'I think Angel and Spike are both Gryffindors as well. Spike's loyalty is pretty much his most featured characteristic. Angel is all Champion-y and self-righteous as well [...] and he is also super loyal'. However, in the novels, loyalty is a trait explicitly associated with Hufflepuff. The idea that Gryffindors are automatically loyal, then, might be considered fanon, an idea viewed as fact within segments of the fan community with implied rather than direct textual evidence. As the Tumblr Pottermoreanalysis explains, 'Gryffindors often take loyalty and justice as traits, but when they claim those traits for Gryffindor, they're wrong – they're basically just stealing Hufflepuff traits from Hufflepuff and claiming they're Gryffindor'. Therefore, depending on which side of this interpretative debate fans land on, their affordance of the Hogwarts Houses might vary.

Slytherin is also subjected to differing interpretations. Because of the stereotypes surrounding it, many fans reserve this House for villains, keeping their favourite characters far from the likes of Lord Voldemort, Draco Malfoy and Bellatrix Lestrange. In ThePsychoticQueen's fic, Spike assumes that he will be put into Slytherin because of his history as the Big Bad: '"Nah, I'm probably a Slytherin," Spike figured. House of the evil and bad. Yeah, that was him. Because as much as he liked to pretend, he was still a bad man.' The story does not contradict prevailing stereotypes of Slytherin as the House of Evil;

instead, Buffy sorts Spike into Gryffindor as an argument for his redemption and an illustration of her love for him. Still, other users have a different interpretation of House Slytherin, and their affordance of it reflects this divergent understanding. As Heymeowmeow notes in a Reddit thread, echoing the Sorting Hat's song, 'Slytherin is not about being evil or mean. Slytherin is about being cunning and ambitious.' This interpretation suggests that Sorting is not a barometer of morality but a consideration of personality traits. Whether you view Slytherin in more or less favourable terms will likely affect the affordance that you make of it.

Some characters clearly match the Hogwarts House archetypes according to most fans: *Hamilton* antagonist Aaron Burr is unequivocally Slytherin, as is *Game of Thrones* schemer Littlefinger. There is no doubt that Buffy is Gryffindor. However, the debate surrounding more ambiguous characters is far more interesting. Because the characters in serial television shows, like *Buffy* and *Game of Thrones*, are complex and well-developed, changing and evolving as the show arcs through its narrative, an argument can be made for characters fitting into multiple Houses and Sorting characters often requires interpretative justifications and textual evidence to support House claims. In the Reddit thread '*Buffy* characters into Hogwarts Houses??', fans debate whether Buffy's bookish mentor Giles belongs in Ravenclaw because of his intelligence and knowledge, or Slytherin because he is 'fairly ruthless and cunning', and doesn't prioritize 'fighting fairly', as GinaZaneburritos writes. Reddit user Clockworklycanthrope notes that '[w]hile he's obviously brilliant he's not into it for the sake of knowledge. It's all about what that knowledge gets him, and he's shown time and time again that he's willing to do whatever it takes to make sure things go according to *his* plan' (original emphasis). Clearly, the debate about Giles's place within the interpretative framework of the Hogwarts Houses requires sophisticated analysis of his characterization and motivation, as well as a nuanced understanding of the Houses.

A similar debate centres around Daenerys Targaryen (Dany). On Tumblr, user Starline Hodge makes the case for Dany as Gryffindor, noting that 'she can be reckless'. The Tumblr Sorting Hat Chats, disagrees, however, suggesting in their post 'Hey I'm *Obsessed* with Your Sorting Methods…' that although Dany has some Gryffindor traits (they view Gryffindor as her secondary alignment), her primary orientation is towards Hufflepuff. In fact, this site has developed its own system for Sorting characters. As it succinctly explains,

Buffy, Hamilton and Jon Snow Go to Hogwarts:
Literary Affordance and the Hogwarts Houses as Interpretative
Framework and Rhetorical Tool
Jessica Hautsch

'[p]rimaries are WHY you do what you do and secondary Houses are HOW you do what you do. Motives and methods. Ends and means. Reasons and skills' ('The Basics'). Kat, one of the authors of this blog, offers a detailed and textually supported explanation of how Dany's Hufflepuff motivations and Gryffindor approach work together:

> with her people-oriented Hufflepuff primary leading her to free the slaves, and her Gryffindor secondary giving her the strength of character to stand against political caution and do what her Hufflepuff feels is right. This is also her flaw [...] she lacks the finesse and strategy for diplomacy, and makes each instance of mercy into a grand statement. And while these are for the most part sound when looked at individually, they lack the foresight of consequence – a great example being her disrespect of the slavers causing economic/welfare troubles.
>
> ('Hey I'm *Obsessed* with Your Sorting Methods...')

Still others disagree with this assessment. Rebecca Felgate, a YouTube personality and *Harry Potter* fan (she identifies as Slytherin), for example, argues that 'while the Sorting Hat probably did think about putting her in Ravenclaw, she is a true Slytherin in bloodline and in ferocity'. Felgate justifies her choice using the text, noting that

> Daenerys is all about making the ultimate power play and disregarding the rules to do so [...] she's not evil, but she's just ready to do what she has to do to win. Only a Slytherin would seek vengeance by locking her enemies into an unopenable vault.

Felgate acknowledges Dany's bravery, a Gryffindor trait, but her interpretation of Dany, in contrast to Kat's, positions the Mother of Dragons as less reckless and more cunning: 'she stops and thinks before she acts. She's calculating, like a Slytherin'. The discussion and debate surrounding the 'correct' Sorting of Dany's characteristics demonstrates how different interpretations can be. Depending on which elements Daenerys's fans emphasize and which they overlook, the text can be used to support her placement in any of the four Houses.

Another polymorphic character is the 'polymath' and 'pain in the ass'

('Take a Break' [2015]) Alexander Hamilton in the beloved 2015 musical by Lin-Manuel Miranda. Fans have made arguments for Hamilton's suitability for Gryffindor, Ravenclaw or Slytherin, depending on their interpretation of the character. Jazmyn Strode, for example, puts Hamilton in Gryffindor. She cites lyrics from the musical to support her claim – 'I wished for a war […] I knew it was the only way to rise up' ('Right Hand Man') and 'I will lay down my life if it sets us free' ('My Shot') – and states that '[t]he man is non-stop and exhibits no restraint. So scrappy. So hungry. So representative of Godric Gryffindor'. In a two-video YouTube series, JonasAlmostFamous makes the case for Alexander's Ravenclaw-ness: 'He's totally a Ravenclaw. He's so up in his head and a nose in a book. And he values, in the people around him, he values being able to banter with them', EliseBeeYT explains in the videos. On Reddit, Animavero-quaerenti agrees that Hamilton would be a Ravenclaw, but 'only because he asked', alluding to Harry's choosing his own House during the Sorting Ceremony. However, the most popular Sorting puts Hamilton in the House that Harry rejected: Slytherin. The Tumblr Hogwarts House Habits insists:

> Hamilton is consistently driven by his ambition – his desire to rise above his station, make a name for himself, help create a nation […] And if the Sorting Hat told Alexander Hamilton 'Slytherin could help you on your way to greatness', he would take it up on that offer in a heartbeat.

Most users, however, acknowledge that Hamilton contains a combination of these characteristics. Some fans propose for themselves and characters Hybrid Houses, such as Gryffinclaw (Gryffindor/Ravenclaw) or Raverin (Ravenclaw/Slytherin), but these are rarely used in relation to characters. Even for a difficult character like Hamilton, part of the challenge of Sorting seems to be to take a stand and commit to a House, albeit with a caveat or two. For example, Aminoapps user Tonks acknowledges Hamilton's 'Ravenclaw qualities in the way that he writes nonstop', but sees those qualities as less dominant than his Slytherin ones: 'his ambition is constantly shown throughout the whole show. He also has a lot of pride because he will do anything to protect his legacy'. On Reddit, Trashymctrashcan argues that while Hamilton is primarily Slytherin, he also has Gryffindor traits: 'ambition and desire for power drive him, but Gryffindors do tend to be reckless, which he's shown to be time and time again'. Kat and Inky of Sorting Hat Chats also posit this combination, noting,

Buffy, Hamilton and Jon Snow Go to Hogwarts:
Literary Affordance and the Hogwarts Houses as Interpretative
Framework and Rhetorical Tool
Jessica Hautsch

'[j]ust look at *Hurricane*. Anyone who sees a brimming political sex scandal and says, "You know what I should do? TELL EVERYONE EVERYTHING" – well, they're probably a Gryffindor Secondary.'

Harry Potter celebrities have also weighed in on Hamilton's House; during interviews, Miranda has asked stars from the film franchise where they would Sort his *Hamilton* characters. Miranda tweeted that Daniel Radcliffe (Harry Potter) had pegged Hamilton as a 'Ravenclaw. Definitely'. The Tweet received 345 replies, most of them evaluating the merits of Radcliffe's Sorting, some of them citing lyrics to question or confirm his assertion. Miranda also sat down with Emma Watson (Hermione) and explained: 'The number one question I get asked, because the fandom is real, is, um, we have to sort the founders into Hogwarts Houses' (see 'Watch Emma Watson Sort the Cast of *Hamilton* into Hogwarts Houses' [2016]). Watson, who has prepared with notes (of course, as she says, 'I'm Hermione'), sorts Hamilton into Gryffindor: 'For me, he is all authenticity. All courage'. Miranda provides some supporting evidence for Watson's argument, citing Hamilton's nickname of 'the Little Lion', connecting Alexander to the Gryffindor's emblematic animal. The affordance of the Hogwarts Houses allows Miranda, and the cast of *Harry Potter*, a way to engage with fans, sharing an interpretive tool and rhetorical shorthand. As Kim explains, 'Miranda is one of us: a creator in a post-*Harry Potter* world who incorporates HP models, allusions, and assumptions into his own work'. With this, his fandom and membership of the fan community is marked by his discursive affordance of the Houses.

During their interview, Miranda informed Watson that Radcliffe had Sorted Hamilton into Ravenclaw, and she was perplexed: 'Why though?' ('Watch Emma Watson Sort the Cast of *Hamilton* into Hogwarts Houses'). Watson's response is likely not dissimilar to that of other fans who encounter Sortings with which they disagree. In fact, the affordance of Hogwarts Houses demonstrates the enormous variety of interpretations between fans and communities. Stanley Fish categorizes interpretative communities as 'made up of those who share interpretive strategies not for reading (in the conventional sense) but for writing texts, for constituting their properties and assigning their intentions'. He argues that the 'interpretative strategies' that we bring to texts 'shape' our understandings of them. People who approach a text with different strategies will not encounter the same text. Discussing the text with members of your interpretative community reinforces your approach to read-

ing and your interpretation. But when discussing a text with members of a different interpretative community, you 'might be tempted to complain to the other that we could not possibly be reading the same' story. That is why Watson cannot understand how Hamilton could be a Ravenclaw and why I can't understand anyone who doesn't put him in Slytherin: our experiences of the text are different.

Character development

In _Harry Potter and the Deathly Hallows_ (book: Rowling, 2007; films: Yates, 2010, 2011), Dumbledore implies that adult Snape, unlike his younger counterpart, should have been placed in Gryffindor. This sort of character development demonstrates a particular challenge for fan Sortings. Some characters stay consistent in their alignment during face/heel or heel/face turns. Hodge, Sennalvera, JackOfTrades, Sopheyrac, Gocereal and Sorting Hat Chats all note that Jamie Lannister, for example, retains Gryffindor traits throughout his arc. Reddit commenter SchroedingersKneazle argues that 'Gryffindor values are chivalry, courage, daring etc… I think Jaime fits perfectly as a flawed Gryffindor'. But in other cases, like Snape's, character development can suggest a shift in House alignment. Although Hodge, for example, sorts Dany into Gryffindor, she does so despite the fact that the Dragon Queen is 'closer to Slytherin later in the series', suggesting that as characters change, so do their Houses. In addition, Donewithwoodenteeth puts the initially young, romantic and naive Sansa Stark in Ravenclaw, noting, however, that,

> To be fair, [her mentor] Littlefinger is teaching her to be more Slytherin in nature. And Sansa is capable of being cunning and shrewd and is certainly ambitious/wanting of power at the start of the series. In fact, the traditionalism of Slytherin is in line with Sansa especially in the first book of the series.

Although Donewithwoodenteeth is adamant that Sansa is 'Ravenclaw 100%', this post suggests that if her Slytherin characteristics were nurtured, her

Buffy, Hamilton and Jon Snow Go to Hogwarts:
Literary Affordance and the Hogwarts Houses as Interpretative
Framework and Rhetorical Tool
Jessica Hautsch

House alignment *could* change. In her conversation with Miranda, Watson makes a similar case for Aaron Burr, whom she controversially suggests could have been a Hufflepuff (much to a laughing Miranda's shock): 'Because, I feel like, as a young man if Aaron, Aaron could have grown or developed [...] He could have gone in Hufflepuff's direction, but didn't' ('Watch Emma Watson Sort the Cast of *Hamilton* into Hogwarts Houses'). Watson suggests that Burr's upbringing *might* have led him to Hufflepuff, suggesting that such traits are not fixed and that House alignment is mutable.

In a similar vein, the vampires of *Buffy* pose Sorting challenges. According to the ontology of *Buffy*, vampires lose their human souls (though protagonists Spike and Angel are notable exceptions). As Buffy explains, when a person becomes a vampire, 'you die. And a demon sets up shop in your old house. It walks and talks and remembers your life but it's not you' because your soul is gone ('Lie to Me', Season 2, Episode 7). Although the vampire mythology of the show grows more nuanced as it progresses, suggesting that some remnants of human traits are extant after the vampiric transformation ('Doppelgangland', Season 3, Episode 16), it continues to draw a clear distinction between vampires with their souls and those without. Because of this, some fans make distinctions between the soul/no-soul version of the vampires. For example, Mysterious Lights asserts that while Angel is Gryffindor because 'he's a Champion of Light who likes beating up the bad guys', Angelus (his unsouled version) is Slytherin:

> It's not just that he's got cruelty to at least *match that of Voldemort himself,* it's that he mixes his cruelty in with this whimsical craftiness, manipulating people to inflict as much psychological trauma as possible before he actually goes to kill them.

(original emphasis)

However, on Reddit, Laceyrock sees greater consistency in Angel's character: 'He is definitely fueled by his ambitions, whether they be for complete

Figure 3:
sortinghatforotherfandoms sorts the Game of Thrones *characters (2017).*

chaos and destruction as Angelus or for redemption as Angel.' Clockworkly-canthrope seconds this idea, arguing that '[w]hen he's evil, it's to destroy the world. When he's good, it's to save it. Angel is the Slytherin'. Spike is also an ambiguous figure; Fool for Buffy on Buffy-Boards, asserts that he is 'too controversial to sort'. Those who try place him in Hufflepuff, Gryffindor or Slytherin. Ravenclaw gets little love, but as Spike admits he doesn't 'have a reputation for being much of a thinker' ('Touched', Season 7, Episode 20). Both WillowfromBuffy and Blaze Sort Spike into Hufflepuff, presumably because of his loyalty, first to his paramour Drusilla and then to Buffy. However, more interesting is the debate about whether he is Gryffindor or Slytherin. S Rou argues that he is the latter because

> he has Slytherin written all over him even after he got a soul. He's ambitious and shady abd [sic] does what he wants to the point he can be kind of ridiculous. He's very obsessed with Buffy and has that dark edge to him that Slytherin have.

In contrast, GinaZaneburritos argues that '[e]ven without a soul, I see Spike as Gryffindor'. Although these fans have differing interpretations of Spike, they are similar in their insistence that his soul/nonsoul House is the same, the affordance of the Hogwarts Houses allowing fans to identify similarities between these two versions of the characters, thereby undercutting the show's insistence that they are completely distinct.

Poking fun through Hufflepuff

Houses are also used to disparage generally disliked characters. For example, Dan Selcke Sorts *Game of Thrones*'s treacherous Theon Greyjoy into Hufflepuff 'on account of his continued incompetence'. Likewise, he questions Sorting both Sansa Stark and her mother Catelyn into Ravenclaw: 'Nothing about Catelyn or Sansa screams Ravenclaw to me. They've both shown cunning, sure, but they've also made their share of bone-headed moves. They're closer to Hufflepuffs.' Selcke's explanation about why he puts Sansa and Catelyn into Hufflepuff has nothing to do with justice, loyalty or other Hufflepuff traits, but rather because he sees them as 'bone-head[s]' or, as Hagrid might say, 'a bunch of duffers'. This use reveals the importance of understanding how the Houses are interpreted by the fan community, the stereotyped

Buffy, Hamilton and Jon Snow Go to Hogwarts:
Literary Affordance and the Hogwarts Houses as Interpretative
Framework and Rhetorical Tool
Jessica Hautsch

biases against certain Houses, and how they can be used, rhetorically, as compliments or slights.

The ultimate insult, however, is to suggest that a character would not be admitted into Hogwarts in the first place. Riley Finn, Buffy's Season 4 and 5 boyfriend and one of the most despised characters in the show, does not even get the Hufflepuff treatment as fans such as GinaZaneburritos dismiss him as a magicless 'muggle', or assert that he wouldn't 'get into hogwarts in the first place' (thosefilthyhobbitses). Certainly, many fans have placed both Riley and Catelyn in Hufflepuff for their stalwart loyalty – in particular, Cat's Tully heritage commits her to 'Family, Duty, Honor'. However, the goal in these particular examples is not character-based but an opportunity for ridicule. While this dismissive approach lacks some of the analytical rigour seen in the analysis of other characters, it is humorous, and it allows fans to discursively unite in their shared dislike of a despised character.

Conclusion

This article's small sampling shows how members of multifandom communities have made affordances of the Hogwarts Houses as an interpretative framework and rhetorical strategy for analysing a range of non-*Harry Potter* characters. Although the discourse of the Hogwarts Houses departs from traditional analysis, it facilitates debates about interpretation, about reading and misreading, not only the primary texts being analysed but also *Harry Potter* and the Houses themselves, opening up a new (and hopefully deeper) understanding of both. The debates about how to Sort different characters suggests a nuanced and close reading, often relying on supporting evidence to bolster or challenge claims. By inventing their own discourse to discuss and analyse popular and canonized works, these rogue readers demonstrate interpretative and rhetorical sophistication and the desire to create new approaches to fiction, to better understand the characters and works they love. The use of the Hogwarts Houses allows fans to not only interrogate works of fiction but to communicate their fandom. Whether they identify as Slytherin, Gryffindor, Ravenclaw or Hufflepuff, their affordance of the Hogwarts Houses asserts their place within the *Harry Potter* fan community. ●

GO FURTHER

Books

Is There a Text in This Class? The Authority of Interpretive Communities
Stanley Fish
(Cambridge: Harvard University Press, 1980)

The Ecological Approach to Perception
James J. Gibson
(Boston: Houghton Mifflin, 1979)

Textual Poachers: Television Fans and Participatory Culture
Henry Jenkins
(Abingdon: Routledge, 1992)

Rhetor Response: A Theory and Practice of Literary Affordance
Peter H. Khost
(Logan: Utah State University Press, 2018)

The Language of Interpretation: Patterns of Discourse in Discussions of Literature
James D. Marshall, Peter Smagorinsky and Michael W. Smith
(Ubrana: National Council of Teachers of English, 1995)

The Reader, the Text, the Poem: The Transactional Theory of the Literary Work
Louise M. Rosenblatt
(Carbondale: Southern Illinois University Press, 1978)

Harry Potter and Philosopher's Stone (20th Anniversary Slytherin edn)
J. K. Rowling
(London: Bloomsbury, [1997] 2017)

Extracts/Essays/Articles
'An Outline of a Theory of Affordances'
Anthony Chemero
In *Ecological Psychology*, 15:2 (2003), pp. 181–95.

Buffy, Hamilton and Jon Snow Go to Hogwarts:
Literary Affordance and the Hogwarts Houses as Interpretative
Framework and Rhetorical Tool
Jessica Hautsch

'The Embodiment of Collective Exclusion: Transcending the Borders of Social Segregation in *Harry Potter*'
Alyssa Hunziker
In *disClosure: A Journal of Social Theory*, 22 (2013), pp 54–60.

'Canon vs. "Fanon": Genre Devices in Contemporary Fanfiction' [MA thesis]
Katherine E. McCain
(Washington, DC: Georgetown University, 2015)

'Patriotism, House Loyalty, and the Obligations of Belonging'
Andrew P. Mills
In G. Bassham (ed.). *The Ultimate* Harry Potter *and Philosophy: Hogwarts for Muggles*
(Hoboken: John Wiley & Sons, 2010), pp 259–300.

'Identity, Rhetoric and Behavior: The Contradictory Communities of Wizard Rock'
[MA thesis]
Keli Rohlmna
(Lubbock: Texas Tech University, 2010)

'Canon, Fantext, and Creativity: An Analysis of Pamela Aidan's Fitzwilliam Darcy, Gentleman as Fanfictional Response to Jane Austen's *Pride and Prejudice*' [MA thesis]
Veerle Van Steenhuyse
(Gent: Ghent University, 2009)

Online
'Comment: What Hogwarts House Do You Think the *Hamilton* Characters Belong to?'
Anima-vero-quaerenti
Reddit. 2017, https://www.reddit.com/r/hamiltonmusical/comments/5p50ex/what_hogwarts_house_do_you_think_the_hamilton/.

'Buffyverse Characters in Every Hogwarts House: Dawn Summers'
Apprenticebard
Tumblr. 17 May 2015, https://apprenticebard.tumblr.com/post/119243116103/buffyverse-characters-in-every-hogwarts-house.

'Comment: Sorting *BtVS* Characters into Hogwarts Houses'
Blaze
Buffy-Boards. 14 July 2017, https://buffy-boards.com/threads/sorting-btvs-characters-into-hogwarts-houses.70365.

'Comment: *Buffy* Characters in Hogwarts Houses??'
Clockworklycanthrope
Reddit. 2015, https://www.reddit.com/r/buffy/comments/2u7h74/buffy_characters_in_hogwarts_houses/#bottom-comments.

'Anonymous Asked: What Hogwarts House Do You Think Best Fits Sansa?'
Donewithwoodenteeth
Tumblr. 5 February 2015, http://asoiafuniversity.tumblr.com/post/110192750270/what-hogwarts-house-do-you-think-best-fits-sansa.

'How the *Harry Potter* Books Saved My Life'
Courtney Ellefson
The Mighty. 29 August 2016, https://themighty.com/2016/08/harry-potter-j-k-rowling-and-how-they-helped-me-battle-depression/.

'*Game of Thrones* Characters Sorted into Hogwarts Houses'
Rebecca Felgate
YouTube. 21 July 2017, https://www.youtube.com/watch?v=__lixRhkTQ.

'Comment: Sorting *BtVS* Characters into Hogwarts Houses'
Fool for Buffy
Buffy-Boards. 13 July 2017, https://buffy-boards.com/threads/sorting-btvs-characters-into-hogwarts-houses.70365.

'Comment: *Buffy* Characters in Hogwarts Houses??'
GinaZaneburritos
Reddit. 2015, https://www.reddit.com/r/buffy/comments/2u7h74/buffy_characters_in_hogwarts_houses/#bottom-comments.

Buffy, Hamilton and Jon Snow Go to Hogwarts:
Literary Affordance and the Hogwarts Houses as Interpretative
Framework and Rhetorical Tool
Jessica Hautsch

'Comment: (Spoilers All) What Hogwarts Houses Would Each of the Characters Get Sorted Into?'
Gocereal
Reddit. 2015, https://www.reddit.com/r/asoiaf/comments/2t6tyt/spoilers_all_what_hogwarts_houses_would_each_of.

'The Blatant Racism of JK Rowling's Ilvermorny Houses'
Samantha Gross
Study Breaks. 31 August 2016, https://studybreaks.com/culture/the-blatant-racism-of-jk-rowlings-ilvermorny-houses.

'Comment: *Buffy* Characters in Hogwarts Houses??'
Heymeowmeow
Reddit. 2015, https://www.reddit.com/r/buffy/comments/2u7h74/buffy_characters_in_hogwarts_houses/#bottom-comments.

'*Hamilton*: Sorted by Madamxpresident'
Hogwarts House Habits
Tumblr. 16 February 2016, http://hogwartshousehabits.tumblr.com/post/139384553644/hamilton.

'Comment: (Spoilers All) What Hogwarts Houses Would Each of the Characters Get Sorted Into?'
JackOfTrades
Reddit. 2015, https://www.reddit.com/r/asoiaf/comments/2t6tyt/spoilers_all_what_hogwarts_houses_would_each_of.

'Sorting *Hamilton* Characters into Hogwarts Houses! (ft. EliseBeeYT)'
JonasAlmostFamous
YouTube. 15 March 2017, https://www.youtube.com/watch?v=mBIzz2Z7bBo&t=359s.

'Sorting *Hamilton*'
Lorrie Kim
Lorriekimcom. 13 July 2016, https://lorriekimcom.wordpress.com/2016/07/13/sorting-hamilton/.

'Comment: *Buffy* Characters in Hogwarts Houses??'
Laceyrock
Reddit. 2015, https://www.reddit.com/r/buffy/comments/2u7h74/buffy_characters_in_hogwarts_houses/#bottom-comments.

'Put *Buffy* Characters in Hogwarts Houses'
Mari
The Slayerettes: Official Forum, Co-Hosted with the Hellmouth Empire. 18 December 2013, http://slayerettes.boards.net/thread/386/put-buffy-characters-hogwarts-houses.

'I Asked This Nice Young Man How He'd Sort Hamilton at Hogwarts. His Answer: "Ravenclaw. Definitely". GNIGHT! *Hides*'
Lin-Manuel Miranda (@lin_Manuel)
Twitter. 26 January 2016, https://twitter.com/Lin_Manuel/status/692196235399319553/photo.

'Ive-Always-Wondered-If-Hufflepuffs-Are-Just-As'
Pottermoreanalysis
Tumblr. 29 May 2013, http://pottermoreanalysis.tumblr.com/post/51694822906/ive-always-wondered-if-hufflepuffs-are-just-as.

'Sorting Hat: *Buffy the Vampire Slayer*'
Robert
Mysterious Lights. 14 April 2012, http://mysteriouslights.blogspot.com/2012/04/sorting-hat-buffy-vampire-slayer.html.

'Watch Emma Watson Sort the Cast of *Hamilton* into Hogwarts Houses'
Joanna Robinson
Vanity Fair. 17 March 2016, https://www.vanityfair.com/hollywood/2016/03/emma-watson-sorts-hamilton-hogwarts-houses.

'If *Game of Thrones* Characters Were in Hogwarts Houses'
Dan Selcke
Fansided. 2016, https://wizardsandwhatnot.com/2016/02/24/if-game-of-thrones-characters-were-in-hogwarts-houses.

**Buffy, Hamilton and Jon Snow Go to Hogwarts:
Literary Affordance and the Hogwarts Houses as Interpretative
Framework and Rhetorical Tool**
Jessica Hautsch

'Comment: *Game of Thrones* Characters Sorted into Hogwarts Houses'
SchroedingersKneazle
Reddit. 2017, https://www.reddit.com/r/harrypotter/comments/5kfdt4/game_of_
thrones_characters_sorted_into_hogwarts.

'Comment: (Spoilers All) What Hogwarts Houses Would Each of the Characters Get
Sorted Into?'
Sennalvera
Reddit. 2015, https://www.reddit.com/r/asoiaf/comments/2t6tyt/spoilers_all_what_
hogwarts_houses_would_each_of.

'Comment: (Spoilers All) What Hogwarts Houses Would Each of the Characters Get
Sorted Into?'
Sopheyrac
Reddit. 2015, https://www.reddit.com/r/asoiaf/comments/2t6tyt/spoilers_all_what_
hogwarts_houses_would_each_of.

'*Hamilton* Sorting'
Sorting Hat Chats
Tumblr. 2016, http://sortinghatchats.tumblr.com/post/96659136178/hey-im-obsessed-
with-your-sorting-methods-and.

'Hey I'm *Obsessed* with Your Sorting Methods...'
Sorting Hat Chats
Tumblr. 2015, http://sortinghatchats.tumblr.com/post/96659136178/hey-im-obsessed-
with-your-sorting-methods-and.

'The Basics'
Sorting Hat Chats
Tumblr. 2015, http://sortinghatchats.tumblr.com/post/121904186113/the-basics.

'The Men of *Game of Thrones*: All House Edition'
Sorting Hat for Other Fandoms
Tumblr. 2017, https://sortinghatforotherfandoms.tumblr.com.

'The Women of *Game of Thrones*: All House Edition'
Sorting Hat for Other Fandoms
Tumblr. 2017, https://sortinghatforotherfandoms.tumblr.com.

'Comment: Sorting *BtVS* Characters into Hogwarts Houses'
S Rou
Buffy-Boards. 27 July 2017, https://buffy-boards.com/threads/sorting-btvs-characters-into-hogwarts-houses.70365/.

'JK Rowling on Her Love of Hufflepuff'
SnitchSeeker.com
YouTube. 12 October 2012, https://www.youtube.com/watch?v=Smu0Rneksxl.

'My *Game of Thrones* Hogwarts House Sorting List'
Starline Hodge
Tumblr. 2014, http://starline.tumblr.com/post/55854560492/my-game-of-thrones-hogwarts-house sorting-list-so.

'*Hamilton* Characters and Their Hogwarts Houses'
Jazmyn Strode
li.stArchive. 2017, https://li.st/jloraines/hamilton-characters-and-their-hogwarts-houses-Og9TYHa1HtlNUZyP4T4L59.

'Better Be... Gryffindor'
ThePsychoticQueen
Archive of Our Own (AO3). 9 May 2016, https://archiveofourown.org/works/6798877.

'Hogwarts: Which House Are You?'
The Second City
YouTube. 5 July 2011, https://www.youtube.com/watch?v=yOZ5_wipT2o.

'Comment: *Buffy* Characters in Hogwarts Houses??'
Thosefilthyhobbitses
Reddit. 2015, https://www.reddit.com/r/buffy/comments/2u7h74/buffy_characters_in_hogwarts_houses/#bottom-comments.

Buffy, Hamilton and Jon Snow Go to Hogwarts:
Literary Affordance and the Hogwarts Houses as Interpretative
Framework and Rhetorical Tool
Jessica Hautsch

'*Hamilton* Characters into Hogwarts Houses Part 1'
Tonks
Amino Apps. 16 April 2017, https://aminoapps.com/c/harry-potter/page/blog/hamil-ton-characters-in-hogwarts-houses-part-1/6KTz_u4d8x0mgvmbKKwlZemgVYaeZ.

'Comment: What Hogwarts House Do You Think *Hamilton* Characters Belong To?'
Trashymctrashcan
Reddit. 2017, https://www.reddit.com/r/hamiltonmusical/comments/5p50ex/what_hogwarts_house_do_you_think_the_hamilton.

'If These Are the Four Houses of America's Hogwarts, They Are Completely Insane'
Katharine Trendacosta
io9. 16 May 2016, https://io9.gizmodo.com/if-these-are-the-four-houses-of-americas-hogwarts-they-1776025194.

'Comment: Sorting *BtVS* Characters into Hogwarts Houses'
WillowfromBuffy
Buffy-Boards. 14 July 2017, https://buffy-boards.com/threads/sorting-btvs-characters-into-hogwarts-houses.70365/.

'Hogwarts Houses vs. Ilvermorny Houses.' Google Trends, 29 April 2018, https://trends.google.com/trends/explore?date=all&q=Hogwarts%20Houses,Ilvermorny%20Houses.

'Home Page.' Pottermore: Wizarding World, 2012, https://www.pottermore.com.

Film/Television
'Lie to Me', Joss Whedon, dir., *Buffy the Vampire Slayer* (USA: Mutant Enemy Productions, 1997).

'Doppelgangland', Joss Whedon, dir., *Buffy the Vampire Slayer* (USA: Mutant Enemy Productions, 1999).

'Touched', David Solomon, dir., *Buffy the Vampire Slayer* (USA: Mutant Enemy Productions, 2003).

Music
'My Shot'
Lin-Manuel Miranda
In *Hamilton: An American Musical*, Original Broadway Cast (Atlantic Recording Corporation, 2015).

'Right Hand Man'
Lin-Manuel Miranda
In *Hamilton: An American Musical*, Original Broadway Cast (Atlantic Recording Corporation, 2015).

'Take a Break'
Lin-Manuel Miranda
In *Hamilton: An American Musical*, Original Broadway Cast (Atlantic Recording Corporation, 2015).

Chapter
08

Harry's Magical Move to Broadway

Valerie Guempel

→ *Harry Potter and the Cursed Child* (Rowling, Thorne and Tiffany, 2016) is both a nightmare and a dream come true for many *Harry Potter* fans. When the script was published on 30 July 2016, *Harry Potter* enthusiasts of all ages, myself included, eagerly began reading it, not knowing what to expect.

Quickly enough, excitement turned to bewilderment and incredulity. Set immediately after the epilogue of *Harry Potter and the Deathly Hallows* (Rowling, 2007), the play features a rather outlandish plot filled with a Time-Turner that can go back years, a centuries-old trolley witch who guards the Hogwarts Express, Voldemort's child and Harry's scar hurting once again. As many fans claim, it reads like bad fanfiction, full of implausible, extravagant ideas that do not adhere well to canon.

Once I saw the play, however, my feelings changed.

On 10 March 2018, I woke up shortly after nine in the morning and, like many people, immediately reached for my phone. One of my most recent e-mails dating from the previous hour announced that they were handing out 1200 tickets, priced $20 each, to the first preview performances of *Cursed Child* to those first in line that day at Broadway's Lyric Theatre box office.

Considering my experience reading the script, I did not jump up and down for joy. Nor did I immediately change my clothes and rush out the door. Instead, I texted my friends, debating whether it would be worth the two-hour-long roundtrip on the subway and day-long wait in line. After all, the script was a mess, even though I had heard better things about the actual West End performances. I exchanged a few texts with my friends, paced my bedroom and conducted a quick introspection, and minutes later I found myself hurriedly getting ready for the day and speed-walking to the subway.

Even if the play itself turned out to be awful, much like the script itself, who could pass up cheap Broadway premiere tickets? As a poor graduate student and lifelong *Harry Potter* fan, I certainly could not pass up this chance.

Luckily, I was not too late. I arrived at the Lyric Theatre just before 11 a.m. and immediately joined the queue. Before I knew it, a few of the theatre's staff, all wearing the new *Cursed Child*-style Hogwarts hats and scarves, placed a gold, plastic wristband with the words 'Cursed Child' and the number 165 around my wrist. I was in! With this, I settled in for the cold, nine-hour wait.

As far as waiting in lines go, this was surprisingly one of my best experiences. Despite the homework I had brought (one of Jane Austen's novels), I soon found myself passing the hours away by talking to the people around me, the majority of whom were also huge *Harry Potter* fans. Over the course of the day, the staff made rounds up and down the queue with free *Cursed Child* buttons (the same kind they give out after the performances), hot chocolate and coffee, bottled water, donuts and even pizza when dinnertime approached. In

Harry's Magical Move
to Broadway
Valerie Guempel

addition, we could take photos with the Hogwarts House banners used onstage, and, shortly after 5 p.m. when they had finished their rehearsal, with some of the *Cursed Child* actors themselves. Still saved to my phone are selfies with the actors who play Hermione Granger (Noma Dumezweni), Ron Weasley (Paul Thornley) and Ginny Weasley (Poppy Miller), all of whom, along with three other main actors, originated their roles in London and came to New York to open the play.

Of course, the majority of this was likely done as publicity for the play – many photos and videos from that day ended up on the play's Twitter page @HPPlayNYC. Nonetheless, no matter the reason, I enjoyed all the free food and photo opportunities. Even more, I loved walking out of the box office with two sets of $20 tickets.

Figure 1: Valerie Guempel at the Cursed Child *New York premiere (2018).*

The next weekend, of course, was even better. One of the things I remember most, besides the performances themselves, is how much time I spent marvelling at the inside of the theatre. I already knew that the outside had been remodelled, moving the theatre's main entrance from 42nd Street to 43rd, mounting a giant nest sculpture on the roof and adding a large black wing beside the play's name. What I had not realized, however, was how much the inside had also been changed.

Looking around the rich and elaborate interior, I could see that the theatre inside had been tailored to a degree I have never seen in any other theatre on or off Broadway. A *New York Times* article by Michael Paulson later reported that the show 'cost about $68.5 million to bring to Broadway, including not only $35.5 million to capitalize the show – more than for any other nonmusical play in history – but also another $33 million to clear out and redo the theatre'. From the gorgeous, monogrammed red carpet containing the letter H for Hogwarts and patterned with leaves, feathers and other designs, to the magnificent wallpapers whose patterns and colours differ slightly throughout the theatre to even the wonderful dragon- and phoenix-themed lights, it was clear that it was intended that the Lyric Theatre would be home to *Cursed Child* for many years to come.

Figure 2: The terrier Patronus
(2018).

Although the entire place is gorgeous, I consider the masterpiece to be the mural of Patronuses, created by artist Peter Strain. Located next to the cloakroom, each Patronus is composed of a quote from the play, the luminous words configured in the shapes of a phoenix, Jack Russell Terrier, horse, otter, stag, cat and doe. That first night, I stared at each Patronus for minutes, marvelling at its beauty and attempting to read the quotes amid the bustle of people walking by. Since I only discovered this near the end of my explorations, I made sure to return first thing the next night, before the majority of the crowd had entered, to drink in more of the sight and to photograph each Patronus.

It was not until examining the photos much later that I realized the full significance of each. The Patronuses belong to some of the more influential adults in the play, and the quotes are said by or about those characters. While there are a few other characters who can produce full, corporeal Patronuses, the only Patronuses pictured in the mural belong to teachers or parents who are relatively positive influences on both fans and the next generation of characters. I use the word 'relatively' because both J. K. Rowling and Jack Thorne have done well in presenting the flaws in each. No one is perfect in the *Potter* universe, even – or perhaps *especially* – the characters who are the most beloved and quoted.

The Patronus mural is beautiful to see, but, like the interactive wands and spell-casting locations at Universal Studio's Wizarding World, it is likely only fully appreciated by the more dedicated fans. It takes time and patience to read and place each quote with the character to whom it belongs. The mu-

**Harry's Magical Move
to Broadway**
Valerie Guempel

ral is thus an homage to the more dedicated fans who, even now, still love to carefully examine each new *Fantastic Beasts* movie or Pottermore article for deeper fanlore.

Overall, the theatre's architecture presents a slightly more obvious interpretation; it acts as an extension of the play itself. Everything from the wallpaper to the design of the lights sets the mood as the audience walks in, reminding fans of Hogwarts and the Wizarding World's timeless nature. As Lyric Theatre designers Christine Jones and Brett J. Banakis, along with Project Director Gary Beestone, state in the play's programme:

We took details from the original Lyric and infused them with the spirit of our show's first home, the Palace Theatre in London, to create this new space that has become part of the world of our story. We also echoed elements of our set design throughout the auditorium, arriving at a theatre that is both bespoke for our production as well as grounded in its own unique identity and integrity.

The theatre, like Universal Studio's Diagon Alley or Hogsmeade, creates a world that touches fiction and in which fans can engage indirectly with elements from the stories.

When describing Universal Studio's Wizarding World of Harry Potter, Henry Jenkins writes:

Make no mistake about it. This is a magical place. Some of the fans spoke of weeping the first time they entered this space. Others described it as a kind of homecoming as they were at last able to enter a world they had previously known only through their imagination.

To a lesser extent, the Lyric Theatre accomplishes this. Although it does not function as a replica location from the books or play, various aspects reference images from Hogwarts itself. For instance, the wallpaper near the upstairs entrances to the balcony suggests the Slytherin common room. The carpet with its H makes an instant association. Lyric Theatre is not Diagon Alley or Hogsmeade, or even a collection of their props as in the London studio tour. Nonetheless, some of the magic from *Harry Potter* is remarkably present in the theatre's design.

The second most surprising thing from that weekend, after the theatre's architecture, was the music. After we took our seats and listened to an opening speech from director John Tiffany, *Cursed Child* began. From the beginning, Imogen Heap's wonderful score filled the background, heightening the emotional landscape, and helping the play transition from one scene to the next. Although very different from John Williams's iconic music associated with the original films, I found Heap's to be well-suited after only a short adjustment.

Often paired with fluid movements and swishes of the characters' robes, the music introduces the audience to the new world glimpsed in *Deathly Hallows*'s epilogue. There is even a part of the play near the beginning of Part 1: Act 1 that I call a dance. Granted, it is not a dance in the traditional sense, but it is a dance nonetheless. A wand dance, in fact, when a variety of Hogwarts students move with their wands. This small scene has become one of my favourite parts of the play, strangely enough. Simple in concept but strange to consider when taken out of context, the wand dance is set to Imogen Heap's 'Cycle Song' and shows the students trying to master the light spell 'Lumos'. It is only after some struggles, during which they dance in unison with their new wands, that they finally conjure light by the end of the song. Even Albus Severus, who has particular difficulty with the spell, manages to cast it alongside his classmates.

I not only love this scene because of its significance in the play, but because I also see it as a metaphor for the fandom experience. The lecture on 'Lumos' transitions to practising with the spell and then to creating light. In a similar way, we read the play's script, discuss it with others, watch it and create various fanworks based off it. Fandom may not always appear in a way that one expects, but it can often be beautiful and is composed of many people operating in unison.

Although I have gone on to see the play twice more, my memories from this first weekend of preview performances are my favourite. This is partly because it was my first time seeing the show and experiencing everything with fresh eyes, but primarily it was the energy that filled the theatre. At least half of us had waited in line for hours the previous weekend just to obtain tickets, and it was clear the majority, if not all, of us were dedicated fans who have been familiar with the stories for years. We applauded as each of the major characters came onstage, excitedly chatted to each other before and after the performances, and eagerly examined the theatre's many beautiful reno-

Harry's Magical Move
to Broadway
Valerie Guempel

vations. Many even wore full Hogwarts cosplay or other themed clothes. We were all ecstatic to be there, and the excitement was contagious.

The actors also felt this energy. The next day Anthony Boyle, who plays Scorpius Malfoy, tweeted that the audience was 'electric' at those first performances. Since then, while audiences from the later performances still gasp and applaud at the appropriate parts, they lack the over-the-top energy that first audience had. It turns out, however, that even these later audiences remain more vocal than those in London. The cast commented on this difference at the play's red carpet premiere a month later on 22 April. Boyle claimed, 'Americans are just so much more up for it. They're just really enthusiastic, and it feels incredible. It just feels amazing to open it over here and be a part of this community'. Paul Thornley (Ron Weasley), Sam Clemmett (Albus Severus Potter), Jamie Parker (Harry Potter) and Noma Dumezweni (Hermione Granger) all echoed his sentiments (cited by Weiss).

Nonetheless, it is also obvious that there are at least a few people at each show who have never read the original books, or at least not in some time, as overheard audience conversations revealed during the second and third times I attended the show. Luckily, the Showbill (in place of the normal Broadway Playbill) contains brief summaries of the first seven books, catching the non-hardcore fans up to speed so they can enjoy the show without too much confusion.

To an extent, the show is just as great for non-hardcore fans. However, *Cursed Child* is not what anyone, except perhaps playwright Jack Thorne, had in mind, for a *Harry Potter* play. After all, any new work for a large fandom cannot meet its millions of expectations. Nonetheless, *Cursed Child* tries to appease both longtime fans and new fans (but does not always succeed in doing so) by cramming many moments into the two-part show: time travel, Harry's scar hurting, the original trio and Ginny teaming up with Draco, dream flashbacks of scenes with the Dursleys and Hagrid, and the next generation at school with McGonagall as headmistress. While entertaining to watch, these elements seem like they were shoved one after another into the script, trying to create a showy, overly dramatic story rather than a well-written one. After all, compared to *Angels in America* (Kushner, 1993), another two-part play whose revival opened the weekend after *Cursed Child*'s first Broadway preview performance, *Cursed Child* is relatively short (5 ¼ hours compared to *Angels in America*'s 7 ½). In other words, *Cursed Child* brims with a variety of characters spanning several generations, incredible special effects and gratuitous plot devices. These elements are both part of the play's allure and its crutch that it relies upon in place of a better-written script.

I cannot deny, however, that that these same features look incredible onstage. I still tell people that the first time I watched the play, I forgot half the time that the laws of physics even existed. The special effects include Polyjuice potion, a working Floo in McGonagall's office, Muggle clothes that transform into robes, a floating hat, papers that organize themselves and a dozen other jaw-dropping works of magic. Even more magical, perhaps, is that these effects looked amazing onstage no matter whether I was seated in the middle of the orchestra or three rows from the back of the balcony. The play's wow factor, evident most in the play's physical appearance, is its greatest strength, keeping the audience's eyes glued to the action the entire time.

The play's second greatest strength is the way it caters to a variety of ages. As the *Potter* fandom has aged, so have the main characters. The original book series saw the trio become teenagers; the *Fantastic Beasts and Where to Find Them* (Yates, 2016) movie stars Newt Scamander in his twenties and *Cursed Child* follows Harry's struggles as a father in his late thirties as well as the next generation's school adventures. Clearly, *Cursed Child* is a story for the kids who grew up with Harry, Ron and Hermione; the adults who chose to read the stories as well; and the present-day children who have recently read the original series for the first time. This is possible because the play, like the original series, serves as a *bildungsroman* (coming-of-age story) through its focus on Albus Severus and Scorpius, but splits its attention with the adult characters who were the heart of the first series. This dual focus caters to a multigenerational audience, inviting fans both new and old to participate once more in the *Potter* fandom.

Despite enjoying seeing the play in person, there are four main elements I could not help but cringe at as I read the script and watched the show. I have decided to discuss them below and offer tentative resolutions or better interpretations.

Harry's scar hurting again

As we know from the seventh book, Harry was a Horcrux, a part of Voldemort's soul. When Harry died, that soul fragment died, ridding Harry of any type of connection to Voldemort, including his ability to speak Parseltongue. Seeing

**Harry's Magical Move
to Broadway**
Valerie Guempel

as children are distinct entities from their parents, biologically and psycho-
logically, Voldemort's daughter Delphi would not have inherited any piece of
Voldemort's soul, only half his DNA.

The only plausible explanation for Harry's scar hurting during the play,
therefore, is that it is psychosomatic pain, caused by Harry's own stress. Harry has likely internalized the rumour that Voldemort may have had a child in
the form of Scorpius Malfoy, causing Harry's PTSD to worsen and triggering
nightmares and the psychosomatic scar pain. The play fails to make this explanation obvious, however, making that particular element of the plot appear
to disagree with the established canon.

Ron's characterization

My second most vexing issue with the play, after the misattributed scar pain,
is Ron's rather one-dimensional characterization – even worse than it is in
the films. As many know, many of Ron's better and more memorable lines
from the books went to Hermione on screen. With this, he goes from being
a cool-headed, intelligent tactician to the person who panics in a crisis. This
was seen movie after movie, starting with *Harry Potter and the Philosopher's
Stone/Sorcerer's Stone* (Columbus, 2001) when the trio encounters devil's
snare. Instead of Ron reminding Hermione that she is a witch who can create
magic fire, as he does in the book (Rowling, 1997), Ron is the one who panics
and needs saving. In *Harry Potter and the Chamber of Secrets* (book: Rowling,
1998; film: Columbus, 2002), book-Ron explains what 'Mudblood' means following the incident with Malfoy, whereas in the film it is Hermione. Then, in
Harry Potter and the Prisoner of Azkaban (book: Rowling, 1999; film: Cuarón,
2004), film-Ron fails to stand up on his broken leg and utter the line, 'if you
want to kill Harry, you'll have to kill us too!' Instead, he remains silently seated
while Hermione steps protectively in front of Harry and says the line. *Cursed
Child* only continues this tradition of ridding the character of some of his best
qualities. In the play, he is reduced to the role of comic relief, the fun uncle
who rarely takes a situation seriously. Although this type of characterization
is evident all throughout the play, it is most obvious in Part 1: Act 1, Scene 7,
when he sends the *Potter* children joke-shop presents, including giving Albus
a love potion.

This love potion is actually the most cringeworthy aspect of Ron's character. One would think, at the very least, that he would have learned not to mess

with love potions after he accidentally dosed himself with one during *Harry Potter and the Half-Blood Prince* (book: Rowling, 2005; film: Yates, 2009). Instead, he gives Albus the potion as a joke, which seems unconscionable as well as out-of-character. Today, it is inexcusable to still pretend that love potions, the lesser version of a date-rape drug, can be considered a joke. More people are heeding what others say about sexual-assault awareness and, the play, set primarily in the 2020–21 Hogwarts school year, fails to acknowledge these serious issues. Although the play was written and first performed in the West End before the #MeToo movement, it does not predate the illegality of date-rape drugs and awareness of sexual harassment and assault. The play could have easily avoided this problem with any other type of potion. Instead, this plot device unwittingly changed Ron's characterization in reprehensible ways.

Time travel
The time travel is one of the most prominent issues fans have with the play, partly because the type of time travel seen in *Cursed Child* is very different from that found in the books. In the play, the characters transform the past to the point of creating alternate timelines, whereas in *Prisoner of Azkaban*, Harry and Hermione actually change nothing. No version of history exists in which they did not travel back and do what they did. Some people may attempt to attribute this discrepancy to the massive scale of how far the characters go back, but logically, the same rules should apply even with the changes in the amount of time travelled.

Rose/Scorpius
The *Harry Potter* franchise has a history of supposed queer subtext that never overtly appears in the primary texts and movies. Even when *Prison of Azkaban*'s director Alfonso Cuarón made the decision to have actor David Thewlis portray Remus Lupin as a gay man, a decision made without consulting Rowling, the end result was not obvious to the audience. Furthermore, when *Half-Blood Prince* revealed Lupin's relationship with Tonks, Thewlis claims he 'changed [his] whole performance after that. Just saw it as a phase he went through' (cited by Vary). Dumbledore is the only character Rowling has confirmed as being LGBT+ despite many fans wishing for more queer characters. And famously, she did so in an author appearance after book seven came out, instead of directly referencing his love for Grindelwald even once in the text.

**Harry's Magical Move
to Broadway**
Valerie Guempel

Considering the amount of time Albus and Scorpius spend together throughout *Cursed Child*, the depth of their (platonic) feelings for each other and the complete lack of any queer *Harry Potter* characters besides Dumbledore, many fans prefer to ship Albus/Scorpius over Rose/Scorpius. This preference is particularly evident on the popular fanfiction site Archive of Our Own (AO3), which currently (as of June 2018) contains 2241 stories with the Scorpius/Albus relationship tag compared to the 849 Scorpius/Rose stories. Even when taking into account the data from FanFiction.net, another popular site (468 Scorpius/Albus versus 1006 Scorpius/Rose), the number of Scorpius/Albus stories is still far greater than that of Scorpius/Rose stories.

In today's world, where LGBT+ identities are becoming more and more recognized and accepted, *Cursed Child* does the queer community an injustice by leaving them out completely, even to the point of deleting a line from the rehearsal edition. Each version of Part 1: Act 2, Scene 16 has Albus admitting that Scorpius makes him stronger and that he wants Scorpius in his life. The rehearsal script, however, also includes a line where Albus claims Scorpius is 'probably the best person I know'. It would have been simple to have left this line in and slightly change the play's ending to imply – keeping with the books' tradition to not state queerness outright – how Scorpius's romantic interests have shifted from Rose to Albus. After all, the majority of the script already shows that the two teenage boys care for each other deeply, while Scorpius and Rose rarely speak together. To change the boys' feelings from platonic to romantic would have been very easy as well as a major achievement for the queer community. Instead, to the disappointment of many, the play largely ignores its queer subtext.

For all of the above reasons and more, countless fans have divorced *Cursed Child* from the rest of the *Potter* franchise, choosing to ignore it in favour of the original series and the *Fantastic Beasts* movies. With the release of Warner Bros. Interactive Entertainment's *Harry Potter: Hogwarts Mystery* app on 25 April 2018, a few fans have even declared the video game to be more canon than the play. Although I feel slightly better about *Cursed Child* after having seen it performed several times, I am still not a large fan of the script and find it difficult to fully accept the story as canon when I have read many better-written fanfictions. There are certain things I like about the play, especially the actual performances, but I continue to view many of the plot points as major departures from the events and characters' personalities in the books.

The publication of *Cursed Child* script (2016) has led more people, such as Daniel Morales Olea, Caroline Bishop and many others, to speak about the Death of the Author phenomenon, a symbolic death first discussed by theorist Roland Barthes in an essay he published in 1967. Ever since *Deathly Hallows*'s publication in 2007 and the eighth film's release in 2011 (Yates, dir.), fan engagement with the texts and the articulation of their own fanon ideas (ones that have been accepted as true among many fans but for which little or no evidence exists in the canon texts) have been gaining more prominence. Add to all of this the ridiculous nature of the play's script, and at this point in many people's minds, J. K. Rowling has ceased to exist. Although not written by her, Rowling endorsed *Cursed Child*, therefore making it an official story. However, fanon ideas rather than new canon ideas have been gaining traction. For instance, more people accept the pairing of Sirius and Remus than they do Albus and Scorpius' adventures with a Time-Turner. Fans are placing more significance on their own readings of the texts rather than on whatever Rowling may declare on Twitter or Pottermore. As new *Fantastic Beasts* movies are released over the next few years, there may be a revival of the author, but as for now she is very much metaphorically dead.

In the end, there are a few things we should remember about *Cursed Child*, which other analyses of the play sometimes forget. First, the play has ushered in more depictions of various *Harry Potter* characters as people of colour. Although Noma Dumezweni being cast as Hermione was not the first time fans could imagine the character as a black woman, for there is fanart that predates the play (showcased by Blay, among others), it reinforced the idea that the character does not have to be white. Her skin colour is never described in the books, and Noma is perfect for her role as the adult Minister for Magic Hermione Granger. Fanart portraying Harry as non-white also predates *Cursed Child* (predominantly dating back to 2015 when racebending various *Potter* characters became noticed), but a canon black Hermione cemented these new depictions of Harry Potter.

On 21 December 2015, months after fanart depicting a black Hermione gained traction in the online community, Pottermore published an article revealing that Jamie Parker, Noma Dumezweni and Paul Thornley had been cast as Harry, Hermione and Ron. Some people immediately pushed back against Noma's casting, but J. K. Rowling responded with the following Tweet she pinned to her Twitter account: 'Canon: brown eyes, frizzy hair and very clever.

**Harry's Magical Move
to Broadway**
Valerie Guempel

White skin was never specified. Rowling loves black Hermione'. Rowling's en-
dorsement of a black Hermione as well as other people's support for the idea
has led to the creation of more fanart portraying various *Potter* characters as
people of colour, while encouraging fans to see themselves in even the most
iconic characters.

The second takeaway regards *Cursed Child*'s themes. *Deathly Hallows* ends
with the lines: 'The scar had not pained Harry for nineteen years. All was well'.
Despite the many deaths and suffering that Harry and the other characters
went through over the course of the series, the epilogue wraps up everything
perfectly with no mention of how they coped in the aftermath. *Cursed Child*
explores the time period after the epilogue and the consequences of the
first seven books, including Harry's PTSD. As Mercedes Lackey notes in her
short essay, '*Harry Potter* and the Post-Traumatic Stress Disorder Counselor'
(2005), Harry has survived a multitude of events – from his imprisonment in
the Dursley's cupboard under the stairs to his own death at Voldemort's hands
– that would be enough to give anyone PTSD. She ends with the observation:

> *Somewhere, out there in the fictional world of Harry Potter, there's a PTSD
> counselor avidly reading the wizarding papers, rubbing his hands and
> thinking happily of how he'll be able to pay the college fees for his kids
> once all this comes back to haunt the Boy Who Lived.*

Cursed Child is ultimately about Harry trying to cope with his post-traumatic
stress, which only worsens when various events are set into motion over the
course of the play. Everything in the play can be viewed through this lens, from
Albus and Scorpius' adventures in the past to the current timeline. The end
of *Cursed Child* even offers Harry a chance to grieve again, perhaps more so
than he ever has, for the loss of his parents and his years of trauma. We now
know that everything in the first seven books happens for a reason, and changing the past, no matter how much we wish we could, would not offer a better
future. The play leaves both Harry and the audience with a sense of finality and
allows us to fully come to terms with the events of the original series.

All in all, *Cursed Child* is a play meant for the stage, not to be read. It is another piece of the overall *Harry Potter* franchise, but one specifically designed
to be performed live. Even with its flaws, it flourishes on the stage with all of
its bells and whistles, at this point having won dozens of awards, including nine

Olivier Awards and six Tony Awards. Although the script still reads like bad fan-fiction, its special effects and acting are what make the magic happen. ●

GO FURTHER

Books
Harry Potter and the Philosopher's Stone/Sorcerer's Stone
J. K. Rowling
(New York: Scholastic, 1997)

Harry Potter and the Chamber of Secrets
J. K. Rowling
(London: Bloomsbury, 1998)

Harry Potter and the Prisoner of Azkaban
J. K. Rowling
(New York: Scholastic, 1999)

Harry Potter and the Half-Blood Prince
J. K. Rowling
(New York: Scholastic, 2005)

Harry Potter and the Deathly Hallows
J. K. Rowling
(New York: Scholastic, 2007)

Harry Potter and the Cursed Child
J. K. Rowling, Jack Thorne and John Tiffany
(Crawfordsville, IN: Pottermore, 2016)

Extracts/Essays/Articles
'The Night of a Thousand Wizards'
Henry Jenkins
In V. Frankel (ed.). *Harry Potter, Still Recruiting* (Allentown PA: Zossima Press, 2012), pp. 94–100.

**Harry's Magical Move
to Broadway**
Valerie Guempel

'*Harry Potter* and the Post-Traumatic Stress Disorder Counselor'
Mercedes Lackey
In M. Lackey (ed.). *Mapping the World of Harry Potter* (Dallas, TX: BenBella, 2005), pp. 157–62.

Online
'Erased by Time and Blockbusters – The Cautionary Tale of Ron Weasley'
Emily Asher-Perrin
Tor.com. 15 January 2014, https://www.tor.com/2014/01/15/erased-by-time-and-block-busters-the-cautionary-tale-of-ron-weasley.

'*Harry Potter* and the Undead Author'
Caroline Bishop
Eidolon. 28 June 2017, https://eidolon.pub/harry-potter-and-the-undead-author-6cb-8cab76720.

'Black Harry Potter Characters Aren't Just Beautiful – They're Revolutionary'
Zeba Blay
Black Voices. 28 July 2015, https://www.huffingtonpost.com/entry/black-harry-pot-ter-characters-are-revolutionary_us_55aea1d5e4b0a9b94852c333.

'One Sentence Sums Up Why *Harry Potter*'s Ron Weasley Is a Billion Times Better in the Books'
Sarah Doran
Radio Times. 24 May 2016, https://www.radiotimes.com/news/2016-05-24/one-sen-tence-sums-up-why-harry-potters-ron-weasley-is-a-billion-times-better-in-the-books.

'Why J. K. Rowling Must Die'
Daniel Morales Olea
Cultura Colectiva. 17 October 2016, https://culturacolectiva.com/books/why-jk-row-ling-must-die.

'Another *Harry Potter* Landmark: At $68 Million, the Most Expensive Broadway Non-Musical Play Ever'
Michael Paulson
New York Times. 14 April 2018, https://www.nytimes.com/2018/04/14/theater/harry-potter-broadway.html.

'Harry, Hermione and Ron Cast in Upcoming Stage Play *Harry Potter and the Cursed Child...* and J. K. Rowling Is Delighted!'
Pottermore Team
Pottermore. 21 December 2015, https://www.pottermore.com/news/cursed-child-play-casts-harry-hermione-and-ron.

'Canon: Brown Eyes, Frizzy Hair and Very Clever. White Skin Was Never Specified. Rowling Loves Black Hermione :-* https://twitter.com/mauvedust /status/67585906528 5812224...'
J. K. Rowling (@jk_rowling)
Twitter. 21 December 2015, https://twitter.com/jk_rowling/status /678888094339366914?lang=en.

'*Harry Potter* Cast Talks Their Favorite Scenes and How Remus Lupin Was Originally Kinda Gay'
Adam B. Vary
Entertainment Weekly. 15 April 2011, http://ew.com/article/2011/04/15/harry-potter-cast-favorite-scenes-remus-lupin-gay.

'We Asked the *Cursed Child* Cast About Hitting Broadway and Apparently Americans Are Much Much Louder'
Josh Weiss
Syfy. 23 April 2018, http://www.syfy.com/syfywire/we-asked-the-cursed-child-cast-about-hitting-broadway-and-apparently-americans-are-much.

**Harry's Magical Move
to Broadway**
Valerie Guempel

Film/Television
Harry Potter and the Philosopher's Stone/Sorcerer's Stone, Chris Columbus, dir. (USA: Warner Bros, 2001).

Harry Potter and the Chamber of Secrets, Chris Columbus, dir. (USA: Warner Bros, 2002).

Harry Potter and the Prisoner of Azkaban, Alfonso Cuarón, dir. (USA: Warner Bros, 2004).

Theatre
Harry Potter and the Cursed Child, J. K. Rowling, Jack Thorne, John Tiffany and Imogen Heap (Palace Theatre, London, 30 July 2016–ongoing; Lyric Theatre, New York, 16 March 2018).

Angels in America, Tony Kushner (Neil Simon Theatre, New York, 25 March–15 July 2018).

'SO YOU'RE TELLING ME THAT THE WHOLE OF HISTORY RESTS ON... NEVILLE LONGBOTTOM? THIS IS WILD'

RON WEASLEY
(HARRY POTTER AND THE CURSED CHILD)

Fan Appreciation #4: Ariel Birdoff
(author, wrocker, librarian and fan)
Valerie Estelle Frankel

Ariel Birdoff with *Nerd!Verse*,
10 December 2014.

Ariel Birdoff was born in New York City some time ago. After attending college in Pennsylvania, she moved back to New York City and now lives with her husband and a lot of books. She is a compulsive crafter, obsessive YA (young adult) reader and enormously enthusiastic librarian. *Harry Potter* has been a huge part of her life since she first read *Harry Potter and the Philosopher's Stone/Sorcerer's Stone* (Rowling, 1997) in 1999.

Valerie Estelle Frankel (VEF): So, Ariel, thanks for joining us. I think we met at your first *Potter* con (huh, mine too) *Phoenix Rising* in 2007. It's been quite a journey, huh? Why don't you tell us a bit about yourself.

Ariel Birdoff (AB): Hi Valerie! Thanks for having me! Yes! *Phoenix Rising*! One of the best cons I've ever been to. It really has been a journey! Well, right now I am working as a school outreach librarian for New York Public Library and living in Queens with my husband. My wizard rock band Madam Pince and the Librarians is celebrating its eighth birthday this year!

VEF: What I find really cool is that you've actually written poetry on the top franchises. What gave you the idea? How have the responses been? Do you see other fans doing anything similar?

AB: I actually studied poetry in college. Verse forms have always fascinated me. A few years ago, I challenged myself to write a poem a day for an entire year. When the year was up, I noticed that a lot of what I wrote was about my favourite shows, books and movies! I'd always wanted to publish my poetry, so I figured the best bet would be to self-publish *Nerd!Verse* [2014]. I was able to completely raise the money through Indiegogo with the help of my friends and family. It's certainly not a bestseller, but I've been invited to book signings, and my book is currently in Muhlenberg College's circulating collection and on WorldCat [a worldwide library catalogue]. I haven't seen a lot of other fan poetry books, but I know there is a wizard literary magazine out there! *Wizards in Space* [2016–ongoing] it's called, I believe.

VEF: A couple of years ago, you and I got together to do fannish readings in Manhattan, I recall. You opened with your poetry and then I read one of my parodies at a delightful pizza party to a room full of applause. How is the big New York fanclub, The Group That Shall Not Be Named (TGTSNBN) going?

Fan Appreciation #4
Ariel Birdoff

AB: Yep! That was so much fun! I had just published *Nerd!Verse* at that time. The Group That Shall Not Be Named is going strong. There are still meetups every month and events all the time!

VEF: What about your library? Have you done cool *Potter* events there?

AB: NYPL (The New York Public Library) has done some wonderful *Harry Potter* events! Sometimes they've even partnered with TGTSNBN. The Brooklyn Public Library does some great events as well. Every year in July they throw a huge birthday party for Harry. Activities can include wand making, spellbook inscription, fortune telling and dramatic readings of *Harry Potter* books by librarians and volunteers. It's a dream to be able to cosplay at the library for my job!

Figure 1: Ariel Birdoff,
Nerd!Verse (2014).

VEF: Since you're the expert, any books to recommend specifically to *Potter* fans?

AB: This is my favourite question! Recommending books is what I live for! I would suggest *An Ember in the Ashes* by Sabaa Tahir (2016) for an incredible fantasy series featuring diverse characters and a captivating plot. Another book that is absolutely delicious is *Carry On* by Rainbow Rowell (2015). If you're a reader of fanfiction, the story of Simon and Baz at a familiar magic school will surely warm your heart. Make sure to read Chapter 61 several times.

VEF: Have you met our great lady, J. K. Rowling?

AB: YES! I met her when she was on tour for *The Casual Vacancy* [2012]. It was an incredible moment. I managed to put as much feeling as I could into a tear-filled 'thank you'. She smiled at me and noticed my Hufflepuff lapel pin. I told her I was Hufflepuff and proud. I then proceeded to cry for hours afterwards. I still can't believe it happened!

Our Ravenclaw & Hufflepuff librarians

Figure 2: Library Day, 31 July: Ariel Birdoff and Jason Woodland teach kids about magic at the Brooklyn Public Library (2017).

VEF: What is it about Harry that you think brings people together?

AB: Magic! Honestly, that's the only way I can explain it. Something about reading those books, makes you want to talk to everyone about it. I can't even imagine how different my life would have been without Harry.

VEF: And you've really brought Harry into your personal life, haven't you? I recall seeing your *Potter*-themed 2016 wedding go by on Facebook with all the bridesmaids in color-matched dresses holding the hardcovers...

AB: Yep! My husband and I are quite the *Potter* fans. That's one of the reasons we started dating. He's the Slytherin to my Hufflepuff! When we were planning our wedding, we tried to slip as much *Potter* in as we could, while still keeping our families happy! Our engagement photos (in the New York Public Library) featured a wand duel, a marauder's map dress and our favourite HP books. Our cake toppers at the wedding were crocheted versions of ourselves as Hogwarts students. We also used the illustrated *Sorcerer's Stone* [2015] as our guest book.

VEF: That's an awesome inspiration for fans everywhere. On another topic, why is Madam Pince your hero? How'd you start playing?

AB: She's not exactly my hero, but she is a lot of fun. Since her canon character is pretty terrible (I appreciate J. K. Rowling's apology to librarians about her), I enjoy writing angry songs from her point of view. I'd also like to think that I can help her reputation just a little bit!
I started Madam Pince and the Librarians at the second Wrockstock – the big wizard rock gathering for *Harry Potter*-related filk bands (roughly, the folk music of the science fiction/fantasy fandom). We had been play-

Fan Appreciation #4
Ariel Birdoff

Figure 3: Madam Pince and the Librarians: Ariel Birdoff, Devon Bennett, Stacy Pisani and Kelly Owen (2017).

ing 'Apples to Apples' in the Cabin of Love, and I casually mentioned that if I ever started a wrock band, it would be called Madam Pince and the Librarians. My fellow wrockstockers asked me seriously, 'why don't you?' I really didn't have a good answer... so I called up my friend Erich as soon as I landed in New York and we started a band! A few years later Kelly became my partner, and soon we were joined by Stacy and then Devon!

VEF: What was the best part about being in your band?

AB: The friendship. The only thing better than having a close group of friends, is having a close group of friends that encourage creativity and boost your self-esteem!

VEF: I know you're one of the many very popular groups. For those who haven't been, could you tell us more about Wrockstock?

AB: Wrockstock is home. I wish it was still going on. It was a three-day wizard rock festival in the heart of the Ozark Mountains put together by Abby Kupferberg. It was like going to the most perfect sleepaway camp. Every afternoon and evening there were wrock shows, and there were activities like arts and crafts and archery for attendees. You ate in a beautiful cafeteria with huge windows overlooking the lake with all your friends and all the bands. If you weren't friends with someone already, you soon became friends. It is one of the most positive and affirming events I've ever had the pleasure of attending. It was the birth of Madam Pince in its second year, and the final year saw Madam Pince playing on the main stage. It was such a magical event, and the friends I made there will be friends for life.

VEF: Who's your favourite band besides your own?

AB: That is a REALLY tough question. Can I just say all of them? If I have to choose just one, I think I'll have to say Swish and Flick. Their lead singer is kind of amazing.

VEF: Do you think wrock is on its way out or still strong? Where can people hear it?

AB: Wrock is definitely still going strong! There is a Facebook group dedicated to a 'Wizard Rock Revival' where new bands are sharing their music all the time. There are also annual compilations coming out featuring music written within the past year! Here is more information on the most recent one: http://wizardrocksampler.tumblr.com. Madam Pince's 'Hufflepride' was featured on the 2016 sampler (https://wizardrock.bandcamp.com/album/2016-wizard-rock-sampler) on Bandcamp!

VEF: Do you see *Cursed Child* [2016] and *Fantastic Beasts* songs happening, or do people stay classic?

AB: I definitely think there will be *Cursed Child* and *Fantastic Beasts* songs! I think there are some already! There's a lot of great inspiration to be found in those stories!

VEF: Where do you see the fandom heading? What is it like now?

AB: I honestly don't know. I hope it continues going strong. For me, *Harry Potter* will be in my heart and my daily life with my family and my friends. I hope there will always be events and cons for us to attend, and if not, we'll make our own.

VEF: Anything new and awesome on your horizon?

AB: I may or may not have some *Cursed Child* Scorpius/Albus lyrics brewing in my head! Stay tuned!

VEF: Wow, we will. Being you sounds kind of amazing – you've definitely thrown yourself into the fandom, and I know it's glad to have you. ●

Fan Appreciation #4
Ariel Birdoff

~~~~~~~~~~~~~~~~

GO FURTHER

Books
Nerd!Verse
Ariel Birdoff
(New York: 'Puff Books, 2014)

Carry On
Rainbow Rowell
(New York: St. Martin's Griffin, 2015)

Harry Potter and the Sorcerer's Stone (Illustrated edn)
J. K. Rowling
(USA: Arthur A. Levine Books, 2015)

An Ember in the Ashes
Sabaa Tahir
(USA: Razorbill, 2016)

Websites
Madam Pince and the Librarians, https://librarywrock.bandcamp.com
The Group That Shall Not Be Named, https://www.meetup.com/TGTSNBN
Wizards in Space, https://wizardsinspacemag.com
Wizard Rock Revival, https://www.facebook.com/groups/1088071511244372
Wizard Rock Sampler, http://wizardrocksampler.tumblr.com.
Wizard Rock Sampler 2016 on Bandcamp, https://wizardrock.bandcamp.com/album/2016-wizard-rock-sampler

'HONESTLY, AM I THE ONLY PERSON WHO'S EVER BOTHERED TO READ *HOGWARTS: A HISTORY*?'

HERMIONE GRANGER
(HARRY POTTER AND THE PRISONER OF AZKABAN)

Part 4
Fictional World

Chapter
09

Tuesdays with Malfoy: The Pain of Sharing Fandoms

Katryn Alessandri

→ As a person with social anxiety, I've always envied fans who can handle con life. A self-described Potterhead, I delight at scrolling through pictures from *LeakyCon*, *Prophecy* and the many locally-sponsored *Yule Balls*, but I could never muster the courage to attend. I sift through cosplay sites, dreaming of the day when I'll throw caution to the wind and order that phenomenal Minerva McGonagall outfit, complete with crooked hat, ornate brooch and lush green velvet robes.

Figure 1: Katryn Alessandri, Gryffindor (2013).

However, I am far too overwhelmed by public fan life, a fate I know many fans like me share due to the rather large centre in the Venn diagram of 'nerds' and 'anxiety'. Even dressing up does nothing to diminish the effect that crowds have on me. To use a *Potter* metaphor, I freeze up like baby Ginny Weasley faced with our favourite lightning-scarred and bespectacled hero. For me, the crowds are a deal-breaker and would most likely find me curled in a foetal ball in Diagon Alley, wand in hand, until the convention ended.

As a result, I find myself mostly online, navigating the fandom with millions of others on sites like Pottermore, in groups on Facebook and in hashtags on Twitter. Unfortunately, in part due to the anonymity of the Internet and social media, I soon found that I was occupying that space with people I *deeply* disagreed with on several fundamental levels. While I had taken the *Harry Potter* books primarily as a social allegory against racism and ethnic cleansing, not unlike Nazi Germany during the Second World War and the Holocaust, I saw that many fans were displaying the very traits that were mirrored in Voldemort's hatred of Muggle-born and half-blood wizards. To my shock, however, many of these individuals did not identify with the Malfoys or even the Dursleys, but the *heroes*. Although the fan conventions have behaviour policies that include prohibiting harassment based on race or disability, the online world is filter-free, and the responses from narrow-minded fans easily slip through the cracks.

In June 2016, previews began for *Harry Potter and the Cursed Child* (Rowling, Thorne and Tiffany, 2016) at the Palace Theatre in London. John Tiffany, the director, had cast Noma Dumezweni as a grown-up Hermione, a black woman whom J. K. Rowling described as 'the best actress for the job' (cited by Ratcliff). Upon the casting announcement, the reactions were immediate. 'Not being racist but how can a black woman play Hermione? This play has lost all credibility', one fan identifying as Sean the Mondasian Cyberman (@WhoPotterVian) wrote on 21 December 2015. Another fan Augustine Jackson (@TheHighnessAJ) said: 'Hermione should be white... it isn't the same to see a black "Hermione" #boycott' (21 December 2015). Many fans also popped in to say that the idea of a black Hermione ruined their image of the character

Tuesdays with Malfoy:
The Pain of Sharing Fandoms
Katryn Alessandri

or the trio as a whole. Most tried to insist within their protest that they were by no means bigoted, but one must wonder what these comments are if *not* racist? How can stating that a beloved character imagined as a black woman *ruins* their perception not a racist sentiment?

When J. K. Rowling saw the response, her comment was immediate: she referred to the fans as 'a bunch of racists' and expressed that she saw Dume-zweni as a perfect choice for the role (cited by Ratcliff). This is in keeping with Rowling's past statements on the theme of mistreatment and bigotry in her books. Rowling has long spoken of the similarities in how Death Eaters look at purity of blood to assess the worth of an individual to the charts Nazis would use to determine Aryan blood during their regime. Despite this clarity, how-ever, Rowling does not expect that reading the *Harry Potter* books will change anyone's deep-seated beliefs. At the *Harry Potter Children's Press Conference Weekend* in 2016, Rowling said:

> *I do not think I am pessimistic, but I think I am realistic about how much you can change deeply entrenched prejudice, so my feeling would be that if someone were a committed racist, possibly Harry Potter is not going to have an effect.*

While many fans who were upset over Dumezweni's casting continued to sug-gest a boycott, Rowling made it clear that she was not shedding many tears about losing their business. This harsh response to the casting of *Cursed Child* on social media made me realize something: I was sharing this wonder-ful *Harry Potter* fandom, which I loved and felt so welcome in, with a bunch of Lucius Malfoys.

The outrage over casting a black woman as Hermione was certainly not the first time such vitriol had been directed at film adaptations of popular fan-doms. It has, I now know, been going on for years, in more and more public arenas. When I started to enter the online world several years ago, eager to connect with other fans, I was shocked to see the level of intolerance in fan-doms online. A friend of mine, Karim Moussally, who has been a Redditor since its formation over a decade ago, and a Wikipedia administrator since the early 2000s, scoffed at my naïveté: 'These people have been around since the In-ternet was born', he told me in 2017. While I had been trained to see people like this as trolls simply trying to get a rise out of people, I came to see that

these narrow-minded people online are not just trolls but *people*. They are daughters, fathers and grandparents. They love their pets. They have the same picture of themselves with a wand at the *Harry Potter and the Philosopher's/ Sorcerer's Stone* (Columbus, 2001) film premiere that I do! Of course, I should have known. Especially in the *Harry Potter* lexicon, a troll is a lot easier to spot than a Death Eater.

The first time I noticed this darker element to fandom was in 2012 when *The Hunger Games* (Ross, dir.) was released. A month before the premiere, a fan of the trilogy (Collins, 2008–10), who called himself 'Adam' to maintain anonymity, posted a series of Tweets he'd collected in reference to the *Hunger Games* film release, dating back several months to the first trailers. Anna Holmes of the *New Yorker* reported on these posts in her article 'White Until Proven Black: Imagining Race in *Hunger Games*' (2012). The collection of tweeted reactions was revealing to say the least: 'I was pumped about the Hunger Games. Until I learned that a black girl was playing Rue', one user named JohnnyKnoxIV said. 'Adam' goes on in the interview with Holmes to note that the most glaring moment to him came with a Tweet from a young woman, close to the film's release. 'Alana's tweet was not the most offensive or nakedly racist of the bunch [...] but perhaps the most telling. "Awkward moment when Rue is some black girl and not the little blonde innocent girl you picture," she wrote.'

I would have to agree that this *is* the most telling reaction. First of all, the character of Rue in the *Hunger Games* trilogy is clearly described as dark-

Tuesdays with Malfoy:
The Pain of Sharing Fandoms
Katryn Alessandri

skinned. In the first book (Collins, 2008), Katniss Everdeen muses on her fellow tributes: 'most hauntingly, a twelve-year-old girl from District 11. She has dark brown skin and eyes, but other than that she's very like Prim in size and demeanor.' Second and most importantly, how does the character being black erase her innocence? The realization that other people who loved these books as I did had these reactions sickened me. I wondered: can someone see in a book something not just different but the *complete opposite* of what I do?

Perhaps it was foolish of me to assume that any fan who thinks this way would automatically identify with Draco Malfoy instead of Harry Potter – that House Slytherin is where fans of this nature would choose to align. As *Cursed Child* touches on even more than the greyer areas of early *Harry Potter*, the House you are Sorted into does not dictate your entire character, just your strengths and qualities. My own sister identifies as Slytherin and she is a lovely person – no Riddle or Lestrange traits at all. After all, there is nothing wrong with being a shrewd, achievement-oriented good leader, which are all traits that many Slytherin possess. This House might also have another pull. American author Angie Thomas writes so passionately about *Harry Potter* as seen through her characters' eyes in her novel *The Hate U Give* (2017) that one can only assume she herself is a Potterhead. One point really struck me, though. The main character, Starr, recalls that when she and her brother were children they all wanted to be Slytherin because that House is synonymous with wealth and prosperity. 'When you're a kid in a one-bedroom in the projects,' Starr says, 'rich is the best thing anybody can be.'

This nuanced House view is touched upon a lot in *Cursed Child*, where we see Scorpius Malfoy and Albus Potter as protagonists. Scorpius Malfoy, in fact, makes one of the most glaring sacrifices of the whole story. When he is cast into an alternate reality where he has everything but knows that this world is cruel to others, he says: 'The world changes and we change with it. I am better off in this world. But the world is not better. And I don't want that' (Act 3, Scene 9). In another nuanced turn, Cedric Diggory, likeable Hufflepuff and all-around great chap, is portrayed in a villainous role. Hufflepuffs are generally portrayed as the 'loyal friends'; this begs the question: can our House traits be twisted towards evil? While loyalty is the most common word associated with Hufflepuffs, one can see that Cedric might have turned to villainy, believing that others had been disloyal to him. Looking at it this way, the very thing that made Cedric a hero could make him a villain. A Gryffindor's reckless bravery could be their downfall, as could the Ravenclaws' tendency to put too much stock in the learning that exists in books. With this, many of these emboldened online racists may actually justify their views as Gryffindors, bravely facing the intolerance of people who don't share *their* viewpoint.

In some ways, longtime *Harry Potter* fans can track the changes in themselves though their House status. Children who grow up with the books and take the numerous quizzes may find themselves Sorted into one House, while two decades later, life experience may find them in a different House altogether. My change in Houses almost seemed to happen overnight. For years, the Sorting quizzes had placed me squarely in Gryffindor, and why not? I was brave, determined and not bound to any silly 'rules' that could keep me from proving myself. After I had a child, however, my House status abruptly changed. It had been a few years since I'd logged into Pottermore, and I'd forgotten my username. So I decided to create a whole new account while juggling a napping newborn (the true mark of any dorky mom) and my Sorting test came back Ravenclaw. I was shocked. *This must be a mistake*, I thought. I took three more outside quizzes. Ravenclaw, Ravenclaw, Ravenclaw.

At first, I was concerned. As a mother, had I lost my sense of bravery and adventure? Was I now doomed to a life of abiding by all the rules, and always opting for intellect over instinct? As I grew into my new self, however, I realized that the traits I now had were actually reflective of my growing as a person. In my youth, I had a lot of talent, but not much of a focus on the hard work and research that led to success. I often found myself skating by as opposed to truly committing myself to anything. Once I became a mother and dedicated myself wholly to parenting, with the hard work and research to boot, I found that I was much more capable in that arena than I ever thought possible. This made me wonder though: how many Potterheads are using their House as a defence? Is House Sorting the new astrology? Similar to those who explain away their flaws and quirks by stating, 'I can't help it, I'm a Taurus!' or 'Sorry I lost my temper – it's the Scorpio in me,' Sorted Potterheads also use their House's characteristics to explain away behaviour. Can a Gryffindor House explain careless comments? Can a Ravenclaw status forgive a know-it-all, paternalistic attitude?

As with anything, a well-placed *Harry Potter* quotation can put it all into place. In *Harry Potter and the Order of the Phoenix* (Rowling, 2003), Sirius Black sums it up best: 'Yes, but the world isn't split up into good people and

Tuesdays with Malfoy:
The Pain of Sharing Fandoms
Katryn Alessandri

Death Eaters.' It's really in *Order of the Phoenix*, the hardest to read for me in the series, that Harry learns about the grey areas. Not all Slytherins will be cartoonishly evil, and not all Gryffindors will be the heroes defeating them. Sirius is an excellent representation of the fact that it's more complicated. He even points out the dichotomy of light and dark in each of us – it's our actions surrounding those qualities that make us *good* or *evil*. Throughout the *Harry Potter* lexicon, Harry is forced to face the idea that even those he respects most once held paternalistic or prejudiced views. As Tiffany L. Walters points out in her master's thesis 'Not So Magical: Issues with Racism, Classism, and Ideology in *Harry Potter*' (2015), Dumbledore himself found himself 'impassioned by the idea of the wizarding community's divine right to dominate over Muggles' for Muggles' 'own good'. Even Arthur Weasley's job title within the Ministry's 'Misuse of Muggle Artifacts Office suggests that to study and work with Muggle objects is to study a primitive culture', Walters writes. In the seventh book, *Harry Potter and the Deathly Hallows* (Rowling, 2007), Harry comes to see that even people and structures that appear to protect Muggle-born and half-blood wizards have a dark past. As he looks up at a statue in the Ministry of Magic, he realizes that

> what he had thought were decoratively carved thrones were actually mounds of carved humans: hundreds and hundreds of naked bodies, men, women, and children, all with rather stupid, ugly faces, twisted and pressed together to support the weight of the handsomely robed wizards.

The ugly support structure of their culture is revealed.

Now armed with the knowledge that it is not our House but our quality of character that makes us good people, how can we as fans argue with those who do not interpret the books through the allegorical lens that Rowling suggests? American author John Green says: 'What I eventually realized is that the real business of books is not done by awards committees or people who turn trees into paper or agents or even writers. We're all just facilitators. The real business is done by readers' (cited by Mancini). Warts and all, this is true. Readers are free to interpret the work in any way they wish, and that is often how we have these flourishing fan communities.

In John Granger's *Harry Potter's Bookshelf: The Great Books Behind the Hogwarts Adventures* (2009), Rowling says:

I think most of us if you were asked to name a very evil regime would think of Nazi Germany. [...] I wanted Harry to leave our world and find exactly the same problems in the Wizarding world. So you have the intent to impose a hierarchy, you have bigotry, and this notion of purity, which is a great fallacy, but it crops up all over the world. People like to think themselves superior and that if they can pride themselves on nothing else, they can pride themselves on perceived purity. [...] The Potter books in general are a prolonged argument for tolerance, a prolonged plea for an end to bigotry, and I think it's one of the reasons that some people don't like the books, but I think that it's a very healthy message to pass on to younger people that you should question authority and you should not assume that the establishment or the press tells you all of the truth.

From this, it's easy to see Rowling's intent in writing these stories, no matter what the interpretation. And, when it comes to *Cursed Child*, Rowling was asked directly and gave her answer. 'Canon: brown eyes, frizzy hair and very clever', she said on Twitter in 2015 when casting was revealed, 'white skin was never specified. Rowling loves black Hermione'. However, many have decided to interpret the text in a very different way and cling to white Hermione as their preferred heroine.

With this staggering wilful ignorance of the creator's intent, I can't help but think of two other fandoms that have had similar issues. The *Star Wars* franchise had its own reckoning of insufferable online racists when previews and trailers showed stormtrooper John Boyega in *Star Wars: The Force Awakens* (Abrams, 2015). Many were downright livid. While many of the accounts have now been suspended and the Tweets deleted, Benjamin Lee of *The Guardian* reported that 'the hashtag #BoycottStarWarsVII was started after trolls were angry over the casting of black actor John Boyega, claiming the film was promoting "genocide"'. While some tried to backpedal their comments by displaying anger that the cloned stormtroopers should all look like Jango Fett, the fact that *Force Awakens* took place two generations after this storyline didn't placate them.

One example is the alt-right Facebook group 'Down with Disney's Treatment of Franchises and Its Fanboys', organizing against Disney to trash reviews and start boycotts when films dare to cast a person of colour or of gender diversity. 'Down with Disney's Treatment of Franchises and Its Fanboys'

Tuesdays with Malfoy:
The Pain of Sharing Fandoms
Katryn Alessandri

claim responsibility for using bots to skew the average critical score of *Force Awakens*. The page was removed from Facebook when the group tried to orchestrate a campaign to trash the Rotten Tomatoes score of Marvel's *Black Panther* (Coogler, 2018), but, to date, the page has been reinstated. Kayleigh Donaldson is right on when she suggests in her article '*Star Wars* Has a White Male Fandom Problem' (2018) that 'the more this attitude is fostered, the more it is allowed to grow and become irrevocably empowered, particularly in online communities where harassment and abuse is euphemized as "trolling"'.

Similarly, when the *Star Trek: Discovery* (2017–ongoing) series trailer was released, featuring an Asian female captain and her black female first officer, alt-right fans were up in arms. Manu Saadia of the *New Yorker* reported on the outrage:

> Many commenters, though, were clearly appalled by the absence of white men in command positions. 'Where is the alpha male that has balls and doesn't take crap from anyone?' one asked. 'Is everything going to have to have females in every fucking thing?' another asked. A third person called Yeoh 'a reject from a overseas customer-support line'. A fourth dubbed the show 'Star Trek: Feminist Lesbian Edition'.

The responses to this franchise are puzzlingly similar to those who attacked the concept of a black Hermione in *Cursed Child*. Throughout the over half-century of *Star Trek*, even from the beginning, the series has favoured diversity. The original series featured people of colour and even broke the mould by showing television's first interracial kiss in 1968. In 'Today in Science' (2016), Creator Roddenberry himself said of the original series (1966–69):

> Star Trek was an attempt to say that humanity will reach maturity and wisdom on the day that it begins not just to tolerate, but take a special delight in differences in ideas and differences in life forms. [...] If we cannot learn to actually enjoy those small differences, to take a positive delight in those small differences between our own kind, here on this planet, then we do not deserve to go out into space and meet the diversity that is almost certainly out there.

Considering that the show has continued to shatter boundaries for decades, it is baffling that anyone could limit this franchise – which shows a nearly utopian future of the human race, having moved past issues like poverty, racism and greed – as only significant for a white space cowboy.

All in all, the question really is, how should we react when faced with fans who veer so far from even the author's interpretation of the text? Some might say we should just ignore the trolls. However, more and more, it's becoming clear that these trolls are actual people who take these beliefs into the world. Donaldson states that 'we are long past the point where "ignoring the trolls" [is] effective, and to pretend to do so merely empowers the bullies'. When uncontested, they may use these intolerant beliefs to suppress, to control and even hurt other fans. This sounds unmistakably like a certain *Harry Potter* villain, as Voldemort *did* use people's fear of Muggle-born wizards to drive his revolution. In many ways, this is mirrored even in our global politics.

This quotation from Draco Malfoy in *Philosopher's Stone/Sorcerer's Stone* provides a chilling mirror to the 2016 election in America, in which Donald Trump used the fear of immigration to win the title of president of the United States:

> *I really don't think they should let the other sort in, do you? They're just not the same, they've never been brought up to know our ways. Some of them have never even heard of Hogwarts until they get the letter, imagine. I think they should keep it in the old wizarding families.*

It doesn't seem like a coincidence that J. K. Rowling has been extremely outspoken about the current US administration, especially when Trump echoes these sentiments so well, as in his 2015 Presidential Announcement speech published in *Time* magazine:

> *When Mexico sends its people, they're not sending their best. They're not sending you. They're not sending you. They're sending people that have lots of problems, and they're bringing those problems with us. They're bringing drugs. They're bringing crime. They're rapists. And some, I assume, are good people.*

Tuesdays with Malfoy:
The Pain of Sharing Fandoms
Katryn Alessandri

In fact, when Rowling was tagged on Twitter in reference to Trump's similarly-spirited Muslim ban, she responded by saying: 'How horrible. Voldemort was nowhere near as bad'. Clearly, she perceives a parallel.

If we, as *Harry Potter* fans, want to answer the question of how we should respond to such vitriol within the sanctuary fandoms that many of us prefer to the real world, we can always find the answer in the books. In *Order of the Phoenix*, Dumbledore says: 'Indifference and neglect often do much more damage than outright dislike […] We wizards have mistreated and abused our followers for far too long, and we are now reaping our reward'. In this quotation, he is actually not talking about the attitude of pureblood wizards, but of Sirius Black's treatment of the house elf, Kreacher. Even in fantasy, the *Harry Potter* lexicon does a lot to mirror our reality as human beings. Even those of us who speak out against corruption and fascism still haven't fully recognized how many of us have benefited from it over the centuries. In book four, *Harry Potter and the Goblet of Fire* (Rowling, 2000), we see Hermione, who is of a marginalized group (Muggle-born), passionately speaking for the rights of the house elves:

> 'S – P – E – W!' said Hermione hotly. 'I was going to put Stop the Outrageous Abuse of Our Fellow Magical Creatures and Campaign for a Change in Their Legal Status – but it wouldn't fit. So that's the heading of our manifesto.'
> She brandished the sheaf of parchment at them.
> 'I've been researching it thoroughly in the library. Elf enslavement goes back centuries. I can't believe no one's done anything about it before now.'
> 'Hermione – open your ears,' said Ron loudly. 'They. Like. It. They like being enslaved!'

Ron, though definitely one of the heroes, still turns a blind eye to the mistreatment of creatures who have been long oppressed because it's the way things have *always* been. Even those of us who are outspoken liberals must realize that there are ways in which we can be as narrow-minded and hurtful as Death Eaters without even realizing our bias.

If we are to take Dumbledore's words to heart, simply ignoring or dismissing the words of blatantly racist fans, pretending they don't exist, is the *worst* thing we can do. J. K. Rowling has been clear in her intent for the story she has written. Despite the fact that fans are free to interpret the text however they like, others also have the right to speak up when they believe the heart of the story is being corrupted by bigoted online comments and trolling. Rowling is a writer, not a wizard, but she has shown bravery in her words, constantly speaking her beliefs even when they are unpopular and unafraid to lose fans when she knows she is on the right side of history. I'd like to be as brave as not just Harry and Hermione, but as Rowling.

Of course, I'm not suggesting a full-scale Battle of Hogwarts at *LeakyCon*, or for us to start waging an actual war with fans who do not share our beliefs, but don't we owe it to ourselves and our wizarding hearts to try and change their minds? Or, failing that, to at least speak up? Consider the following scene from *Harry Potter and the Chamber of Secrets* (Rowling, 1998):

> *The smug look on Malfoy's face flickered. 'No one asked your opinion, you filthy Mudblood,' he spat. Harry knew at once that Malfoy had said something really bad because there was an instant uproar at his words. Flint had to dive in front of Malfoy to stop Fred and George jumping on him, Alicia shrieked, 'How dare you!' and Ron plunged his hand into his robes, pulling out his wand, yelling, 'You'll pay for that one, Malfoy!' and pointing it furiously under Flint's arm at Malfoy's face.*

Right at this moment in the books, we become aware that 'Mudblood' is the equivalent of a searing racial epithet. While Draco carelessly tosses out the words, what if everyone around Hermione had simply shifted uncomfortably and tried to change the subject? What if others had immediately jumped to Draco's defence, claiming that the word wasn't that big of a deal, or that *Hermione* was the hurtful one for overreacting. Obviously, in the text, we see that the word 'Mudblood' has wide-reaching connotations. People who are identified as 'Mudbloods' and even those who sympathize with Muggles are actually *killed* after Voldemort's takeover. If we hope to fully immerse ourselves in this world, then we must act as our heroes do and stand up to bullies.

If we merely ignore hateful remarks from fans like us, pretending they are insignificant, how are we any different from the propaganda machine of Cornelius Fudge or the *Daily Prophet*? Pretending these hateful remarks are bots or trolls diminishes the powerful and negative effect they have on our fellow fans, who are often the target. Even if we can't wave our wands and 'Imperio!' racist fans into behaving better, we should use those House traits that this

Tuesdays with Malfoy:
The Pain of Sharing Fandoms
Katryn Alessandri

wonderful fandom offers us to make a difference. We can use words, much like wands, to show allyship with fans from all backgrounds. To do so is not only true to the books and to J. K. Rowling, but to Harry Potter himself. ●

~~~~~~~~~~~~~~

GO FURTHER

Book
The Hunger Games
Suzanne Collins
(New York: Scholastic Press, 2008)

Harry Potter's Bookshelf: The Great Books Behind the Hogwarts Adventures
John Granger
(London: Penguin Group, 2009)

Harry Potter and the Philosopher's Stone
J. K. Rowling
(London: Bloomsbury, 1997)

Harry Potter and the Chamber of Secrets
J. K. Rowling
(London: Bloomsbury, 1998)

Harry Potter and the Goblet of Fire
J. K. Rowling
(New York: Scholastic, 2000)

Harry Potter and the Order of the Phoenix
J. K. Rowling
(New York: Scholastic, 2003)

Harry Potter and the Deathly Hallows
J. K. Rowling
(New York: Scholastic, 2007)

Harry Potter and the Cursed Child
J. K. Rowling, Jack Thorne and John Tiffany
(Crawfordsville, IN: Pottermore, 2016)

The Hate U Give
Angie Thomas
(New York: Balzer + Bray, 2017)

Extracts/Essays/Articles
'Not So Magical: Issues with Racism, Classism, and Ideology in Harry Potter'
Tiffany L. Walters
In *All NMU Master's Theses*, 42 (2015) [Online], https://commons.nmu.edu/theses/42.

Online
'Today in Science: Gene Roddenberry'
Daniela Breitman
EarthSky. 19 August 2016, http://earthsky.org/human-world/today-in-science-gene-roddenberry.

'*Star Wars* Has a White Male Fandom Problem'
Kayleigh Donaldson
SyfyWire. 6 June 2018, http://www.syfy.com/syfywire/star-wars-has-a-white-male-fandom-problem.

'Facebook Shuts Down *Black Panther* Troll Group'
Matt Fernandez
Variety. 2 February 2018, https://variety.com/2018/film/news/black-panther-rotten-tomatoes-facebook-1202685658.

'White Until Proven Black: Imagining Race in *Hunger Games*'
Anna Holmes
New Yorker. 30 March 2012, https://www.newyorker.com/books/page-turner/white-until-proven-black-imagining-race-in-hunger-games.

Tuesdays with Malfoy:
The Pain of Sharing Fandoms
Katryn Alessandri

'@HPPlayLDN Hermione Should Be White… It Isn't the Same to See a Black "Hermione" #Boycott'

Augustine Jackson (@TheHighnessAJ)

Twitter. 21 December 2015, https://twitter.com/TheHighnessAJ/status /678924737209323521?ref_src=twsrc%5Etfw&ref_url=https%3A%2F%2Fmic.com%- 2Farticles%2F130853%2Fblack-hermione-casting-in-harry-potter-and-the-cursed- child-sparks-twitter-debate.

'Twitter Trolls Urge Boycott of *Star Wars* Over Black Character'

Benjamin Lee

The Guardian. 20 October 2015, https://www.theguardian.com/film/2015/oct/20/ twitter-trolls-boycott-star-wars-black-character-force-awakens-john-boyega.

'14 Quotes About Writing from John Green'

Mark Mancini

Mental Floss. 15 January 2014, http://mentalfloss.com/article/54511/14-quotes-about- writing-john-green.

'JK Rowling Tells of Anger at Attacks on Casting of Black Hermione'

Rebecca Ratcliff

The Guardian. 5 June 2016, https://www.theguardian.com/stage/2016/jun/05/harry- potter-jk--rowling-black-hermione.

'How horrible. Voldemort was nowhere near as bad'

J.K Rowling (@jk_rowling)

Twitter. 8 December 2015, https://twitter.com/jk_rowling/ status/674196610683940864.

'Canon: Brown Eyes, Frizzy Hair and Very Clever. White Skin Was Never Specified. Row- ling Loves Black Hermione :-* https://twitter.com/mauvedust /status/67585906528 5812224…'

J. K. Rowling (@jk_rowling)

Twitter. 21 December 2015, https://twitter.com/jk_rowling/status /6788880094339366914?lang=en.

'For Alt-Right Trolls, *Star Trek: Discovery* Is an Unsafe Space'
Manu Saadia
New Yorker. 26 May 2017, https://www.newyorker.com/tech/elements/for-alt-right-trolls-star-trek-discovery-is-an-unsafe-space.

'Not Being Racist but How Can a Black Woman Play Hermione? This Play Has Lost All Credibility'
Sean the Mondasian Cyberman (@WhoPotterVian)
Twitter. 21 December 2015, https://twitter.com/WhoPotterVian/status/678878957475864576?ref_src=twsrc%5Etfw&ref_url=https%3A%2F%2Fwww.huffing-tonpost.com%2Fentry%2Fjk-rowling-black-hermione-noma-dumezweni_us_57551b-0ce4b0ed593f14c4f1.

'Here's Donald Trump's Presidential Announcement Speech'
Time Staff
Time. 16 June 2015, http://time.com/3923128/donald-trump-announcement-speech.

'Transcript of the *Harry Potter Children's Press Conference Weekend*.' Wayback Machine, 18 October 2006, https://web.archive.org.

Websites
Pottermore, https://www.pottermore.com

Theatre
Harry Potter and the Cursed Child, J. K. Rowling, Jack Thorne, John Tiffany and Imogen Heap (Palace Theatre, London, 30 July 2016–ongoing; Lyric Theatre, New York, 16 March 2018).

Chapter
10

Recharming the Fans? The Expanded Works and Why They Don't Hold Up

Valerie Estelle Frankel

→ Many wizard school series rode *Harry Potter*'s coat-tails to bestseller status. Some, like Ursula K. Le Guin's *Earthsea* (1964-2018) and Tamora Pierce's *Circle of Magic* (1997-2013), were reissued. Similar novels, like *Secrets of the Immortal Nicholas Flammel* (Scott, 2007) and *Charlie Bone and the Red Knight* (Nimmo, 2009), were clearly trying to co-opt the audience. Percy Jackson, Harry's heir with a demigod camp in place of a wizard school, arguably succeeded the most, beginning with *The Lighting Thief* (Riordan, 2005).

However, Rowling's own spin-off projects become interesting in this context. One would expect the bestselling author to be able to capture lightning in a bottle twice – particularly with her reputation. However, the many spin-offs just don't have the same charm. Strangely, the issue is that many are too close: the computer games, theme parks and even Pottermore and *Harry Potter and the Cursed Child* (Rowling, Thorne and Tiffany, 2016) revisit and replay too many of the familiar storylines without the surprises and fresh new world of the originals. Other projects, from the Cormoran Strike novels (2013-18) to *Fantastic Beasts and Where to Find Them* (Yates, 2016), are darker adult stories meant for a far different audience. Is there any chance of getting more *Potter*? Or has the well been basically dry since 2007?

New mediums, same elements
Fans crowded the movie theatres for the first film directed by Chris Columbus in 2001. They were awed by the candlelit ceiling of Hogwarts, the adorable child characters. When the bricks parted one by one to welcome Harry to Diagon Alley, fans grinned in delight. This was the period when the books had just splashed into public awareness, but before the far darker *Harry Potter and the Order of the Phoenix* (Rowling, 2003) had been published. There were fanmade items circulating (including costumes and Sorting Hats that didn't yet match the films' vision), but Warner Brothers's official merchandizing was just beginning. Fans were charmed. In fact, *Harry Potter and the Philosopher's Stone/Sorcerer's Stone* (titled and scripted both ways to appease two different brandings) was the highest-grossing film of 2001 and second of all time at the time of its release. The films continued steadily, though attendance dropped around the scarier, weightier adaptations of books five and six. Dividing book seven to expand the franchise still further felt like a desperate attempt to make money – and indeed, *Harry Potter and the Deathly Hallows – Part 1* (Yates, 2010) was slow as well as grim. Still, *Harry Potter and the Deathly Hallows – Part 2* (Yates, 2011) claimed the worldwide opening weekend record, earning much more than any other instalment – presumably because fans wanted to finally see Voldemort's comeuppance. All the films brought delightful new moments but were remarkably close to the books – for those keeping up with the novels, they were celebrations but not surprises.

The movies were overshadowed by the releases of books five through seven, since these were the real stories with the real twist endings. They cre-

Recharming the Fans?
The Expanded Works and Why They Don't Hold Up
Valerie Estelle Frankel

ated the midnight release parties, and the publishers were eager to keep capi-
talizing. Back in 2001, Rowling's two Harry Potter schoolbooks – *Quidditch
through the Ages* and *Fantastic Beasts* – had been greeted with mild delight
and major sales by children seeking 'more *Potter*'. Rowling quickly followed
the seventh book's release with a similar tie-in book, *The Tales of Beedle the
Bard* (2008). All three offered scribbled comments from Harry and his friends
for added fannish amusement.

However, unlike the schoolbooks, the new content of *Beedle* had very little
relevance to Harry's world. None of the tales get more than a quick mention
in *Harry Potter and the Deathly Hallows* (Rowling, 2007), aside from the all-
important 'The Tale of the Three Brothers'. They don't reveal depths about the
main series and feel very loosely affiliated with Harry's world, aside from the
characters' snarky comments.

Some of the latter are fun of course. In his added commentary, Dumble-
dore offers a satire of the competing collection, *Beatrix Bloxam's Toadstool
Tales* (a clear parody of Beatrix Potter's works). As 'Beatrix Bloxam' rewrites
'The Wizard and the Hopping Pot', it reads:

> Then the little golden pot danced with delight – hoppitty hoppitty hop! –
> on its tiny rosy toes! Wee Willykins had cured all the dollies of their poorly
> tum-tums, and the little pot was so happy that it filled up with sweeties for
> Wee Willykins and the dollies!
> 'But don't forget to brush your teethy-pegs!' cried the pot.
> And Wee Willykins kissed and huggled the hoppitty pot and promised al-
> ways to help the dollies and never to be an old grumpy-wumpkins again.

As Dumbledore sardonically concludes, 'Mrs Bloxam's tale has met the same
response from generations of wizarding children: uncontrollable retching,
followed by an immediate demand to have the book taken from them and
mashed into pulp.'

Despite moments of cuteness like this, the five moralistic fairytales – of
which only 'The Tale of the Three Brothers' has any real bearing on Harry's
universe – lack the same fannish enthusiasm as the novels received. After a giant release party night and a few scattered fanvids and puppet shows, the piles
of books were consigned to dust-gathering on library shelves. Rumour has it
there's a *Beedle* shadow puppet show at the theme park... if anyone's love for

Harry can be expanded to these awkward fairytales.

Of course, the theme parks were the great gift to the fans. As the eight movies were finishing (with the last in 2011), the parks opened at last (the first at Universal's Islands of Adventure in Orlando in 2010, and then others in Japan and California). These were licensed by Warner Brothers and built to resemble the film sets. Fans can walk through the castle, dine at the Hog's Head, buy a special wand at Ollivander's, discover new fragments of story on Harry Potter and the Forbidden Journey and later on the Escape from Gringotts ride. The parks are a place to experience the love of the Potterverse, much like the ongoing fan conventions; a venue where the park workers joke about a fan's Slytherin T-shirt or let a visitor kiss a toad in the performing chorus. As professor of fandom studies Henry Jenkins describes it:

> [...] the Wizarding World is not about rides and attractions: it's about an environment which conveys through sights, sounds, taste, smell and touch, which makes tangible what had felt so vivid in our minds before, and as the fans said again and again all night, they really cared about the details. You can sip the Butterbeer (a concoction which mixes Root Beer and Butterscotch); you can smell the steam coming out of the train; you can feel the speed of a Quidditch match; you can see the wonders of the magical school; and everything is accompanied by the movie's soundtrack.

However, the park is closer to the video games and movies than to new content – only the Gringotts and Forbidden Journey rides have new stories. For the rest, from the Hogwarts Express to Weasleys' Wizard Wheezes, it's a nos-

Recharming the Fans?
The Expanded Works and Why They Don't Hold Up
Valerie Estelle Frankel

talgic place to celebrate the path that Harry has already trod.

Cursed Child (analysed in far more detail in other chapters of this book) struck many as a sort of fanfiction. Despite the new theatrical medium and (at last) new licensed fiction, it echoed some of the feel of Pottermore or the theme parks – retreading the storyline once again. There were surprises and fun adventures, but the Potterverse (much like the audience) felt stuck in an endless loop.

The play revisits some of the most beloved scenes of the original series, though through the eyes of Albus Potter and Scorpius Malfoy. There's also the alt-world twist with Voldemort winning the war and establishing dominance over the world, leaving Snape and Hermione, among others, in unaccustomed roles. Meanwhile, the boys' fast friendship pleases the Drarry shippers, who often saw Harry's obsession with his nemesis as being far more obsessive than his relationship with Cho or Ginny (a pattern Albus and Scorpius follow). The boys have new personalities, pushing back against the weight of the past instead of being defined by it.

However, close for some meant too close. With the Potter, Weasley and Malfoy families mulling over the mistakes and what-ifs of the seven-book series, from saving Cedric to revisiting James and Lily's sacrifice, the play lacks originality. Like Pottermore, the play places too much emphasis on beloved novel scenes – not just Hogwarts but the Triwizard Tournament, the return of Dumbledore and Snape, even Harry's childhood with the Dursleys. Fans saw the Time-Turners, Dumbledore's Army, Polyjuice potion, Lily's Patronus, and felt sceptical. With its mystery villain and rumours that Scorpius is Voldemort's son, the story tries for the style of twists that framed Snape and Sirius Black as villains, only to reveal stuttering Quirrell and Scabbers the rat. However, Voldemort's true child – basically the only new character in the franchise – doesn't bring Rowling's magical misdirection into the tale. The published script got its own 2016 midnight release, trying once more to capture the magic, but those who only read the book without seeing the more magical stage version couldn't truly feel its place in the Potterverse.

Gritty urbanity: *Casual Vacancy* and Cormoran Strike

With the Dumbledore prequel epic hinted at but not arriving, Rowling turned her work to more realistic adult fiction. *The Casual Vacancy* (2012) had a great deal of pre-release buzz. However, once more *Potter* fans were disappointed.

Rowling had set out to write a grim, truthful literary novel about ordinary citizens failed by the system, as she had been.

The novel delves into the horrific underbelly of the idyllic town of Pagford. As one daughter thinks of her mother: 'She knew that nearly everything of value in Terri Weedon's life had been sucked into the black hole of her addiction; that it had cost her two children; that she barely clung to two more; that she prostituted herself to pay for heroin'. Sukhvinder, a high schooler, pretends all is well, but behind closed doors endures horrific cyber-bullying, leaving her suicidal. The story begins with community leader Barry Fairbrother's death, and with it the suggestion that all the good he was doing to aid the needy citizens will now fade away. Many of their community's problems have no solutions, and the story acknowledges that, presenting a disturbingly accurate picture.

It's an insightful, tear-jerking look at those who most need help, an exploration that may in fact have aided some in the real world. However, it's not light, funny or magical. The theme of the novel could be said to be: 'Life stinks and no matter what you do, you may not ever be able to better your life'. Since this is the exact opposite of the boy wizard's empowering message, it's not surprising this book failed to resonate with fans.

For her subsequent mystery writing – *The Cuckoo's Calling* (2013), the first of the Cormoran Strike books – Rowling used the pseudonym of Robert Galbraith, as she was curious after the jarring response to *Casual Vacancy* how the books would do without her star power. For some reason, she described Robert Galbraith in the author bio as a former military cop now working in private security. Reviews were polite, but if she was hoping for another spontaneous fannish explosion, it never came. The critic Maureen Corrigan writes:

An unknown author trying to break into an overcrowded genre needs more than approving clichés to make an impact. In the U.K., a mere 1,500 copies had been sold. By last week, the novel was deader than a firecracker stand on a rainy Fifth of July.

Rowling's authorship was revealed by Brooks in the *Sunday Times* on 13 July 2013 after it investigated how a first-time author, 'with a background in the army and the civilian security industry', could write such an assured debut novel. *The Times*, checking a tip, ran *Cuckoo's Calling* through forensic 'stylo-

Recharming the Fans?
The Expanded Works and Why They Don't Hold Up
Valerie Estelle Frankel

metric' software and found a strong match with the *Harry Potter* series (1997–2007). Corrigan adds:

> As soon as the news of Rowling's ruse broke this past Sunday, sales of The Cuckoo's Calling soared. The novel has shot to No. 1 in online Amazon sales and an additional 300,000 hard covers have been rushed into print. Signed first editions of The Cuckoo's Calling are selling for around $1,000 on eBay; I think my unsigned first edition probably got packed off in one of the shopping bags full of unwanted review copies I donated to the library a few weeks ago.

(original emphasis)

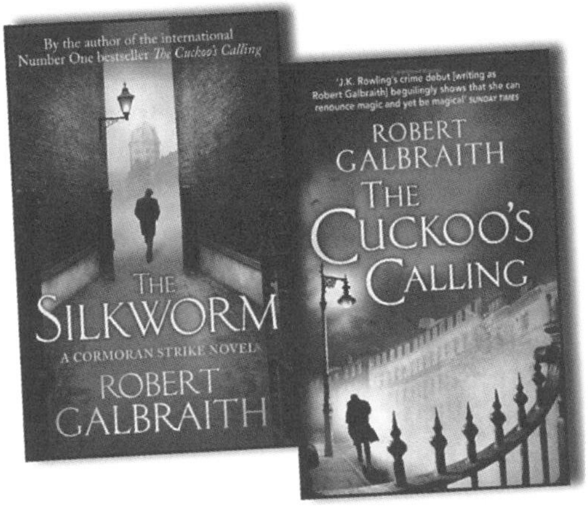

Figure 2: The Cuckoo's Calling and The Silkworm by Robert Galbraith. (2013, 2014).

Rowling responded: 'I had hoped to keep this secret a little longer because being Robert Galbraith has been such a liberating experience. It has been wonderful to publish without hype or expectation, and pure pleasure to get feedback under a different name' (cited by Brooks). Since sales soared after the revelation, some fans were sceptical that the leak had been an accident.

Still, the book was regarded as only an adequate offering. Corrigan adds:

> Rowling has written a respectable urban example of what's been called the 'Mayhem Parva' school of British detective fiction: The story takes place in a circumscribed setting, it's full of oddball suspects, and the killer is affably lurking in plain sight throughout much of the action.

Sequels followed with *The Silkworm* (2014) and *Career of Evil* (2015), once again to unexcited reviews.

The mysteries might be conventional, but they are jarringly distant from the Potterverse in tone. In both *Casual Vacancy* and the Cormoran Strike books, Rowling has her characters swear a blue streak. The mysteries offer drug dens, hacked-off limbs and abusive boyfriends. Someone in *The Silkworm* is advocating for transgender rights. In short, everything she held back from the *Potter* novels ends up here. They're like inverse shadows of the children's books, but as such, they certainly don't draw the same audience.

In *Cuckoo's Calling*, Strike walks down the street smoking, drinking beer in cheap pubs and suffering from his amputated leg. Sweating and swearing at the pain of pushing a camp bed up to the second floor, he then heats up Pot Noodle and thinks, '[h]e had slept in worse places. There had been the stone floor of a multistory car park in Angola, and the bombed-out metal factory where they had erected tents and woken coughing up black soot in the mornings.' While Harry's closet isn't much better, the layer of goofy fantasy makes it far more digestible. Here there is no candy coating – only dark realism.

True, there remain a few echoes of Potterverse themes. Lula Landry, the gorgeous victim, is mixed race (an upgrade from *Potter*) and shares Harry's obsession with investigating her parentage. Cormoran Strike, while a war veteran, shies from celebrity and shares Hagrid's gruff kindness. His brilliant new secretary has a touch of Hermione. *The Silkworm* has a novelist go missing, so Strike reads his blog and thus discovers quite a lot of Rowling's autobiographical thoughts about being a writer. One character explains:

> *That's the thing about traditional publishing, you know, they don't want to take a chance on something that hasn't been seen before, it's all about what fits their sales categories, and if you're blending several genres, if you're creating something entirely new, they're afraid to take a chance.*

Considering Rowling's efforts to sell a children's humorous fantasy mystery boarding school story, her complaint here seems personal. Still, while the books were written for her and perhaps for a traditional mystery audience, they failed to connect with the *Potter* crowd.

Pottermore: A new kind of platform but what exactly is it?

Even while the mystery novels suggested she was done with Harry, Rowling continued her old franchise on a unique platform – her interactive web world of Pottermore. In a new model for authors, she even flipped the new ebook craze by announcing she would be selling ebooks herself, without being bound by Amazon's restrictive deals. Rowling said as Pottermore launched, '[p]ersonally I love print and paper, [but] very recently for the first time I downloaded an ebook and it is miraculous, for travel and for children. I feel great about taking *Harry Potter* into this new medium' (cited by Flood and Brown). The literary agent Jonny Geller, of Curtis Brown, said:

Recharming the Fans?
The Expanded Works and Why They Don't Hold Up
Valerie Estelle Frankel

This does feel like a significant moment. If I was a brand author I would be asking my publisher how to get to the online communities that JK Rowling is getting to. It might be a wakeup call to think of a new way of getting to readers.

(cited by Flood and Brown)

He calls it 'a gamechanger in how global brands, the authors, can reach their readers'.

The beloved Stephen Fry- and Jim Dale-narrated *Harry Potter* audiobooks – originally released on CD and even tape (each created 1997–2007 with Fry reading the British version and Dale the American one) – were repackaged and sold for mobile devices in 2015. The interactive world was free, working more as advertising or a gift to fans than a product, and encouraging fans to keep participating with an online world that could infinitely expand while offering years of entertainment. 'For me, this is such a great way to give something back to *Harry Potter* fans who made the books such in incredible success', Rowling said. 'I still receive a phenomenal number of letters, drawings and stories from fans. This is [the] way for *Harry Potter* to live on in a medium that didn't exist when I started writing the books' (cited by Solon).

Pottermore began with a limited release – only the first million fans who had registered to complete the Magical Quill challenge got to try it out in 2012. First came the Sorting, based on a personality quiz (at this, the fans, all of whom had made firm House choices previously, were largely disappointed at being Sorted contrary to their expectations). *Wired* writer Olivia Solon writes that Rowling had written the algorithm for the Sorting, and another for choosing each player's individual wand. After this, Gryffindor students followed Harry's plot, while the others discovered different common rooms and prefects. Like in the video games, players were guided to follow Harry's adventures more than embark on their own.

In fact, the book plots launched sequentially on Pottermore – a player underwent Harry's adventures chapter by chapter with releases of each book that could make a splash in the news. The other big draw for longtime fans was the long-promised 20,000 words of unpublished lore – the minor characters' wand types, backstories, locations and so on. 'I had more than half of the new material already written or in note form', Rowling said. 'I dug some out of boxes' (cited by Flood and Brown).

With new illustrations, fans could interact with the scenes, finding Chocolate Frog cards, potion ingredients, schoolbooks, money and so on to keep in a wizard trunk. In each chapter, interactive 'moments' appeared where a player could pick up cash at Gringotts or select a wand. Learning spells and potions mimicked the school experience. On a bigger scale, actions earned House points, leading to a massive prize for the winners each year. Players, even those too young for the books, could experience the stories in a new way, and even comment and add their own drawings and content. Since the world was designed to be safe for kids, it featured the prewritten storyline more than interaction with other users.

Pottermore split with Sony in April 2014 and launched a new site on 22 September 2015. Ashley Ross of *Time* magazine reports:

> *The updated fansite – which still features original writing from Rowling in addition to new articles by an unnamed 'Pottermore correspondent' like '11 times Snape was the hardest teacher to please' and 'The 5 Death Eaters you'll never forget' – has some fans feeling a bit frustrated.*

The new site was more news-driven, with articles and interviews made for sharing online. The popular duelling had vanished, along with other interactions like the Moment illustrations, House Cup and Sorting ceremony (restored in January 2016). The new version felt more like Rowling's author site than a game. Fans on Twitter protested: 'What on earth happened to @pottermore? @jk_rowling, I absolutely adore you, but why would have us lose access to tons of additional info?' and '[n]ot impressed w/ the new @pottermore at all. ALL of the interactive stuff is gone. Should've been MORE not removed interaction. Disappointed'; another fan said it was 'like Buzzfeed for *Harry Potter*', Ross reports. The site continued evolving, with some well-publicized releases of new content, but these were more notes and snippets released than stories or interaction. Like *Beedle*, or the post-book-seven interviews Rowling had given, there was backstory here but not story.

Just before the *Fantastic Beasts* film arrived in 2016, Rowling released long pages on the other wizarding schools, especially the History of Ilvermorny and its fairytale founder Isolt Sayre. However, the backstories, dictionaries, history books and folklore of the extended universe have never offered quite the charm of the original novels (as George R.R. Martin is currently discovering

Recharming the Fans?
The Expanded Works and Why They Don't Hold Up
Valerie Estelle Frankel

with his own 2014 and 2018 *Game of Thrones* histories in lieu of the last two novels). Isolt Sayre's touching struggle to defend her mixed-blood family from her evil stepmother is all summary, lacking in moment-to-moment scenes. Like *Beedle*, the background is only slightly relevant to the main series, since the *Fantastic Beasts* characters mention Ilvermorny once but its history and Houses, not at all. Fans enjoyed the backstory briefly (albeit amid cries of insensitivity concerning the Native American religions Rowling had co-opted) and then moved on.

Pottermore was still famously the place to get new content, including three ebooks in 2016. These were titled *Hogwarts: An Incomplete and Unreliable Guide, Short Stories from Hogwarts of Power, Politics and Pesky Poltergeists* and *Short Stories from Hogwarts of Heroism, Hardship and Dangerous Hobbies*. Despite the titling, these were not true stories, but more backstory – summaries without scenes. Many fans were also irritated that all the material was straight from Pottermore, merely collected in book form.

The texts also stay quite close to the published books with little information far beyond the stories. For instance, in *Short Stories from Hogwarts*, lists of classes offered and the abilities of the Sorting Hat are already known. 'J.K. Rowling's Thoughts' as the sections are called, are likewise rather obvious. For instance, she writes: 'A slightly different list of school subjects appears in my earliest notes. Herbology is called "Herbalism", Divination is compulsory from the first year, as are Alchemy and a subject called simply "Beasts", whereas Transfiguration is called "Transfiguration/Metamorphosis"'. Interesting to fans but hardly revelatory. The tantalizing chapter titled 'Secrets of the Castle' only contains information on the Mirror of Erised that was revealed in book one – quite a disappointment.

Heroism, Hardship and Dangerous Hobbies is quite short with only four biographies: Lupin, McGonagall, Trelawny and Kettleburn. Certainly, much of the information is interesting for fans:

Minerva drew unusual attention to herself on her very first evening, when she was revealed to be a Hatstall. After five and a half minutes, the Sorting Hat, which had been vacillating between the houses of Ravenclaw and Gryffindor, placed Minerva in the latter. (In later years, this circumstance was a subject of gentle humour between Minerva and her colleague Filius Flitwick, over whom the Sorting Hat suffered the same confusion, but

Figure 3: Jean Martin and Sonya Jew as Delegate Ya Zhou and President Seraphina Picquery, at the Peers Ball (2018).

reached the opposite conclusion. The two Heads of House were amused to think that they might, but for those crucial moments in their youths, have exchanged positions).

Still, more than furthering her arc, this backstory appears to rather defensively address fannish scepticism that saw McGonagall as a perfect Ravenclaw more than Gryffindor. It's interesting lore, but the entire 'story' is written like a biography or Rowling's notes – which in fact they are. The five backstories in *Power, Politics and Pesky Poltergeists*, covering the antagonists from Slughorn to Umbridge, are no better. Fans who thought they were purchasing books of original stories got quite a disheartening surprise.

Fantastic beasts and how to mismatch them

Since the *Fantastic Beasts* franchise sprang from Harry Potter's 2001 schoolbook, it seemed primed to be the next iteration of *Potter*. Set in 1926 New York, it promised to reveal Dumbledore's backstory and his great love of and betrayal by Grindelwald against the Second World War. Of course, fans of Dobby, Hedwig and Crookshanks were just as excited about the new creatures.

With the American setting, many fans had hoped for greater diversity. In this, they were disappointed, as the all-white hero team of Newt, Jacob, Tina and Queenie broke into two heteronormative couples. True, the sisters are Jewish by all indications and Newt appears to be on the autistic spectrum, but like Dumbledore's queerness, this is all presented covertly. The gorgeous and elaborately gowned Madam President Seraphina Picquery only gets a minor role, though her tokenism emphasizes wizardly inclusion at the highest levels.

On the Wizarding War, fans are still waiting. The first film is setup, establishing the growing tension between the Wizarding and Muggle worlds. While the

Recharming the Fans?
The Expanded Works and Why They Don't Hold Up
Valerie Estelle Frankel

Second Salemers protest corruption, the wizards withdraw into secrecy and Grindelwald finds willing ears for his wizard supremacy campaign. The first film has a brief namedrop of Dumbledore and a quick peak of a Hufflepuff scarf, but otherwise stays firmly in America. Grindelwald only reveals himself at the end and lays out no clearer plan than his vague quest for dominance. Basically, this independent story didn't lay the ground for much of Harry and Voldemort's – or even Dumbledore's – war.

Fans of the animals were more satisfied. Newt's secret suitcase-world delighted audiences, with gentle tentacled graphorns saved from extinction; a crowd of friendly mooncalves; and blossoms that blow into insects. Newt cuddles Frank the Thunderbird and hands his new friend Jacob a baby occamy, while Jacob, the audience stand-in, gazes in loving wonder. Outside the suitcase, Newt flirts with a massive erumpent to pacify it; uses his bowtruckle to pick locks; unleashes the brilliantly blue swooping evil; and of course scolds his exasperating niffler as it loads up its pouch. For magical animal lovers, it's a dream. Of course, Newt's menagerie is arguably a subplot, allowing comic bumbling against a background of rising bigotry. It seems a gesture to those seeking the Potterverse's family-friendly elements, or worse, those wanting to capitalize off of them. As Manohla Dargis decides in her *New York Times* review:

> Given the expanding Potter universe – this is the first of five projected Fantastic Beasts features – the book could pass for a product catalog for potential merch, one that Ms. Rowling embellishes with comedic passages, glimmers of romance and parallel action scenes.

Indeed, licensed nifflers and animal guidebooks soon crowded the shops.

The two plots seem mismatched. The cute animals would fit well in a G-rated film or the early *Potter* adventures with their light-hearted joking. However, the four adults facing forcible memory erasure even as the Second Salemers call for them to be burned at the stake is far darker. Dargis writes, '[u]nlike the *Potter* movies, which grew darker and heavier as Harry and the series developed, *Fantastic Beasts* is playing peekaboo with the abyss right from the start'. Poor Credence Barebone begins the story, abused by his adoptive puritanical mother, Mary Lou, 'an anti-magic proselytizer spreading old-fashioned fire, brimstone and intolerance on city streets' (Dargis). At last, after he is manipulated by Grindelwald, who entices his allegiance with suggestively predatory scenes, a despairing Credence turns into a ball of seething black energy in a metaphor for the worst effects of child abuse. Grindelwald wants to use him, the wizards are willing to destroy him and Credence becomes collateral damage in their rising war. All this savagery reveals why the film was finally rated PG-13.

The characters each work through pain, from Newt's expulsion from Hogwarts to Credence's searing torture. In her review, titled 'The *Harry Potter* Franchise Is Stuck Between Adulthood and Adolescence', (2016), Tasha Robinson explains that the tropes seen here – from obsession with transformation to awkward bureaucracy – appeared in both the *Harry Potter* series and *Casual Vacancy*, leaving both series as she says, 'in an awkward twilight between adolescence and maturity'. While the mysteries and realistic novels admit the failures of society, Harry's world suggests it can still be fixed. As she concludes:

> *Not all of those story elements fit together, conceptually or tonally. This is a movie that centers equally on vicious beatings of affection-starved children, and a sort of cute, gold-hungry magical platypus (called a Niffler) that wants to cram all the world's valuables into its bottomless flesh-pouch [...] It's not just a serious adventure with comic elements, or vice versa: it's a grab bag of world-building wonder and awkward absurdist humor, with violence and childish giddiness tossed around in equal measure. It reads as though Rowling's version of an adult world is still dependent on the patronage of kids. In other words, it's a standard blockbuster movie, trying to grab adults and children at the same time, and not entirely serving either audience.*

A final twist: Creating mobile games

While Pottermore had turned into more of an announcements page, the popularity of smartphones offered another possibility for expansion. *Fantastic Beasts: Cases from the Wizarding World* launched on 17 November 2016, a day before the film. The game is developed by Mediatonic and has the player join the Ministry of Magic, check out reports of monsters and protect Muggles and creatures from one another throughout modern Britain. Mary Casey, a proud Slytherin and avid *Harry Potter* fan, is one of the creators. Casey describes how much the creators of the games love working in this world, which she calls made 'for fans, by fans', though with new plots and characters:

Recharming the Fans?
The Expanded Works and Why They Don't Hold Up
Valerie Estelle Frankel

'It was important for us to create something new, fresh, and interesting for players. Rather than revisiting the books and movies that people know and love, we decided to take those elements and create a new slice of life inspired by all the wonderful, imaginative things that J.K. Rowling has written both for Newt and for Harry,' said Casey. 'And I think by placing it in the Ministry, we kind of opened the door a little bit on something that is mentioned and is important in the original books but seeing it from a different perspective.'

(cited by Lewis)

There's lots to do. When a monster menaces Muggles, the player investigates. At crime scenes, particular objects must be found in a treasure hunt against time (admittedly a staple of many online games). After solving a location, a mirror-flipped version or one with a few items removed may appear for an additional challenge. These clues then need further investigation with *Potter* spells like 'Alohomora', 'Scurgefy', 'Reparo', etc. The player casts these by tracing and then solving a simple puzzle. Of course, nearly the entire game is about treasure-hunting. Simon Reed writes in his review: 'It still has the same problems that can make hidden object games incredibly off-putting for some – and all the magical creatures in the world can't make up for that'.

Locations, from deep forests to underwater realms, have a magical feel, though they're also cluttered with random items. Exploring well-known locations like the Ministry of Magic and Zonko's Joke Shop, beside new ones like deep forests and lake bottoms, emphasizes the breadth of the world and lets fans travel beyond the book and film locations. The creatures of course are the bowtruckles, erumpets, dragons and so forth of the series, with lots of trivia and a story arc as well. The player must put together clues from case files to work out exactly which beast is rampaging and then work to contain it. The characters are all new, without a mention of Harry's or Newt's friends (and only a few of celebrities like Gilderoy Lockheart). Still, it definitely feels like Harry's world – schoolbooks and monsters are straight from Rowling, and the first investigation takes place at the Chudley Cannons training ground, while the second visits the Leaky Cauldron, where a mountain troll has got loose. Bursts of the theme music helps the player feel truly immersed in Harry's world.

The game is energy based – replenished over time – with additional long time-outs when an NPC (non-player character) takes six or twelve hours to investigate something and report back. One can work with Facebook friends to share energy and compare scores, but otherwise there's not much teamwork. As in a real mystery, the clues and evidence are pre-set but can be investigated in any order. One can also go back to a previous case to earn more points. In a small twist, rare ingredients lie around crime scenes, to be brewed into helpful potions or 'upgrades'. An invigoration draught, for instance, sets hints to maximum, while a wit-sharpening potion slows the countdown.

It's a perfectly fine independent game and works for those even barely familiar with Rowling's original or prequel universes (though those who know the animals quite well may have a slight advantage when it comes time to guess whodunit). Still, *Fantastic Beasts* just isn't as popular as the original Potterverse, so those seeking that world's original charm won't find it in a game this far removed from Hogwarts. As Reed concludes:

> It's just another hidden object game, albeit with a lick of paint that elevates it slightly above the more generic spooky additions to the genre. It's just nice to be in the Leaky Cauldron looking for rats or stacks of books or pieces of Quidditch equipment.

Another game followed. On 25 April 2018, *Harry Potter: Hogwarts Mystery* launched from Portkey Games, the new label from Warner Bros. Interactive Entertainment. The game takes place before Harry's arrival, when Bill Weasley and Tonks are students. This timing allows Snape and Dumbledore to fill their customary roles, alongside other beloved professors. As Pottermore Staff explain:

> Hogwarts Mystery *is set in a different time period for players to create their own alternative Wizarding World timeline, the 1980s. In this role-playing mobile game, players will be able to immerse themselves in those authentic Wizarding World settings. For the very first time, they can create their own personalised student character, visit their house's common room and make choices that will define their own Hogwarts story.*

Recharming the Fans?
The Expanded Works and Why They Don't Hold Up
Valerie Estelle Frankel

The new player indeed chooses a name and appearance, with diversity fully enabled. The player's brother has vanished under mysterious circumstances while seeking a lost treasure at Hogwarts. As the player investigates the rumoured Cursed Vaults of Hogwarts, fans finally find a new story at their beloved setting. While befriending characters highly reminiscent of Hermione and Neville, and tangling with Merula, a female bully quite similar to Draco, the young hero must solve the mystery, all while staying out of trouble.

The player casts spells by finger-tracing and attends classes, there choosing whether to watch other students, research, observe the teacher, ask questions, etc. While speaking with others, the player decides which answer to give, earning knowledge, bravery or empathy points. Many of the questions are trivia from the books, allowing a knowledgeable player to soar. Spending money, energy and gems allows the hero to act, even while also buying wizardly clothes and accessories. Weekly contests throw in wizard beachwear, cursebreaker uniforms, punk outfits and more. Still, unlike many games, the player cannot go everywhere or talk to everyone as many characters aren't clickable and locations are often blocked off. Reviewer Nick Fernandez adds:

> If you're familiar with Kim Kardashian: Hollywood (there are more than 10 million of you, somewhere), Harry Potter: Hogwarts Mystery will feel familiar – it's essentially the same game with a Hogwarts reskin […] The tasks themselves are where the game leaves a lot to be desired. Each task has a time limit ranging from an hour to nearly half a day, and is completed by tapping on highlighted objects on the screen. Each tap will deplete your energy, which can only be regenerated by waiting long periods of time or purchasing gems through in-app purchases.

Some of the mistakes of Potttermore are fixed here – the story is original, instead of Harry's over-told quest, but features many of the beloved Hogwarts characters along with music and even actors from the films. In addition, the art really does feel immersive enough to take players into the Potterverse.

With all this, both of the mobile games, more than perhaps the theme parks, truly give a sense of entering Harry's world while being able to be oneself, embarking on new adventures. Even as *Fantastic Beasts* struggles to balance its fandom while the original seven novels reach out to a new generation, it's nice to see that the franchise is still adapting. ●

GO FURTHER

Books

The Cuckoo's Calling
Robert Galbraith
(New York: Little, Brown, and Co., 2013)

The Silkworm
Robert Galbraith
(New York: Little, Brown, and Co., 2014)

Career of Evil
Robert Galbraith
(New York: Little, Brown, and Co., 2015)

Fantastic Beasts and Where to Find Them
J. K. Rowling
(New York: Arthur A. Levine Books, 2001)

Quidditch Through the Ages
J. K. Rowling
(New York: Arthur A. Levine Books, 2001)

The Tales of Beedle the Bard
J. K. Rowling
(New York: Scholastic, 2008)

The Casual Vacancy
J. K. Rowling
(New York: Little, Brown, and Co, 2012)

Hogwarts: An Incomplete and Unreliable Guide. (Kindle edn)
J. K. Rowling
(USA: Pottermore, 2016)

Recharming the Fans?
The Expanded Works and Why They Don't Hold Up
Valerie Estelle Frankel

Short Stories from Hogwarts of Heroism, Hardship and Dangerous Hobbies
(Kindle edn)
J. K. Rowling
(USA: Pottermore, 2016)

Short Stories from Hogwarts of Power, Politics and Pesky Poltergeists
J. K. Rowling
(USA: Pottermore, 2016)

Harry Potter and the Cursed Child
J. K. Rowling, Jack Thorne and John Tiffany
(Crawfordsville, IN: Pottermore, 2016)

Extracts/Essays/Articles
'The Night of a Thousand Wizards'
Henry Jenkins
In V. Frankel (ed.). *Harry Potter, Still Recruiting* (Allentown, PA: Zossima Press, 2012),
pp. 94–100.

Online
'Whodunnit? JK Rowling's Secret Life as Wizard Crime Writer Revealed'
Richard Brooks
Sunday Times. 14 July 2013, https://www.thetimes.co.uk/article/whodunnit-jk-row-
lings-secret-life-as-wizard-crime-writer-revealed-vfxzwf72jzh.

'The Only Surprise in Rowling's *Cuckoo's Calling* Is the Author'
Maureen Corrigan
NPR. 18 July 2013, https://www.npr.org/2013/07/18/202732292/the-only-surprise-in-
rowlings-cuckoos-calling-is-the-author.

'Review: *Fantastic Beasts* Unleashes J.K. Rowling's Magic on Old New York'
Manohla Dargis
New York Times. 17 November 2016, https://www.nytimes.com/2016/11/18/movies/fan-
tastic-beasts-and-where-to-find-them-review-eddie-redmayne-j-k-rowling.html.

'*Harry Potter: Hogwarts Mystery* Review – *Harry Potter* and the Prisoner of Microtransactions'
Nick Fernandez
Android Authority. 27 February 2018, https://www.androidauthority.com/harry-potter-hogwarts-mystery-review-859269.

'*Harry Potter* Next Chapter? Wizard Website Tells and Sells All'
Alison Flood and Mark Brown
The Guardian. 23 June 2011, https://www.theguardian.com/books/2011/jun/23/harry-potter-website-pottermore.

'*Fantastic Beasts: Cases from the Wizarding World*, New Case Released!'
Haley Lewis
MuggleNet. 26 January 2017, http://www.mugglenet.com/2017/01/fantastic-beasts-cases-wizarding-world-new-case-released.

'A Guide to Portkey Games' Place in the Wizarding World™'
Pottermore Staff
Pottermore. 25 April 2018, https://www.pottermore.com/news/a-guide-to-portkey-games-place-in-the-wizarding-world.

'*Fantastic Beasts: Cases from the Wizarding World* Review: Sense of Wander'
Simon Reed
Gamezebo. 24 November 2016, https://www.gamezebo.com/2016/11/24/fantastic-beast-cases-wizarding-world-review-sense-wander.

'*Fantastic Beasts* Review: The *Harry Potter* Franchise Is Stuck Between Adulthood and Adolescence'
Tasha Robinson
The Verge. 18 November 2016, https://www.theverge.com/2016/11/18/13676696/fantastic-beasts-harry-potter-rowling-eddie-redmayne-film-review.

Recharming the Fans?
The Expanded Works and Why They Don't Hold Up
Valerie Estelle Frankel

'Here's Why Some Harry Potter Fans Are Unhappy with the New Pottermore'
Ashley Ross
Time. 22 Sept 2015, http://time.com/4044232/harry-potter-pottermore-new-site.

'Ilvermorny School of Witchcraft and Wizardry'
J. K. Rowling
Pottermore. 2016, https://www.pottermore.com/writing-by-jk-rowling/ilvermorny.

'J. K. Rowling's Pottermore Details Revealed: *Harry Potter* E-Books and More'
Olivia Solon
Wired. 23 June 2011, https://www.wired.com/2011/06/pottermore-details.

Video games
Fantastic Beasts: Cases from the Wizarding World [Android, iOS]
(Warner Bros. Interactive Entertainment, 2016).

Harry Potter: Hogwarts Mystery [Android, iOS]
(Warner Bros. Interactive Entertainment, 2018).

'WORDS ARE, IN MY NOT-SO-HUMBLE OPINION, OUR MOST INEXHAUSTIBLE SOURCE OF MAGIC. CAPABLE OF BOTH INFLICTING INJURY AND REMEDYING IT'

ALBUS DUMBLEDORE
(HARRY POTTER AND THE DEATHLY HALLOWS)

Contributor Details

EDITOR

Valerie Estelle Frankel is the author and editor of many books on pop culture, including *Superheroines and the Epic Journey* (McFarland, 2017); *Harry Potter: Still Recruiting* (Zossima Press. 2012); *Teaching with Harry Potter* (McFarland, 2017) and *How Game of Thrones Will End* (Thought Catalog, 2014). Many of her books focus on women's roles in fiction, from her McFarland Heroine's Journey guides *From Girl to Goddess* (2010) and *Buffy and the Heroine's Journey* (2012), to books like *Women in Game of Thrones* (McFarland, 2014) and *The Many Faces of Katniss Everdeen* (Zossima Press, 2013). A lecturer at Mission College and San Jose City College, she's a frequent speaker at conferences and lives in Sunnyvale, California. Come explore her research at vefrankel.com.

~~~~~~~~~~~~~~~~~~~

CONTRIBUTORS

Katryn Alessandri has been a writer since the age of 5, although her controversial debut, 'Amy and the Elf Who Stole Christmas', was not the breakout hit she had hoped. You can find her humour writing on the Hit Job on Medium. com, where her articles have been featured in the 'Editor's Pick' section; her fiction in *Suspense Magazine* and her serialized fiction in *The Sleuth*. When she isn't writing, Katryn spends her time with her husband and child nerding out in Oakland, California. She may or may not be wanted in five states for grand theft sandwich.

Lisa Gomez is a Los Angeles-based singer/songwriter in a duo group with her twin sister Gina called Gemeni. Gemeni have a song called 'A Stake in My Heart' (2011), inspired by *Buffy*, on sale on iTunes. In addition to their debut album *More Than Me* (2011), Gemeni have a YouTube channel with over 30,000 views, including the YouTube Geek Week hit video 'Thorsday', which Marvel Entertainment featured on their channel. Lisa is obsessed with Joss Whedon, Marvel, the BBC's *Sherlock* and tea, and is in the middle of writing her second full-length album, two novels and her first screenplay. You can visit Gemeni's website at Facebook.com/GemeniTwins.

Valerie Guempel is an English MA student at Fordham University, located in New York City. Her academic interests include nineteenth-century British literature, queer and disability theory and fan studies. In 2017, she received her BA in English and women's & gender studies from Saint Louis University. A lifelong fan of both theatre and *Harry Potter*, she has spent her spare time this past year seeing over a dozen Broadway shows, including *Harry Potter and the Cursed Child*, which she has now seen three times. When not entering Broadway lotteries for cheap tickets, she reads fanfiction and attends events with NYC's meetup group, The Group That Shall Not Be Named, the largest *Harry Potter* fanclub in the world.

Jessica Hautsch is a Ph.D. student at Stony Brook University, focusing on the reading and writing practices of online fandom. She has published and presented on fanfiction, fan use of animated GIFs, the Hogwarts Houses as interpretative frameworks and gendered and racialized representations in *Buffy the Vampire Slayer*.

Aya Esther Hayashi holds a Ph.D. in music from the Graduate Center, City University of New York. Her dissertation, 'Musicking, Discourse, and Identity in Participatory Media Fandom' (2018), focused on the musicians and communities surrounding filk (roughly, the folk music of the science fiction/fantasy fandom), wizard rock (a punk-inspired, DIY-music movement inspired by J. K. Rowling's *Harry Potter* novels), and the YouTube musicals of Team StarKid and AVbyte. With Jessica Getman, she edited and wrote the introduction to the *Journal of Fandom Studies*'s special issue 'Musicking in Media Fandom' (4:2, 2016). She currently lives in New York City and serves as development associate at Pan Asian Repertory Theatre, the pioneer Asian American theatre company on the East Coast.

Joel Hawkes is a lecturer in English literature at the University of Victoria, British Columbia. His work is particularly interested in the practices and performances that create the physical and literary spaces we inhabit. He can't seem to stop writing about popular culture, especially the world of science fiction and fantasy, of which he's a huge fan. Recent publications include chapters in *The Comics of Joss Whedon* (McFarland, 2015) and *Joss Whedon and Race* (McFarland, 2016); forthcoming papers look at the movie *Serenity* and Jeff Lemire's comic *Essex County*.

S. Evan Kreider is an associate professor of philosophy at the University of Wisconsin Oshkosh, Fox Valley campus. His areas of research interest include ethics, aesthetics and popular culture. He is the co-editor of and contributing author for *The Philosophy of Joss Whedon* (University Press of Kentucky, 2012), and a contributing author for *The Philosophy of the X-Files* (University Press of Kentucky, 2009), *Homer Simpson Ponders Politics: Popular Culture as Political Theory* (University Press of Kentucky, 2013), *Jim Henson and Philosophy* (Rowman and Littlefield, 2015) and *The Who and Philosophy* (Lexington Books, 2016).

César Alfonso Marino graduated from the University of Buenos Aires (UBA) in the Facultad de Filosofía y Letras (Faculty of Philosophy and Letters). He is dedicated to participating in conferences on the relationship of pop culture with literature, music, films and video games. He has published articles in Argentinian at Luthor magazine. He has published essays in *The Comics of Joss Whedon* (McFarland, 2015), edited by Valerie Estelle Frankel; *Dick Grayson, Boy Wonder: Scholars and Creators on 75 Years of Robin, Nightwing and Batman* (2015), edited by Kristen Geaman; *The Ages of the Incredible Hulk* (2016), edited by Joseph Darowski and *Screening the Nonhuman: Representations of Animal Others in the Media* (2016), edited by Amber E. George and J. L. Schatz.

Erin Pyne is an author (*The Ultimate Guide to the Harry Potter Fandom* [Rowan Tree Books, 2011]) and theme park design writer. She has created dozens of attractions and shows at theme parks around the world including Universal Studios, Sea World and Motiongate Dubai. If you've ever visited the Wizarding World of Harry Potter then you've probably experienced her work. Erin ran the Orlando Harry Potter Club for over a decade and lives in Orlando with her three sons (wizards).

Emily E. Roach is a doctoral candidate in the Department of English and Related Literature at the University of York; a pop culture freelance writer and an LGBT activist. Emily researches fandom and post-Stonewall American LGBT fiction, including performance poetry and young adult fiction. Emily's research is currently focused on online creative communities, theorizing online space and LGBT fiction hosted online, specifically queer poetry and fanfiction. A writer of slash fiction and a longtime writer and community moderator in the *Harry Potter* fandom, Emily has published several articles on *Harry Potter* and has articles forthcoming on real person fiction in pop music fandoms; the meta-textual fangirl in *Supernatural* and the queer subtext of *Stranger Things*.

Madeline Wilson has been a *Harry Potter* fan since she first read the books in 2000, but she became involved in the larger fandom when she attended *LeakyCon 2009*. She is a co-creator of a dance workshop called Dance Against the Dark Arts, a fanfiction author, a cosplayer, an avid wizard rock fan and a member and former co-president of 'hp-ohio', a *Harry Potter* fan group for adults in Ohio and the surrounding area.

Image Credits

Introduction	Fig. 1 p. 6 San Diego, CA, 2018. Photo by Valerie Estelle Frankel. Fig. 2 p. 7 San Diego, CA, 2018. Photo by Valerie Estelle Frankel.
Chapter 1	Fig. 1 p. 17 Orlando, Florida, 2014. Photo by Erin Pyne. Fig. 2 p. 18 Wizarding World of Harry Potter, Orlando, Florida, 2010. Photo © Erin Pyne. Fig. 3 p. 21 Wizarding World of Harry Potter, Orlando, Florida, 2010. Photo © Erin Pyne.
Chapter 2	Fig. 1 p. 38 © Madeline Wilson, 2010. Fig. 2 p. 40 Universal Orlando Royal Pacific Hotel, Orlando, Florida, 2011.
Fan Appreciation #1	Title image p. 48 © A. J. Holmes, 2009.
Chapter 3	Fig. 1 p. 61 Ontario, CA, 2017. Photo by Michael Benedict. Fig. 2 p. 66 Baycon, San Mateo, CA, 2018. Photo by David Price.
Chapter 4	Fig. 1 p. 84 © Electronic Arts, 2003. Fig. 2 p. 87 © Warner Bros. Interactive Entertainment, 2018.
Fan Appreciation #2	Title image p. 92 © Justin Zagri, 2016. Fig. 1 p. 93 © Broad Strokes, 2013. Fig. 2 p. 96 © Broad Strokes, 2016.
Chapter 5	Fig. 1 p. 103 © Tactical Studies Rules, Inc., 1974. Fig. 2 p. 110 © Evil Hat Productions, 2013.
Chapter 6	Fig. 1 p. 117 © DC Comics, 2013. Fig. 2 p. 123 Licensed under CC BY 2.0. https://www.flickr.com/photos/52611380@N05/13965622827, 2014. Photo by City.and.Color.